T0329555

THE

PUBLICATIONS

OF THE

Lincoln Record Society

FOUNDED IN THE YEAR

1910

VOLUME 63

FOR THE YEAR ENDING 31st AUGUST 1968

THE RECORDS OF
THE COMMISSIONERS
OF SEWERS

IN THE

PARTS OF HOLLAND

1547—1603

EDITED BY

A. E. B. OWEN, M.A.

UNDER-LIBRARIAN, CAMBRIDGE UNIVERSITY LIBRARY

Volume II

PRINTED FOR

THE LINCOLN RECORD SOCIETY

BY

J. W. RUDDOCK & SONS LTD., LINCOLN

1968

This volume has been produced
with the assistance of a grant from
The British Academy

General Editor's Preface

Miss Mary Kirkus, the editor of the first volume of these Records, died, to the regret of her colleagues and friends, in 1959, still relatively young, when work on the second volume was not far advanced. The Society has been fortunate enough to find a continuator of her work in Mr. Arthur Owen, who has made a study of the records of Commissioners of Sewers in various localities and was himself brought up in the south of the Parts of Lindsey at no great distance from the countryside with which the records deal.

KATHLEEN MAJOR

CONTENTS

Introduction to Volume II

Before writing her introduction to volume I Miss Kirkus had already transcribed from microfilms, and typed, all the documents she proposed to include in this edition. The present editor expected to do no more than verify the text and prepare indexes for the remaining volumes and see them through the press. It became evident, however, that some departures from the original plan were necessary, and an explanation of these is given below.

But first, something must be said of Miss Kirkus's own work. She herself was reticent about the technical problems presented by these records, and only those who have handled the originals can appreciate the nature of the difficulties which confronted her. The handwriting of the verdicts, which she described as "in general cursive, seemingly put down hurriedly with little punctuation and often not easy to read"—a fine piece of understatement—is one such difficulty. Another is the spelling, which at times is so eccentric as almost to defy comprehension. But besides these physical difficulties, which are daunting enough, Miss Kirkus had also to face problems of interpretation with very little in the way of precedent to guide her. The extensive and valuable bibliography she provided in the first volume tends to conceal the fact that her own study of the workings of the courts of sewers was very much a pioneer one. Until it appeared, the records of land drainage had been little studied and less published.[1] Her introduction to this edition has already shown itself of the utmost value to students; and her successor as editor is glad to acknowledge his personal indebtedness to Miss Kirkus's work, which has illuminated his own research at many points. Such changes as he has ventured to introduce into the remainder of the edition are intended only to increase its usefulness for others.

Scope of the edition. At the outset Miss Kirkus may have hoped to print almost all the surviving records of the Holland Courts of Sewers down to 1603, but as work proceeded the need for some curtailment became evident. An outline scheme for publication in four volumes, drawn up when the first volume was nearly ready, shows that she had decided not to print any verdicts or laws later than 1587, and only selected later documents, none after 1598, from other classes. A list at the end of this scheme, of items left out, includes verdicts from 1589 to 1600 and several further laws from 1588 to 1599: against the first of these laws is a note "interesting row . . . try to get in". But a review of the material still to be printed made it clear to the present editor that, on the contrary, still further curtailment was needed. As projected by Miss Kirkus the whole of volume II and the greater part of volumes III and IV would have

[1]A few additions to Miss Kirkus's bibliography of land drainage history will be found in A. E. B. Owen: "Land Drainage Authorities and their Records", *Journal of the Society of Archivists* vol. II no. 9 (April 1964), pp. 417-423.

consisted of verdicts. But the form of these is well enough shown
by those already printed in volume I; and in her introduction to this
Miss Kirkus had in fact effectively extracted all that this class of
documents can be made to yield concerning the administrative
history of the sewers courts. Their further interest would seem to
lie mainly in their wealth of topographical detail, but even this tends
to be repeated from one verdict to the next, while many pages
consist only of names of landholders with a record of the amount
of bank for whose upkeep each was responsible. Therefore, since
verdicts survive for almost every year in this period, it seemed
better to make a selection and so render it practicable (some of the
omitted verdicts being of considerable length) to complete the edition
in three volumes instead of four. The editor has endeavoured to
make such a selection as will fairly represent the whole of this class,
both chronologically and in intrinsic interest, without sacrificing
anything of importance for the history of the sewers courts. Brief
descriptions of items intended for printing by Miss Kirkus but now
omitted are inserted in the text, since they are referred to in her
introduction.

At the same time these omissions make possible the inclusion of
some additional material from the class of accounts, only one example
of which was proposed for printing in Miss Kirkus's scheme. Verdicts
and laws record what was not done and what ought to be done; but
the value of accounts is that they record what actually *was* done to
repair the banks and drains, and they thus show land drainage in
action when other documents only give us, as it were, the theory.
The early Holland records unfortunately contain very few accounts
but a comparison with the East Lindsey courts, among whose
records accounts survive in abundance, indicates that this is just an
accident of preservation. The present volume includes extracts
from accounts concerning the diking of the Welland in 1567 (165a):
in volume III it is proposed to include specimens of dikereeves'
accounts.

Arrangement of text. The documents in volume I are printed
consecutively with no breaks other than between folios or sections.
This means that the user is given the impression of a single con-
tinuous text, whereas in fact verdicts or portions of verdicts for six
different years seem to be represented. Admittedly these early
verdicts are not always easy to distinguish from each other. Owing
to past confusion, and the lack of any date on most folios, parts of
different verdicts have been put together, and folios misplaced or
lost, so that a modern file does not necessarily represent one original
verdict. This needs to be said in fairness to Miss Kirkus, since it is a
difficulty she did not emphasize as she might have done. However,
the present editor has attempted to disentangle these verdicts and
an analysis of the contents of volume I is now printed (p. viii).
In addition, all documents hereafter printed have been given ex-
planatory headings so that the nature of each may be clearly seen.

Method of transcription. Special symbols were used in volume I to indicate matter interlined, cancelled or deleted in the original, or supplied by the editor, all such matter being placed within brackets. This system has now been simplified. *Interlined* matter is now printed without special indication save in a few instances which are the subject of footnotes. *Cancelled* or *deleted* matter is for the most part omitted without remark, or else consigned to a footnote; where it has been allowed to stand in the text, a footnote records the fact of cancellation or deletion. The vast majority of such corrections are due to mere scribal carelessness and in themselves are of no interest whatever. Matter *supplied* by the editor is printed as before within square brackets, but since this is a common editorial convention, the symbol "s" is now omitted as superfluous. It is hoped that these changes and the omission of the special symbols, resulting in a less cluttered text, will make the documents easier to follow. The *conventions* employed in transcription are otherwise the same as in volume I.

Numbering. As the dual system of numbering employed in this edition has been found somewhat confusing, it may be as well to explain it afresh. The running number on the *right* is that assigned by Miss Kirkus for internal reference within the edition. In general, each such number relates to one folio of the original, but in certain cases Miss Kirkus broke up lengthy blocks of text into numbered sections which do not correspond to folios, e.g. sections 501-506; in other cases one number comprehends more than one folio, as may be seen in sections 205-213. These numbers are therefore best regarded as section, rather than folio, references. The few documents not intended for printing by Miss Kirkus but added by the present editor have been allotted section numbers to fit them into this system, e.g. 165a. The number in square brackets on the *left* is that assigned by Miss Eileen Brown who put the documents into order while they were at County Hall, Boston. It is these numbers which actually appear on the documents and which are used in the catalogues at the Lincolnshire Archives Office, and which should therefore be quoted by anyone wishing to consult or cite the originals.

I greatly appreciate the care which the printers have taken with the text at all stages.

A. E. B. OWEN

DOCUMENTS PRINTED IN VOLUME I

[1]In a footnote to volume I, p. vii, section 65 is referred to as a joyce book. This is incorrect. Though incorporating information from a joyce book, it is not itself such a document but is, in fact, the first (surviving) folio of the verdict which follows. No original joyce book of a date early enough to include in this edition has been found. It should be noted that the old numeration of this verdict shows the present order of the folios to be incorrect and at least one folio to be missing.

SYNOPSIS OF DOCUMENTS IN VOLUME II

(*An entry in italics signifies that the document is briefly described but not printed, or printed only in part*)

VERDICT FOR KIRTON AND ELLOE WAPENTAKES, 1565

[473.VIII.1][1]   146

[2]Item the sayd jurie sayethe that the heade drean of Allgarkyrke
& Fosdyke is in great rewynge and decaye in dyvers & sundrye
places for lake of roodynge scouryng & dykynge and the same to be
dykyd & scouryd soo ofte as nyde shall require by the lordes free
hollders & copie holders by acare sylver, and the same to be roodyd
& hoked yerlye be them that leyethe & adioynethe agaynst ytt as
alwayes haythe bene accustomyde from tyme to tyme.

(*See bankes*) Item thay saye further that the see bankes belongynge to the same towens be in dyvers & sondrye places defectyve in
the defalte of theis persones folowynge fyrste

[3]Rychard Brandon & Thomas Welbie	x fote
the hayres of Thomas & Nycholas Armon	xiij fote
the hayres of Goodynges	xvj fote
Thomas Hunnynge	xij fote
John Armon	vj fote
Castell & Ellegar	xx fote
[4]our soveraynge ladie the quen	iij roodes
[5]George Claymon	v fote
the hayres of Christofer Gryne	xxv fote
divers cotages	xxij fote
James Ratlyfe	xl fote
Mr Harryngton	xx fote
Thomas Rooper	xx fote
Renold Hall	xx fote
Mr Wellowbie	x fote
[6]landes layt Mr Wollmers	xvij fote

(*Kyme dyke bankes by Sott' Allgar' Fosdyke Wygtoft & Swynshed*)
Item the sayd jurie sayethe that whereas there is a certayn banke
callyd Kyme Dyke Banke begyngynge at the Horne & soo to Wyllowbothe & soo to Pykelbeke Bouthe belongynge to the VIII Hundrethe
Fene which is in rewinge & decaye for that yt is not in hyght &
brede wherbie the fresshe waters dothe overflowe the sayd fene to
the great hyndraunce & undoynge of the commeners of the sayd
VIII Hundrethe and yt owght to be mayd by iiij[or] Hundrethes
that is to saye frome the Horne to Wyllowbothe by Sotterton Allgarkyrke & Fosdyke by commaund mynworke and from Wyllowbothe
to Pykkelbeke Bowthe by Swynshed & Wygtofte whiche banke we

---

[1] This folio is numbered in the left margin " quart' ". Other folios in this file
seem to have borne similar numbers, of which the following can be deciphered :
" [s]eptimo " (now 4), " decimo " (7), " undecimo " (8), " duodecimo " (9), " tercio-
decimo " (10), " quartodecimo " (11) ; others are missing or illegible. Folios 12,
13 and 14b are numbered at the foot " 21 ", " 22 ", " 23 ". Thus the first three
folios, and others between the present numbers 11 and 12, are missing from this
verdict.

[2] The top left-hand corner of this folio is missing.

[3] The following entries are written on the left-hand half of the folio.

[4] This is the last entry on the left-hand half of the folio.

[5] The following entries are written on the right-hand half of the folio.

[6] This is the last entry on the right-hand half of the folio.

payn to be made before the feste of All Sayntes next commynge yf so be that yt be possypell that menoure may be gotte for the makynge of the same uppon payne of everye hundrethe nott mayd x li.

(*Sotterton Goote*) Item the sayd jurye sayethe uppon theire othes thatt the goote callyd Sotterton Goote lyenge there in Sotterton to drean theire waters leyethe to heye by one fotte wherby the fresshe waters that comethe owte of the fene & the waters of the towen m[ay]¹ nott issew owte of ytt except itt be of suche a great surge & hyght, unto the great hy[ndrance]² & undoyynge of the towens and neyghboures next adioynynge unto them wherfore we p[resent] that ytt may be layd lower except some other juste cawse may be . . . your worsshypes discressions beynge nowe Commissioners for that porpose to survaye & . . .

(*A brydge att Symon Were by S[o]t' Allga' & Fosd'*) Item the sayd jurye doo thynke uppon there othes yt is verye requis[ite] that ther be one foote brydge mayd & erectyd new over the commonde sewer nyghe Symone Were that the quens subiectes may passe whiche ledynge over ther horsse & other cattell save . . . towne to markyt towne & the sayd brydge to be mayd by two hundrethes . . . saye Sotterton Hundrethe & Fosdyke Hundrethe.

[473.VIII.2]   147
By Thomas Roper yoman and hys felowes etc.

(1 *Sott' towne dreane*) In primis the sayde jurye sayithe that a drenn or common sewer begynnes at a place called Symon Werie and frome thens by the est syde of a gatte called Mores Gatte to a place called Acrelande Stowe in Sutterton and from thens to a brydge in Fyschemerend called Wasse Brydge in Sutterton aforesayd & frome thens to a place called John Dycconson House and from thens to the sowthe end of a pasture in Sutterton aforesayd the which pasture ys called Squyertofte and buttes of a waye called Boston Gatt or Strugges Waye and so from the sayd Strugges Waye to the gotte of Algerkyrke and Fosdycke the which sewer is in decaye for lacke of dyckinge as well in brede as in deapnis by the space of iij^{xx} rooedes at the least from Symonde Were to a bredge in Sutterton aforesayd callede Wasse Brigge and oughte to be dycked in breade x fotte and in deapnys two fotte by the inabitauntes of Sutterton Algerkyrke and Fosdycke by common menwarke accordynge to ther olde custome that ys to saye Algarkirke and Fosdycke two pens or two rodes or els two spaydes & Sutterton one penye or j rode or els one spayd and from the sayd brigge in Fyschmerend called Wasse Brigge to a howsse called John Dycconson Howsse is in decaye for lacke of dyckinge aswell in brede as in deapenes the space of xx^{ti} rodes and ought to be dycked in brede x fotte and in deapnes ij fotte more then yt ys nowe by the inhabitauntes of Algerkyrke and Fosdycke by common menwarke and from the sayde house called John Dycconson House to the sowthe end of a pasture called Squyertofte

¹ There is a small hole in the folio here.
² The right-hand bottom corner of this folio is defective.

is in ruin and decaye for lacke of dyckinge scowrynge & clensinge as
well in brede as in deapnis by the space of xx^{ti} rodes and ought to
be dycked the brede of x fotte and in deapens two fotte by the
inhabitauntes of Sutterton aforesayd by common menwarke and
from the sayd sowthe end of Squyertofte to the gotte of Algerkyrke
& Fosdicke ought to by dycked roded scowred and clensed by the
inhabitauntes of Algerkyrke and Fosdicke from tyme to tyme as
ofte as ned shall requeryth by the lordes freholderes & copiholders
by acrey selver and from John Dyckenson housse aforesaid to a
gotte called Sutterton Gotte ought to by dycked roded and scowred
and clensed from tyme to tyme as oft as neade shall requyre by
the lordes frey holders and coppeholders of Sutterton aforesayd by
acrey seyver.

(2 *The stoune brigge in [Fys]chemerend*) Also the sayde jury
sayeth that ther ys a serteyne brigge of stoune in Fyschmerend in
Sutterton aforesayd called Wasse Brigge over the common sewer
of Sutterton Algerkyrke and Fosdycke is in ruin & decaye for lacke
of amendynge and ought to be repared nowe and from tyme to tyme
by the inhabitauntes of Sutterton Algerkyrke and Fosdycke
accordynge to ther olde custom as is aforesayd.

(3 *Gookshorne Laune*) Also they saye that one lyttell layne
called Gookshorm Laune commynge from Symmon Were to Gookshorne and from Gookshone to a housse of one William Howson of
Wigtofte is in ruin and decaye for lacke of exalltynge and amendynge
and for lacke of repareynge in sertine placys by the space of iij^{xx}
roodes from Symmon Were to the forsaide William Howson of
Wygtofte house wiche house is sett in Sutterton in a place called
Fyshmerende and ought to be exallted reparede and amended nowe
and from tyme to tyme as ofte as nead shall requeyrre by the
inhabitauntes of Sutterton Algerkyrke and Fosdycke by common
menwarke as ys aforsayde accordynge to ther olde custome.

[473.VIII.3]   148
                        Anno domini 1565
[1]Also they saye uppon ther othes a sertenne drove waye lyenge
in Wygtoft and Sutterton begynninge at Strugges and from Strugges
to a laynne called Squyer Launne and from Squyer Launne to a
stoune bridge in Fyschmerend in Sutterton aforsaide called Wasse
Brygge and from thens to a place called Acrelande Stowe in Sutterton
aforsayde and from thens into a waye called Mores Gatte in Wigtofte
aforsaide to a place called Symonde Were the whiche drove waye is
in ruin and decaye for lacke of exaltinge reparynge and amendynge
in serten placys the space of a C roodes at the least form[2] Symonde
Were to Acrelande Stowe and ought to be repared exalted and
amended nowe and from tyme to tyme as ofte as neade shall requyre
by the inhabitauntes of Sutterton Algerkyrke and Fosdycke by
common menwarke as ys aforsayde accordynge to ther olde
coustomme.

[1] The left-hand margin of this folio is defective.   [2] *Sic.*

(5 *The west cawsey & the west banke*) The sayde jurye sayeth
that the parte of the West Cawsey leadynge from Swynshed to
Heckenton belongen to Sutterton Algerkyrke and Fosdycke and
also one bancke called the West Bancke from the mydest of the
Mydle Dycke of Willowebowthe to the Hornne ys in ruine and
decaye for lacke of exaltynge reparynge and amendinge the west
cawsey in xl^ti roodes at the least and also the west bancke in xx^ti
roodes and ought to be repared exalted and amended nowe and
from tyme to tyme as ofte as nead shall requyre by the inhabitauntes
of Sutterton Algerkyrke and Fosdycke by common menwarke as ys
aforsaid accordyng to ther olde coustomme.

(6 *Broundedycke Kyme Dycke & the Scott Pyttes   The begynnyng
endyng . . . Scott . . . a . . . dyke*) Also the sayde jury sayth that
the parte of Brounde Dycke of Kyme Dycke and of the Scotte
Pyttes bylongynne to Sutterton Algerkyrke and Fosdycke ys
defectyve for lacke of dyckynge bothe in breade and in deapnes
and Brounde Dycke ought to be dycked the space of xij roodes at
the leaste and to be dycked in breade x footte and two spyttes deaper
then yt is nowe and the parte of the Scotte Pyttes belongynge to
Sutterton Algerkyrke and Fosdycke begynninge at a sertenne round
at the west end of an olde wathe called the Fennehouse Wathe and
from thens to a gutter or drenn at Kyrton Holme goinge towardes
Symonde Were the whiche Scotte Pyttes ys defectyve by the space
of iij^xx roodes at the least and ought to be dyked the brede of xvj
fote & in depnes ij spytes deper & [*sic*] it is att this day by the
inhabitans of Sotterton Allgarkyrke & Fosdyke as is aforesayd to
the olde custome.

[473.VIII.4]   149
Thomas Rop[e]r & his felowes

([*Sw*]*ynshed* [*Wi*]*gtoft*) In primis the said jurye saith upon ther
othes that the banckes of an comman suer called Kyme Dycke
from a place called Wyllowghbothe unto Flete Ende howght to be
repayred by thainhabitunce of Swynshed.

Item they the sayd jurye dothe say that the bancke of the sayd
comman suer from Flete Ende unto Pykelbeke[1] Bowthe howght to
be repayred by thenhabitunce of Wigtoft.

(3) Item the jurye dothe say that the comman dreyne lyenge
betwexe Swynshed and Wigtoft from a place called the Rendell
unto Catcate Brydge howght to be dycked by the lande holderes
of Swynshed and Wigtoft.

(4) Item the jurye doth say that ther is three bridges over the
est & west dreynes that is to say Catcate Bridge Mussyldycke
Bridge & Asperton Bridge and owght to be repayred as oft as nede
requyryth by theinhabitunce of Swynshed.

(5) Item the sayd jurye doth say that ther ys a syke called
Hubbard Syke from Androe Gravye into the Haven & owght to be

---

[1] " Goysegole " cancelled.

dycked & clensed by theinhabitunce of Docdyc' Hyll belonghenge to Swynshed & also by the hole inhabitunce of Brothertoft.

(6)　Item the jurye doth say that the inhabitance of Swynshed & Wigtoft howght to dycke rode skowre & clense a comman suer called Hamond Becke from a dycke called Brande Dycke unto a wayth called Dreyton Wayth.

(7)　Item the sayd jurye doth say that the gote belongeng unto Swynshed & Wigtoft is sufficiently mayd by the land holderes of Swynshed & Wigtoft by acre sylver.

(8)　Item the jurye doth say that the fense at the west end of Symondwer Yate owght to be mayde by the inhabitunce of Fenhowse belonghenge unto Swynshed & Wigtoft when & as oft as nede requyryth.

(9)　Item the jurye doth say that nether Gosberkyrke Quadryng Donyngton & Bycker nor enye of the Eyght Hundryth shall cast eny dammes in Hamond Becke from Gosbertone Cloves unto Skyrbyckgoyte.

(10)　Item the jurye doth say that ther is a staw or damme called Acraland Staw in a place called Fyshmerende within the parrish of Suttertun & hath bene alway accustomed to be kept open from myd Marche day unto myd Apryll for the spedye conveyghance of the water of Swynshed & Wigtoft unto the dreyne of Suttertun Algarkyrke & Fosdycke accordynge to the old & awncie[nt] custome.

[473.VIII.4a][1]
(11)　Item the jurye doth say that ther is an bridge called the Hygh Bridge over Hamand Becke & sufficiently mayde by the inhabitunce of Swynshed & Wigtoft accordyng unto the old custome.

([12])　Item the jurye doth say that Kyme Dyke from Wyllowghboth to Gorsgaull ought to be clensed dycked [&] roded by the commaneres of the Eyght Townes evere man his part . . .

[473.VIII.5][2]　　　　　　　　　　　　　　　　　　　　　　　　　150
. . . performe one goote in stede of theyre ij gootes as we have . . . verdytes.

Item the sayd jurye sayethe that wheras ther is a banke or calsaye extendynge frome Swynshed Hey Fene Brydge over whert the West Fene to a place callyd Hole Dyke wher nott the quenes subiectes onelye have theyre passages frome & oute of Holland & other places unto Lyncoln & other places of the seyd countie but also haythe bene a defence for the fresshe waters dessendynge dowen frome the heye countre towardes Holland Fene which is nowe in greatt ruyng & decaye and the same calsay ought of ryght to be mayd by the holle viij Hundrethe of Kyrkton Wyberton Frantone Sotterton & Allgarkyrke Fosdike Wygtofte & Swynshed accordynge to old verdytes & custome.

---

[1] This is a strip of paper in poor condition, probably the head of a larger sheet.
[2] The head of this folio is missing and the marginal notes are almost illegible.

B

Item they saye that one banke extendyng frome the sayd calcey ende by the sayde Hole Dyke to a place callyd the Parkes & soo to the Horne leynge in Holland Fene & ought to be bankyd for the defence of the fresshe waters by the sayd viij^te Hundrethe ys lykwyse defectyve to the great hyndraunce of the sayd comaunders of the sayd viij^te Hundrethe.

Item the sayd jurye sayethe that ther is one drean belongynge to the viij^te Hundreth Fene callyd the Skyrthe begyngnynge att a place callyd Bacon Tofte & so goynge to a place callyd Androwe Grave which is in reuynge & decaye & owght to be dykyd rodyd & scouryd as ofte as nyde shall require by the inhabitaunces of the viij^te Hundrethe every hundrethe his equall parte as haythe bene accustomyd of olde.

Item thay saye further that the sayd drean frome Andrew Grave unto Hoberd Syke Ende & so issewynge into the Haven callyd Wythome is lykwysse defectyve & owght to be dyked roodyd & scouryd frome tyme to tyme soo ofte as nyd shall require by the inhabitaunce of Docdyke belongynge to the parrysshe of Swynshed & the inhabitaunce of Brothertofte as haythe bene paynyd by other verdytes hertofore mayd.

(*Clowes by Boston*) Item the sayd jurye sayethe that the inhabitaunce of the west syde of Boston ought to erecte sett and mayntayne one pare of clowes contaynynge in bred syxe fote in the corner of the bytes next unto the Skyrthe within the forsayd syke callyd Hoberd Syke as apperethe by verdyt of George Hylton & his fellow sworne in the syxt yere of Edward the syxt and as yett nott mayd to the great hyndraunce of the commeners of the viij^te Hundrethe by reson that the salt wate[r] doothe over flow the sayd command in the somer tyme wherfore we pray that the same may be sett accordynglye.

[473.VIII.6]   151
[1]Item we saye that wheras the holle viij Hundrethe is chargyd with ij smale gootes leynge att the syke ende att Langrake for the drenynge of the fene and . . . Brothertofte ought to damme rame & exalte the same gootes as ofte as nyde shall require as thay be chargyd uppon payn of everye defalte iiij^or li. by sertayne verdytes which thay have nott done to the great hyndraunce of the sayd viij^te Hundrethe & to the great daunger & peryll of decaynge & leasynge of same gootes.

(*Fysshermene*) Item the sayd jurye sayethe that ther shall no fysshermen of none of all the viij^te Hundrethe nor Brothertoft nor none other persone shall make eny whersted purpastures or dammes for any maner of nettes or leppes in any drean or petie drean in the sayd viij^te Hundrethe Fene uppon payn of everye werested purpasture or dame so mayd to forfyt v li.

([*Hem*]*pe* & [*fla*]*xe*) Item the sayd jurye thynkythe yt very

---

[1] The left-hand margin of this folio is defective.

nesserye & convenient for the commaund wealthe of the hole
countre that no maner of persone or persones att any tyme herafter
shall ley cast stepe or synke any hempe or flaxe in any dytche pytte
pole or water place by the heye wayes or commaund wayes within
the wepontake of Kyrkton wher the quens subiectes have ther
passages by the space of iiijᵒʳ hundrethe fote att the leste nor in no
commaund sewer petie drean or any other water cources within the
sayd wepontake that be for the conveaunces of the waters uppon
payn of every one soo doynge fyve markes.

(8 *Eliz.* . . . [g]*ootes* . . . *Inquisitions*) Item we saye that wher
there was iij inquisicions hertofore passyd & founde one by Thomas
Cave the yonger of Kyrkton charged & sworne the iiij day of August
in the xxxvj yere of kynge Henrye the viijᵗᵉ and a nother inquisicion
by George Hylton of Donyngton gent' the xvij day of Septemper
in the fyrst yere of Edward the syxt and the thyrd was passyd by
Robert Stevenson of Kyrkton chargyd & sworn in the 3 & 4 yeres
of kynge Philype & quen Marye yt was found & presentyd that was
nydfull & profytable for the safegard of the countre to have viij
smalle gootes layd & mayd uppon the banke of the haven att Langrake in the syke ende issewynge owte of the Lawe Fen & Hey Fene
callyd the viijᵗᵉ Hundrethe Fene to drean shuch waters as passythe
by the sayd fenes unto the sayd syke & the sayd gootes & everye
one of the sayd gootes contayne in lenght xx fote & in brede or
depnes ij fote att the lest & foure of the same gootes to be mayd layd
& kept by the holle inhabitaunce of the viij C & two of the same to
be mayd & layd & kept by the inhabitaunce of Quadrynge Donyngton & Byker & the other two to be layd mayd & kept by the inhabitaunce of Swaton Byllyngborrow & Horblynge, wherof we saye
uppon our othes that the towens of the viij Hundrethe have layd
two and that Quadrynge Donnyngton & Byker have layd one in
parte of performaunce of thos verdytes before rehersyd but the
towens of [K]esten as Byllyngborrow Swaton & Horblynge have not
in no maner of wyse [acco]mplyshed any kynde of thynge in the
verdytes hertofore mayd to the great undoynge of the hole countre
wherfore we pray that the same towens may be chargyd with some
parte as the other towens be accordyng to the sayd old verdytes.

[473.VIII.7]   152
Gosbertown & Surflet

(1) Fyrst Henry Death & Rychard Hunyngham of Gosbertown
and Thomas Margerson & Jhon Pett of Surflet sworn upon ther
othes do say that ther is a pare of clowes in Surflet standyng at a
place called Lowgate which is greatly decayd & broken and it is
meet necessarye & convenyent that the said clowes be newly made
erected & sett up in the same place where they now stand or nyghe
therunto. And the same clowes owght to be mayd repared and
amended from tyme to tyme by the lordes & landes holderes of
Gosbertown & Surflet by acre sylver as of old tyme they have ben
accustomed.

(2)   Item the sayd jurey say that ther is an other pare of clows at Rusgate whych is in ruen & decay & owght to be amendid & reparid by the lordes & land holders of Gosbertown & Surflet by acre sylver.

(3)   Item the sayd jury say that ther is a common sewer calid the Drean under the sedyke wythin the shyfe of Surflet whyche is defectyve in serteyn playces as herafter foloweth for lack of dykyng and the same places owght to be dyked by those persones herafter folowyng that is to say at a place nygh unto the gote by the space of xij rodes by Robert Merkin esqyuer.   And at an other place in the same ryver nygh Common Hyrn xxxix rodes whych owght to be dyked & clensed by the landholders of late Sir Jhon Tempest knyght & ther next adioynyng abowt ten roodes whych owght to be dyked by the landholders of Robert Paygnham esquyer.

(4)   Item the sayd jurye say that ther is a brygg over the common sewer called the Becche at a place callid Hawkenges which is defectyve & owght to be mayd repared and amendid by the lordes & landholders of Gosbertown & Surflet.

(5)   Item the sayd jury say ther is a pare of clowes at Wryghtbold whych is in ruen & decay whyche doth great anoyaunce to the townes of Gosbertown & Surflet whych owght to be mayd & repayrid from tyme to tyme by the inhabytantes of Burn Dyke Morton & Cawthorpe.

(6)   Item the sayd jurye say ther is a lode called Poynton Lode whych is in ruen & decay and owght to be dyked & clensed by the lordes & inhabeyters of Gosberkerk & Surflet as hathe bene accustomed of long tyme.

(7)   Item the sayd jurye say that ther is certayne places in the mayne dreane w[it]hin the parysshe of Gosberkerk under the see bank which owght to be amended by the lordes of Gosberkerk.

(8)   Item the sayd jurye say ther is a brygg called the Fen End Brygg which is in ruen [&] decay & owght to be repared & amended by the inhabyters of Gosberkerk & Surflet as hath bene accustomed.

(9)   Item the sayd jury say that ther is a bank called the North Bank that goeth from Westhrop Barres to the fen[1] . . . whych is in ruen & decay and owght to be mayd by the lordes & landholders thereof abut[ting.]

(10)   Item the sayd jurye say that ther is a bank called the Beche Banke whyche is in ruen . . . in certayn places from the clowes at Wryghtbold to the Park Corner & owght to [be repaired] and amended by Lawrence Robynson for Wryghtbold & Mr. Zouche.

[473.VIII.8]   153

[2]Fyrste the jury saythe that one comen sewere called Hamonde Becke or the Newedyke extendyng frome Surflyte Fyne to one place called Marlode is defyctyve in deveres places for lacke of dekyng

---

[1] The bottom right-hand corner of this folio is defective.
[2] The top left-hand corner of this folio is defective.

rodyng & scoweryng & it owghte to be dekyed roded & scowered frome tyme to tyme as ofte as nede shall requer by the cheffe lordes & the lande honeres of Quadryng & the hundrythe of Quadryng.

(*[Ne]we[dy]ke Banke*) Also the sayd jury saythe that one banke called the Newdyke Banke is defyctyve in devers places as herafter shall apere more at large & it oughte to be bankyed & mayd frome tyme to tyme as ofte as nede shall requere as is aforesayd & the sayd banke extendes frome one style standyng betwyxte Surflyte Drove & us to one place called Marlode as a jouse boke doithe apere.

(*The Upfyn Banke*) Also the sayd jury saythe that one banke called the Upfyne Banke is defyctyve in devers places for lacke of brede & heyghte as it oughte to be & it oughte to be mayde & amendyd frome tyme to tyme as ofte as nede shall requer by the honeres of the landes leyng & buttyng of the sayme banke accordyng to the olde custome ther ussed & it extyndes frome one place called Wesstrope Bares to a place called Strop Hyrne.

(*The tondam of the north syd of the eye*) Also the sayd jury saythe that one tondam leyng of the north syd the eye for the defynce of Donyngton waters is defyctyve for lake of hyghte in devers places as it oughte to be & it oughte to be mayd & amynded frome tyme to tyme as ofte as nede shall requer by the lande honers leyng nexte to the saym tondam & it extyndes from one place called the Strope Hyrne to a place called Garly Halstedes at Quadryng Eyedyke which is to the greate hurte of the inhabetance there & the northe parte of Gosbertowne.

(*The tondam of the southe syde of the eye*) Also the sayd jury saythe that one tondam leynge of the southe syde of Quadryng Eye is defyctyve in devers places for lacke of brede & heyghte & it oughte to be mayd & repared frome tyme to tyme as ofte as nede shall requer by the honeres of the landes leyng & buttyng of the sayme.

(*Baram Lode*) Also the said jury saythe that one pete drene called Baram Lode is in rewyng & decake for lacke of dykyng scowryng & clynsyng & it oughte to be dekyed scowered & clynsed as ofte as nede shall requere from tyme to tyme by the land honeres leyng & buttyng nexte to the saym lode of boithe sydes by eyvne porciones & the sayde lode begynes at the weste syd of a paster called Baram to a place called Chyntofte Stone & ther overe the way by comene mynwarke & so to a brydge called Cole Brydge & frome thynce [to] a place called the Lowe Gayte & of the north syde of the saym gayte & so to Angote.

(*Colle Brydge*) Also the sayd jury saythe that one brydge called Colle Brydge leyng in the northende of Gosbertowne is defyctyve for lacke of brede & depnes & it oughte to be mayd repared & amended frome tyme to tym as ofte as nede shalle requer by the northe parte of Gosbertowne.

(*The Drall*) Also the sayd jury saythe that one pete drene called the Dralle desyndyng frome the wyste syde of Stonges . . . is in rewyng & decake for lake of dykyng scowryng & clynsyng & it oughte to be dekyed scowered & clyn[sed][1] frome tyme to tyme as ofte as ned shall requere by the land honeres leyng & buttyng nexte to the say[d] Dralle of boith sydes by evne porciones & it goythe thoro the landes layte Thomas Pasmer & at his howse . . . the way by comene mynwarke & so bytwyxte a paster called Wydetofte & the landes layte the fo[rsay]d Thomas & so thorghte the sayd paster to a fote way called the Dralle & overe the quenes hey way by [common]e mynwarke & to the Pasnyche Layth & overe the way there by comen mynworke & so frome th . . . to Alldyke Lode.

(*Alldyke Lode*) Also the sayd jury saythe that one petey dryne called Aldyke Lode is in rewynge & decake for lacke of dekyng scowryng & clynsyng & it oughte to be deked scowered & clensed frome tym to tyme as ofte as nede shall requer by the honers of the landes leyng & buttyng nexte to the sayme lode of boythe sydes by ewyne porciones & it bygynes at the weste syde of a paster called Podholle & so bytwyxte the landes of our sowerayng layde the quenes maistes bylonggyne to Monkes Halle & the landes layte Andrew Nowell esquer in the tener of William Wylson & so it goyeth by the southe syde of Alldyke Fyllede & so to the Lowe Gayte of the northe syde of the sayme gayte & so to Angote.

[473.VIII.9] 154

[2][Also] the sayd jury saythe that one gote called Angotte is defyctyve for lacke [of] pychynge & other thynges & it oughte to be mayd repared & amended frome tyme to tyme as ofte as nede shall requer by acare sylvere of the landes within Quadryng & the northe parte of Gosbertowne as it haith byne of old tym.

[A]lso the sayd jury saythe that ther is a sartayne fylde drene leyng at Angotte for the convauunces of the fylde wateres to the sey & it is defyctyve in deveres places for lacke that it is not dekyed of brede & deptenes as it oughte to be and it oughte to be dekeyd scowered & clensyde frome tyme to tyme as ofte as nede shalle requere by the chyufe lordes & the lande honeres of Quadryng & Quadryng Hundrythe & all the landes that drene be it.

([*B*]*oston* [*B*]*rydge*) Also the sayd jury saythe that one brydge called Boston Brydge leyng at the saltcotes is newely repared & amended & so oughte to be kypete from tyme to tyme as is aforsayd.

([*T*]*he new gotte*) Also the sayd jury saythe that one gote called the Newgote is defyctyv for lacke of pychyng & landyng and it oughte to be mayd repared & amended frome tyme to tym as ofte as nede shall requer by acar selvere as is aforsayd.

(*The oute fale*) Also the sayd jury saythe the oute fale frome the sayd gotte to the sey is defyctyve in deveres places for lacke of dykyng scoweryng & clynsyng & it oughte to be dekyed scowered & clensed from tym to tym as ofte as need shall requere by comenwarke by the inhabetance aforsayd.

[1] Two small pieces are missing from the right-hand side of this folio.
[2] The top left-hand corner and part of the left-hand margin of this folio are missing.

(*Defaytes in the Newdyke Banke*) The greate defaytes in the
Newdyke Banke & of whome

[1]Inprimis Mr Awdryne Stokes	ij rodes
Item of Mr Schouch	ij rodes ij fote
Item the quenes mayistee for the chauntry of Gosbortowne	j rode
The saym for Monkes Halle	v rodes di.
The sayme for the chauntry of Quadryng	iiij rodes
Item Thomas Bolles gnetell [*sic*]	ij rodes
Item John Toplyche	j rode
Item Thomas Browne for Kyme landes	di. rode
Item Mr Cawode	iiij rodes di.

(*Defaytes in the Upfyn Banke*) In the Upfyne Banke

Inprimis Mr Thomas Bolles	iiij rodes
[2]Item the heares of John Shepard	iiij rodes

[3]Defaytes of the tondam of the northe syde of the eye
Inprimis Rycharde Ormeshed for a heydyng at Wilowtofte
Item Symonde Snell for my layde Meares lande
Item the quenes maiste agaynste a pynggell in the tener of Richard
  Ormeshed.
[4]Item Jamys Harryman for a paster in the tener of Adam Nese.

[473.VIII.10]   155

[5]. . . jure sayth that ther ys a dicke called Newdicke extendynge
from Hellpringham Becke to a place called Cranmer which is defictyve for lacke of rodyng, scowring, dikyng and clensinge, and
which ought to be mayd, rowdid, scowred, clensed, diked, and
sufficiently banked, by the inhabitors of Biker.

Item the sayd jury dothe saye that ther ys one dreane called
Hammond Becke extendinge from Cranmer to Swane Warth which
ys difectyve for lacke of roding, dikyng, clensing and banking and
which ought to be diked, rodid, banked, scowred and clensed, by
the lordes and land houlders of Byker by acrege.

(*Swane Warth*) Item the sayd jure saythe that ther ys a ryver extending from Swane Warth to Mr Holand Rought with the syxt parte
of Mr Holand Rought whyche ys defícktive for lacke of roding,
dickinge, clensing and scowring and ought to be dicked, clensed,
rodid, and scowred by the inhabitors of Bicker by common menwarke.

(*Pete d[rean]*) Item the sayd jure saythe that ther ys a pete drean
extending from Grene Gotte End and cometh owre a way at a place
called the loyes of Henry Jackson, and so to Horsomgate, and so
fawlleth into the eaye at Beriges Dore, which ys defective for lacke

---

[1] The following entries are written in the left-hand half of the folio.
[2] This is the last entry in the left-hand half of the folio.
[3] The following entries are written in the right-hand half of the folio ; the distances
have not been entered by the clerk.
[4] This is the last entry in the right-hand half of the folio.
[5] Part of the top left-hand corner of this folio is missing.

of roding and scowring and so owght to be roded s[c]owred and clensed from tyme to tyme so oft as ned shal require by the inhabitors of Byker by common menwark.

(*Mr Holand Rought*)   Item the sayd jure doth say that the one half of Mr Holand Rowght ys defictyve for lacke of diking, bankyng, rodynge, clensinge and scowringe, and owght to be diked, banked, roded, scowred and clensed by the inhabitors of Horbling, Hell-pringham and Swaton, from tyme to tyme as ofte as ned shal require which they do not to the utter undoing of the country.

(*Tha [sic] wersted*)   Item the sayd jure sayth that ther ys thre wers or dammes kept in the same rowght by George Carre, the which remaneth but ix foute wide at the most, the which ought to be equall with the common sure called Hamond Becke both ther and in al other places which owght to be xiiij fote wide at the least wherfore we pray that the same maye be pullyd upp or ells mayd wyder so that the waters which passythe throwghe the same may nott be molestyd & troblyd but have the ryght course to the see.

Finis Byker

[473.VIII.11]   156

[1]. . . [th]er ys a common way for the passage of the quenes subiectes out of the partes of Holand . . . within the partes of Kesten and Holand extendyng from a place or house at Brigend called [Saint S]aviours in the partes of Kesten unto a place called the Hye Brig of Brigdike in Donington in the partes of Holand . . . hye way or common way called Brigdike ys greatly in ruen and decay and many briges in sundry places . . . cawuse as wel for the convaynce of waters as for the passwage of the quenes subiectes and that . . . frustrate and brokyng decaed and clearly gone to the great noyanes let desturbans and hendrans of [th]e quenes subiectes which forsayd hye way cawuse or commonway from the sayd place or house at Brigend called Saint Saviours in the partes of Kesten unto the meadest of the sayd Hye Brige of Brigdike in the partes of Holand owght to be mayd repared and amended with certane other briges in certane places of [the] sayd cawuse or hye way . . . the howse of Saint Savers at Brigend aforsayd with the landes and tenementes to the same house belonging and appertaining now in possision of the quenes majestie.

(. . . *gges Hamonbeck*)   Item the sayd jure saye that ther ys a common sewer within the paryshe of Sweinnished called Mr Holand Roughtes parcel & parte of Hammonbeke which ys in ruen and defective for lake of dyking rodyng and clensyng and bankinge as hath bene appoynted and assigned to bene diked roded and clensed by the inhabitance of Quadringe Donington and Biker in the partes of Holand and Byllynborrowe Horblynge and Swaton in the partes of Kesten, and the forsayd inhabitance of Quadringe Donington and Biker have diked and scowared ther partes thereof and the sayd

---

[1] Part of the top left-hand corner of this folio is missing.

inhabitance of Byllyngborrow Horblenge and Swaton hath done nothynge at the other part therof, that should have bene done by the sayd townes of Byllyngborrow Horblyng and Swaton, wherof the sayd jure doth saye that the sayd townes of Billingborrow Horbling and Swaton owght to do the sayme as by other ould verdetes hath bene assigned befor forasmuch as the same place in the sayd common suer ys so greatly landed that nether the water that should have the passwage and course by the same cannot passe nor also such persons that should have passwage throwght the same with ther caregges to the great noyance of the contry both of the water course and caregges.

(*Sowth Yng Dicke*) And further the sayd jure doth saye that ther ys one bancke called the Sowth Ynge Bank whych ys by extemation one mile and a half extending from a place called Kinnitoftstyll unto a place called Wissmans House which ys in ruen and decay and ought to be heaned and banked by the lordes and land houlders of Donington.

(*Goldik Banke*) Item the sayd jure doth saye that ther ys one bancke called Goldike Banke which ys by extimation one mile extendyng from a place called Marlode unto a place called the Hye Brig of Brigdike and ys defictive in certayne places and ought to be mayd by the lordes and land houlder [*sic*] of in [*sic*] the paryshe of Donington.

(*Shofe and South Yng Banke*) Item the sayd jure saye that ther ys a banke called Shoffe and Sowth Yng Banke which ys by extimation one mile and a quarter extendyng from Kynnitoftstyll to Marlod Cornar and ys defictive in certane places and ought to be mayd and mayntened so ofte as nedd shal require by the common menwarke of Donington.

(*Cranmer Banke*) And further the sayd jure doth say that ther ys one bank called Cranmer Banke and Parke Bank extendyng from Havertoft Styl to Biker Cranmer which ys by extimation one mile and halfe which ys defictive in certane places and owght to be banked and mayd by the comman menwarkes of the townshypp of Donington.

(*The [Eaye] and [Par]kdike*) Item the sayd jure saye that there ys one dike called the Eaye and Parkdike which extendeth from Brownistoft End to the Roughtes End and so doth proced within iiij roudes of the chappel of Brigd[ike] which ys by extemation iij miles and ys defictive in certane places and owght to be diked scowered and clensed when ned shal require by the common menwarkes of the townshep of Donington.

[473.VIII.12] 157

Serten artyckles of the . . . here after dothe folow. Dated the xxj of October anno 1565 by ther othes.

(*The queens banke from Brotherhouse*) Item that ther is one banck lyinge frome Brother Housse unto Croylande one the easte syde of Wealand the which is defeatyce in many places & ought for to be repared & mad by our soferaygn lady the quenes majesty for the late monastarye of Croyland.

(*And her . . . banke to Dowsedale*) Item the sead jury seayth that ther is another banck lyinge or beynge from Croyland unto Dousdayll upon the east syde on the water of Nene which is faulty in many places & ought for to be repared & made by our soferanyg ladye the quenes majesty for the aforsead monestory of Croyland.

(*The streeme to xxx Acre Barre by William Gabye*) Item the same jurye dothe seaye that the streme from Dowsdall unto Thertye Acare Bare is allso fauty which ought for to be repared & made cleane by William Gabye the tennante & fermer ther of wythe rodeynge & haffyng.

(*thens to Seynt Guthlac Crosse by John Pinder*) Item the aforesead jurye seath that the same streme from Thertye Acare Bare unto a place caled Sente Goodlackes Crose is in lyke defaute wher of the on halfe ought for to be repared [by] John Pynder for the towneshype of Croyland & the other halfe by Mores Bexwell for the lordshyp of Tharnnye.

[*Numbered at the bottom:*] 21

[473.VIII.13]   158

(22 . . . *bank betwene Brotherhouse & Catchecold*) Item the same jurye seathe that ther is a banck betwene Brother Housse & Kash-could called Newe Bancke which is iij myles in lenthe that is fautye in many places and ought for to be repared by our soferang lady the quenes majesty for her tennantes in Croyland.

(*Betwene Catchcold & Shepe Ee Stowe*) Item the same jurey seathe that ther ys a banck betwene Kachcould & Shyppestowe one myle in lenthe the whiche is in default in many places and ought for to be repared & amendyd by our sofaryng lady the quene for the mentynance of her tennantes in Croyland and for the safttye of Holand.

(*Partycler defaltes*) Item the jurye seathe that ther ys defectyve of the bancke betwene Brother Howsse and Croyland aforsead that ther is, 50 rodes of the preestes, 3 rodes of Wylliam Cottes and a halfe, of the heres of Wylliam Pynnders 5 rodes, of John Dorante 2 rodes & a halfe, Jhames Robynsones 20 rodes, Thomas Rogers the yongare fyve rodes, of the heres of Wylliam Pynder aforsead 5 rodes, Wylliam Colyere 5 rodes, Richard Weche the yonger aforesead 10 rodes fautye and ought for to be mendyd.

[*Numbered at the bottom:*] 22

[473.VIII.14a]   159

(*Dreynes in Alderlod the Old Lode*) Item the same jury seayth that ther is a pettye drene called the Owld Lode extendyng from a pl[ace] called the Greynes unto the water of Nene the which ought for to be clenesed and kepe by Roger Banker the fysher ther of.

(*A dreyn frome Greynes to Folwerd Stakyng & so to Southlake*) Item the same jury dothe seaye that ther is another pettye drene

extendyng from the place called the Grenynes as well unto a place
called Foulleares Stacke ¹& so to South Lake by . . . Syngle Sole
& so to Thorney¹ the which ought for to be clensed by John Dorant
& Robert Anarton the fyshares ther of² . . . Grenes & the other to
. . . by the proffyt takers of . . . within the partes of Borow Soke and
that from Folwerd Stakyng to Weyland there ys a lyke drene called
Sowthlake to be repayred by the . . . thereof and ys . . . stopped as
more att large appereth in the other verdytt of the

³[473.VIII.14b]   160
presentment of the deg'.²

(*South Eye to Perkyns Cote by the lord of Bedford or his tenantes*)
Item the same jurye seathe that the commone swere called Southe
Eye extendyng from Dowssdall southe syde unto a place called
Perkynes Cote is in great ruyng & decaye for lacke of hafyng
rodyng clensyng & scowryng which ought to be done by the lord of
Bedforthe, or by his tennantes or fermmers of Thornay.
[*Numbered at the bottom:*] 23

[473.VIII.15]   161
⁴[T]he vardett of the degreffes for the townshepe of Molltone at
the sessions of [the]sewars holden at Bostone the viij day of October
in the yeare . . . [G]od 1565 in the sevent yeare of the rayng of owre
sovrun lade Elezabayth by the gras of God of Yngland France &
Irland quene.

[Fi]rst the jury saith upone ther othes that ther ys one dyck or
bank in Molltone called the Lowe Dycck ys in rewyng & decaye in
dyvars places [that is] to say our soverane lade the quene for v
rodes Rychard Boolls esquiar for v rodes John Bygott of Molltone
in too bankes of . . . said Lowe Dycck for x rod & the ayres of
Scarlytes in the same dycck iiij rodes John Blanke in the same dycck
iiij rod Robert [Dor]bagge in the same dycck iiij rod & the fefers of
the scolle of Molltone for iiij rodes & the Collegge of Saynct Johns in
Cambrig . . . Cranwels landes iiij rodes.

Item the sayd jury sayth that ther ys on other dyccke or bank
called the Goole Dycck in Mollton ys defecttyve in dyvars places
that ys to say the quines maieste in the same dycck xx rod Thomas
Halle in the same dycck iiij rod Thomas Kynge sennior in the same
dyck iiij rod Jhone Martyng in the same dycck iiij rodes John
Bygott in the same dyk for ij bankes viij rod & the ayres of Sanders
iiij rodes Gylbart Lynsay in the sam dycck iiij rodes Robert Dor-
bagge of Molton in the same dycck iiij rodes.

Item the sayd jury sayth that ther ys on other dyck or bank in
Moltone called Garners Dycck otherwyse cald Ravensdyke ys
defectyve in dyvars places that ys to say the quines maieste in the

---

¹⁻¹, ²⁻² These sections have been added in another hand which is almost illegible.
³ 14a and 14b appear to have been one folio. A cut has been made through the
middle of what is now the bottom line on 14a.
⁴ Part of the left-hand margin of this folio is missing.

same dyck x rod & the lordes of Molton Halle in the same dycck xx
rod Rychard Bolls esquier [in] the same dyck vj rod William Tasche
junior Thomas Dawsone for v rod in the same dyck for Marrettes
landes.

[Item] the sayd jury sayth that ther ys one heddyng betwext the
comone sewer of Molton & the Lowe Felld of the est syd of the sayd
. . . the sayd sewere ys defecttyve ij rod in length & bredth the sayd
hedyng owght to be repared in brydth & lyngth by on Wylliam
. . . rkare of Ufyngtone.

Item the sayd jury sayth that ther ys one other heddyng betwixt
the sayd comone sewer & Lowe Feld on the est syd of the sayd seware
ys defecttyv in length & bredth iij rod & owght to be repared & mayd
by Robert Tego of Molltone.

Item the sayd jury sayth that ther ys on other heddyng betwyxt
the sayd sewar & the sayd Lowe Feld on the est syd of the sayd
seware ys defecttyve xx rodes & owght to be repayred in bredth &
hyght be John Bygott of Mollton.

. . . the sayd jury sayth that ther ys one other heddyng betwyxt
the sayd seware & Fowr Knobll Medowe of the est syd of the sayd
sewar . . . in bredth & hayght xx rod & owght to be repayred & mayd
by Thomes Kyng sennior & Thomes Kyng junior.

. . . sayth that ther ys on dyck or banke called the Doledycck ys
defecttyve & owght to be repared & mayd by . . . that ther owght to
be sett one payr of barres at the end of the sayd dyck . . . owghte to
. . .

[*Endorsed*:] Verd^t 1565

VERDICT FOR KIRTON WAPENTAKE, RIVER WELLAND ETC., 1566

[473.IX.1–7]   *Part printed*   162–168

[162 relates to Skirbeck Quarter, 163 to Frampton and Holland
Fen, 164 to Wyberton and Kirton, 165 to the River Welland, 166–8
to the River Glen and the Bourne Ea. Much of the verdict is in
poor physical condition and it might have been omitted altogether.
165 however gives the background to 165a which follows, and has
therefore been included despite the incomplete state of the text.]

[473.IX.4]   165

[1]The vardet of John Covell & his fellows maid the ix daye of
J . . . 1566 . . . the eyght yer of the reigne of our soverang lady
quene . . .

. . . that the rever of Weyland from Brother Hous to John
Clo . . . nd conteyneth in length nyne hundred and xxx rodes after
six score . . . inge xx^{ti} foot which rever cannot be dyked by reason
that yt is . . . stand in it to dyke. And haffe hath so instratened
the same rever . . . but by that means ys so stoppid that yt will
sor . . . rever to the great undoinge of the quens maiesties tennauntes

[1] The condition of this folio is poor ; the right margin is missing, and the left
half of the folio is much stained and almost illegible.

and ot[her] . . . the said rever from Brother House untyll Clonys Ho[use] . . . to the hard bothom, and mayd of the wid[nes] . . . thus to be done will cost ij s. viij d. the rode which . . . which is the quens mayesties charge as for her severall fi[shing] . . . belonginge to the late monestarie of Spalding and from Cloyne[s] . . . [con]teyneth in lenght syx hundreth and xij rodes after six score . . . rod which must be dyked from the said place aforsayd of the depth of iij foo[t] . . . the widnes of xl^{ti} foote untill the metinge of the watt[ers] . . . to be of the widnes of thirti foote and this ch . . . which amounteth to the sum, nyne score, and iij^{li} which . . . as for her severall fysshinge in the same rever belonging to . . . [Sp]alding And from Peck Bridge douneward to the see for the . . . is to be dikid one spit deper then it is now, and of . . . and this to be done at the charge of Deping Croulond Spalding . . . [Mo]ulton and all other commoners in Depinge and Spaldinge Fenne, and . . . done for the summe of xxx^{ti} vj li. and so the same rever of Weylond . . . stratened of the widnes of xxiiij^{ti} foote from thend of the iij Hundreth . . . aforsayd in divers places as shalbe thought met bevew untill . . . at Surflet toune end, and the said jettes to be may[d] . . . only will so instrat the rever and mak the owt fall so depe . . . so soround the bankes as it hath done hertofor and allso . . . in such pereil of drowninge as it will do yf this be not with all sp[eed] . . . this so dowing the diking of the rever of Weylond . . . of this jetteinge aforsaid must be done at the char[ge] of the inhabytaunts [of] D[eping Cro]wland Spalding Pinchbek Weston and Moulton and all other . . . Spalding Fenne.

. . . said juri saith that befor this rever of Weylond be dikid, a da[m] . . . substanncially mayd at John Cloynes house for the staynge of the wa[ter] . . . dyked from thenc to Pecke Bridge & so forther as is . . . as much as the substaunciall making and takinge upp of . . . the quenes maiesties charg to do, yet the inhabitaunce of Deping . . . [Pinchb]eck Weston and Moulton and all other commeners in Dep[ing] . . . contented for this time onely to be at the charg of . . . Weylond and of the taking yt up agayn And allso the . . . Deping and Spalding Fenn to be at the charge of . . . upp of all thos dammes in the fenne dreans that fall into W . . . after the dyking of Weylond the same dammes to be by them clenn . . . that ther may be a slaker mayd at the hed of the great d . . . Cloynys House or else in some other convenient place apon vew mayd that the watter of . . . in Depyng & Spalding Fenne duringe the tim that the dame . . .

[*The endorsement is illegible.*]

ACCOUNTS FOR DIKING THE RIVER WELLAND, 1567

[490.I.1–12]   *Part printed*   165a

[This document, actually a wages book, is in form nothing but a list of names and payments comprising nearly 800 individual entries. To print these *in extenso* could scarcely be justified in this edition ; and it was doubtless this that decided Miss Kirkus to omit the document from her scheme of publication. Yet it ought not to be passed over without a mention, for it is one of the very few Holland

records surviving from this period which show how the works of
sewers called for by the sewers juries were actually carried out.
Verdicts and "laws" serve, as it were, to illustrate the theory of
land drainage, but we need also to see it in practice, and this the
accounts enable us to do.   Accordingly the contents of the first two
folios and a small part of the third, which record the first week's
wages for all the labourers from Pinchbeck and Spalding—the two
places which bore the brunt of the work—are printed to illustrate
the form of entry, together with the concluding entries on folio 11.
The information available from the accounts is then analysed on
pages 21-4.]

[490.I.1]
Thaccompt of John Gamblin and William Atkinson for the dykinge
of Weylond 1567
    [1] . . . Walpoll Mr Antro . . .

[490.I.1*d*]
                    1567° anno ix° regine Elizabethe
The chardge of John Gamlyn William Atkynson William Wylsbye
Robert Iden Nicholas Worliche John Hynde John Weldon & John
Tygh receyvores & surveyores and paymasters for the som of cc li.
delyvered to them in prest out of her majesties tresure cc li. wherof
payd as followeth

[490.I.2]
The quenes maiestyes charge for the dykyng of the ryver of
Weyland frome Spaldyng Hyghe Bridge to Cubbytt churche anno
1567
(The laboreres in the weypontake of Ello)

	Deyes	Wages	Bord
John Styles	6	ij s.	ij s. viij d.
Richard Glover	6	ij s.	ij s. viij d.
(Pynchebecke laboreres)			
John Darwyne	6	ij s.	ij s. viij d.
Thomas Vassell	6	ij s.	ij s. viij d.
Roberd Ireland	6	ij s.	ij s. viij d.
Christofer Harlewyn	6	ij s.	ij s. viij d.
John Storkes	6	ij s.	ij s. viij d.
John Whiteacres	6	ij s.	ij s. viij d.
William Totteridge	2	viij d.	x d.
George Mason	2	viij d.	x d.
Anthony Munforth	2	viij d.	x d.
James Ammone	2	viij d.	x d.
William Whippe	2	viij d.	x d.
John Criplyne	2	viii d.	x d.
George Bate	2	viij d.	x d.
Richard Foster	2	viij d.	x d.

[1] Words obscured by repair paper.

John Carter	2	viij d.	x d.
Richard Clerke	2	viij d.	x d.
Symon Mylner	2	viij d.	x d.
[1]John Foster	2	viij d.	x d.
[2]William Caster	2	viij d.	x d.
Richard Rey	2	viij d.	x d.
John Wryght	2	viij d.	x d.
William Tylson	2	viij d.	x d.
William Lancaster	2	viij d.	x d.
John Pattenson	2	viij d.	x d.
John Wylson	2	viij d.	x d.
Roberd Styles	2	viij d.	x d.
Thomas Allythorpe	2	viij d.	x d.
Thomas Elland	2	viij d.	x d.
John Heyres	2	viij d.	x d.
John Drope	2	viij d.	x d.
Gylberd Glover	2	viij d.	x d.
Thomas Wylford	2	viij d.	x d.
Richard Gilberd	2	viij d.	x d.
John Averye	2	viij d.	x d.
Richard Walker	2	viij d.	x d.
Thomas Nicolles	2	viij d.	x d.
Richard Steynthorpe[3]		viij d.	x d.
[4]Roberd White	2	viij d.	x d.

Sum' of the wages   xxxvij s. iiij d.   Sum' of the bord   xlviij s.
 Sum' t'   iiij li. v s. iiij d.

[490.I.2*d*]

(*Spaldyng*)	Deyes	Wages	Bord
Richard Horner	4	xvj d.	xxj d.
Nicholas Stanwell	3	xij d.	xvj d.
Thomas Fyssher	5	xx d.	ij s. ij d.
Thomas Pococke	7	ij s. iiij d.	iij s. j d.
Anthony Burgh	5	xx d.	ij s. ij d.
Thomas Pettryll	6	ij s.	ij s. viij d.
Nicholas Heynsworth	1	iiij d.	v d.
Roberd Harecastle	6	ij s.	ij s. viij d.
William Kendale	5	xx d.	ij s. ij d.
Thomas Attkynson	6	ij s.	ij s. viij d.
John Kylche	6	ij s.	ij s. viij d.
John Parratt	6	ij s.	ij s. viij d.
Thomas Blaby	6	ij s.	ij s. viij d.
William Gannesby	7	ij s. iiij d.	iij s. j d.
Richard Attkynson	6	ij s.	ij s. viij d.

[1] This entry has " 20 " written before it.
[2] This entry has " 21 " written before it.
[3] Number of days omitted, presumably because the surname runs into the days column.
[4] This entry has " 41 " written before it.

Thomas Richardson	3	xij d.	xvj d.
Henry Treylewman	6	ij s.	ij s. viij d.
Roberd Wylson	6	ij s.	ij s.
George Richardson	5	xx d.	ij s. ij d.
John Colles	6	ij s.	ij s. viij d.
William Parratt	4	xvj d.	xxj d.
Thomas Gunne	6	ij s.	ij s. viij d.
William Styberd	3	xij d.	xvj d.
William Stanwell	8	ij s. viij d.	iij s. vj d.
William Claxby	2	viij d.	x d.
Edward Attkynson	2	viij d.	x d.
Richard Smythe	1	iiij d.	v d.
William Deyne	1	iiij d.	v d.
Henry Barnes	1	iiij d.	v d.
Roberd Thacker	1	iiij d.	v d.
Richard Harryson	1	iiij d.	v d.
John Rawson	1	iiij d.	v d.
Thomas Burname	1	iiij d.	v d.
Thomas Penwell	1	iiij d.	v d.
William Cole	1	iiij d.	v d.
John Burton	2	viij d.	x d.
Adame Trenche	2	viij d.	x d.
Gilberd Browne	2	viij d.	x d.
William White	1	iiij d.	ij d.
Christopher Crosdale	1	iiij d.	v d.
John Procter	2	viij d.	x d.
John Obrey	2	viij d.	x d.

Sum' of the wages l s. iiij d.
Sum' of the bord lxv s. j d.
Secunda pagina Sum' pagine cxv s. v d.

[490.I.3]	Deyes	Wages	Bord
George Wylson	3	xij d.	xvj d.
Richard Roos	1	iiij d.	v d.
John Whiteney	1	iiij d.	v d.
John Rydesdale	2	viij d.	x d.
Edmond Claxson	1	iiij d.	v d.
Roberd Attkynson	1	iiij d.	v d.
Thomas Jeyes	1	iiij d.	iiij d.
John Jeyes	1	iiij d.	iiij d.
Martyne Grene	2	viij d.	x d.
William Gregory	2	viij d.	x d.
Roberd Gilberd	2	viij d.	x d.
William Calwell	6	ij s.	ij s. viij d.
Edward Medowes	4	xvj d.	xxj d.
Thomas Hytchecocke	2	viij d.	x d.[1]

[1] This completes the entries for Spalding on this folio, which continues with entries for other parishes.

[490.I.11*d*]

[1]Sum of all the wages and bord for one moneth   Clij li. xxiij d.[2]

And so remayneth   xlvij li. xviij s. j d.

Allowed to John Burton thentry of this accompte   v s.

William Attkynson deysyryth to be allowed for xxiiij days abowt
the surveyng of the work abovesaid at xvj d. per diem xxxij s.

John Gamblelyng for the lyke xxxij s.

[3][William] Wyllesby for the lyke   x . . .[3]

[Robert] Idon for the lyke   xx . . .

[John Hy]nd for the lyke   iij s. iiij [d.]

. . . e senr. for the lyke   nihil

. . . the lyke   nihil

. . . the said William Atkynson John Gamlyn & others . . . 1575   xlj
li. xvj d.

. . . Watson Alexr. Skynner[4]

[The accounts cover four weeks' work, a balance being struck
weekly: the first accounting period comprises eight working days.
(The time of year is not mentioned.)   The entries for each week are
arranged by wapentakes and parishes, the order of wapentakes in
each case being Elloe, Kirton, Skirbeck ; the parish order, with
minor variations, is also constant and is that shown in the table
below.[5]   The standard wage paid to a labourer was 4d. a day, with
an allowance for board of 5d. a day and an extra 1d. for the third
and sixth days respectively, making a total board allowance of
2s. 8d. for a working week of six days.   In the second week one
half-day was evidently worked : labourers engaged for six days
that week received a wage of only 1s. 10d. instead of 2s., for five
days only 1s. 6d. instead of 1s. 8d.   In the same week four Spalding
men were each paid 6d. for " one night watching the dam ", and
in the following week four Cowbit men received, in addition to their
day's wage, 8d. for " one night " (for what purpose is not stated) :
these are the only entries which depart from the standard form,
apart from those at the very end of the account which are printed
above.

Assessment for the work seems to have been relatively simple,
since the entire charge fell upon the Crown as owner of the fishing
in the Welland (165), and a sum of £200 was made available from
the Exchequer for the purpose.   Perhaps the chief interest of the
accounts is in the light they throw on arrangements for the provision
of labour services.   The information can best be presented in
tabular form.

[1] The beginning of this folio contains the last few entries for the fourth week of
the accounts.

[2] It may be noted that this total does not agree either with the sum of the figures
for individual weeks as given by the original accountant, or with the sum of the
corrected figures inserted below them by an auditor.

[3] Both margins of the folio are missing at the foot.

[4] These two names are signatures.

[5] As will be seen, the order is a geographical one. In the last two weeks it is reversed
in Elloe and Kirton so as to read from east to west and from north to south respectively.

Weekly Totals of Labourers Employed

ELLOE	I	II	III	IV	Total Man-Days for Month
Pinchbeck	38	13	4	28	318
Spalding	56	24	24	31	562½
Cowbit	24	11	11	17	267
Crowland	1	—	16	16	138
Weston	22	8	4	4	165
Moulton	13	11	5	3	177
Whaplode	7	10	4	5	143
Holbeach	7	10	6	1	139
Fleet	4	6	3	3	96
Gedney	6	8	6	3	138
(Long) Sutton	3	} 9	4	4	138
¹Lutton	3				
Sutton St James	3	4	2	2	66
Sutton St Edmund	3	4	2	2	66
Tydd St Mary	3	4	2	2	64
	193	122	95	121	

KIRTON	I	II	III	IV	Total Man-Days for Month
Surfleet	—	6	3	3	66
Gosberton	—	8	4	—	70
Quadring	—	6	2	2	60
Donington	6	8	4	—	96
Bicker	4	—	4	—	48
Swineshead	6	10	—	—	96
Wigtoft	4	4	2	—	60
Sutterton	—	6	3	2	65
Algarkirk	4	6	2	} 3	102
²Fosdyke	2	—	—		
Kirton	3	9	2	2	95
³Brothertoft	4	—	—	—	24
Frampton	—	6	3	1	60
Wyberton	—	3	—	2	30
⁴(Unidentified)				4	24
	33	72	29	19	

¹ Lutton is named separately in the first week. In subsequent weeks there is a single heading for "Sutton and Lutton".

² Fosdyke is named separately in the first week, and not at all in the second and third. In the fourth week there is a single heading for " Fosdyke and Algarkirk ".

³ Although Brothertoft is named only in the first week, subsequent contributions to the work may be concealed in the entry for Kirton, of which it was a chapelry.

⁴ Possibly Gosberton, but the place-name has been torn away. It comes between Algarkirk and Surfleet in the list.

SKIRBECK

Wrangle	4	4	2	—	60
Leake	8	6	2	—	91
Butterwick	4	4	1	—	54
Benington	5	5	2	6	108
Leverton	5	5	2	2	79
Frieston	8	6	2	—	96
Fishtoft	5	5	2	—	72
Skirbeck	4	5	2	—	66
	43	40	15	8	

The accounts show that with the exception of Boston every parish in Holland contributed labour to the work. The contribution of each parish is only partly shown by the number of individuals engaged, since many men from the parishes nearest to the river worked only for one or two days in the week, as may be seen from the Pinchbeck and Spalding lists above, whereas the smaller contingents from more distant places nearly all worked a full six days in each week. A truer picture of the labour services provided by each parish may be had from the total of " man-days " worked. It will be seen that Spalding bore the brunt of the work, with substantial help from Pinchbeck and Cowbit. At the other end of the scale, the smallest contribution (chapelries excepted) was made by Wyberton, but it is surprising to find distant parishes in Skirbeck wapentake such as Leake and Benington contributing as largely as they did.

Neither the verdict of 1566 which seems to govern these operations, nor that of 1552 which relates to similar work on the Welland, refers to drawing on the whole of Holland for labour. The verdict of 1552 says only that the river should be repaired, diked and scoured " by them accustomed to do the same " (52) ; that of 1566, so far as it can be read, appears to limit the responsibility for diking the river to the inhabitants of Deeping, Crowland, Spalding, Pinchbeck, Weston and Moulton " and all other commoners in Deeping and Spalding Fen " (165). Indeed, apart from the southern parishes of Kirton wapentake, no direct benefit could accrue to other parts of Holland from this work. But although no other instance occurs in these records, there are precedents earlier in the century for such action taken by the Commissioners. In 1500, and again in 1542, the whole of Holland was assessed towards the repair of Boston sluice : on the second of these occasions the three wapentakes and Boston were each made severally responsible for a quarter of the cost.[1] Here again, only Boston itself and the parishes of Skirbeck and Kirton wapentakes adjoining the Witham can have derived any direct benefit from the work. We should perhaps see in these cases the occasional exercise by the Commissioners of a

[1] For particulars of these assessments see vol. 1, pp. 105-129, of the *Fens Antiquities* collection at the Lindsey County Library, Lincoln.

reserve power secured to them both by custom and by the law, which authorized them to do everything requisite to their purpose " by all ways and means after your discretions " (5).]

VERDICT FOR ELLOE AND KIRTON WAPENTAKES, 1567

[473.X.1–9]   *Not printed*   169–177

[169–171 relate to Elloe wapentake, chiefly Whaplode, 172 to Brothertoft and Holland Fen, 173–7 to Kirton wapentake and south-east Kesteven, apparently in connection with the River Glen. The whole verdict is in poor condition and only fragments remain of 175–7.]

VERDICT FOR SKIRBECK, KIRTON AND ELLOE WAPENTAKES, 1568

[473.XI.1]   178

The verdit of the dykegraves and peterelles inquest within the weypentack of Skyrbeck in the parties of Holland in the countie of Lincoln maid before the quenes maiesties justices of sewers at Boston the last day of June in the tenth yeare of of [*sic*] the reine of our sovereing ladie quene Elizabeth by the othes of Fraunces Read gent. Richard Busshie and ther fellowes.

(*Wrangle*) Which say uppon ther othes that one gote in Wrangle called Pell Gote is defective in dyking and hedging frome John Parker his howse unto the out end of the hedging next the sea and ought to be repared and amended by the oweners of the landes ther.

Item that one bridge called Bennyson Bridge one clowe lyeng in Bellerettie Fendick and thre other clowes at Gowle Fendick in Wrangle aforesaid ar in decay and ought to be repared and amended by the oweners of the landes ther.

Item they saie that certeyn places in Damen Fendick in Wrangle ar defective and in decay and ought to be repared and amended by the severall charges and lotes of theis persons following first Osias Benne one gadd

[1]The gyld of Boston one gadd
Mr Fraunces Read one gadd
Osias Benne iiij[or] gaddes
Mr Fraunces Read ij gaddes
the same for his con' vj gaddes
Salomon Clarkeson one gadd
Osias Benne ⎫
John Watson ⎬ for Howitson ij gades
John Knight for Willoughby iij gaddes
Lord Sheffeld iij gaddes di.
[2]Osias Benne ij gaddes
[3]Salomon Clarkeson ij gades
Mr Kyme for Winges toft ij gaddes

---

[1] The following entries are written in the left-hand half of the folio.
[2] This is the last entry in the left-hand half of the folio.
[3] The following entries are written in the right-hand half of the folio.

Thomas Hynd ⎫
Osias Benne ⎬ for Prat Howse ij gades
Pryor of Sempringham one gadd
Walter Hoppester iiij gaddes
Mr Bartie ij gaddes
The lord Shefeld xij gaddes
Mr Fraunces Read . . .[1]
The same for Dymoc . . . ij . . .
Walter Hoppester xv fo . . .
[2]Mr Hanby xvj ga[d]
And must be repared and amended in sufficient height and bre[dth]
before [blank] next that the water do not over flow . . . the same
sub pena.

[473.XI.1d]   179
Item they say that certeyne places in the Infendick in Wrangle
ar in decay and ought to be repared and amended by the severall
charges and partes of theis persons following
[3]First Mr Hanby xix partes
Mr Fraunces Read v partes
William Read gen' iiij[or] partes
[4]The lord Sheffeld x partes
[5]John Cutt ij partes
The quene for landes late belonging to Freston Abbey one part
And must be repared and amended in sufficient height and bredth
befor [blank] that the water do not overflowe the same sub pena.

Item they say that Freskeney Fendicke adioyning uppon Symon
Gote is so in decay that the landes in Wrangle is therby verie muche
drowned and hurt with water and the same ought to be repared by
the inhabitaunt and owners of Friskney.

(Leake) Item they say that the north syd of the seagote head ther
with the crike therto belonging is in decay and ought to be repared
and dyked by the owners of the landes in Leake.

Item that in a banke called Wickehering Banke ther is in decay
lv[ti] gaddes and ought to be repared by the oners of the landes lyeng
without Cockesteight.

Item that ther ar certeyn lotes and partes defective in the [sa]me
banke which ar to be maid and repared by theis persons following
[6]Robert Turpine   viij gaddes
Richard Geator   ij gaddes
John Anthony   iij gaddes
[7]William Fynn   iiij gaddes

---

[1] A piece of the folio is missing.
[2] This is the last entry written in the right-hand half of the folio.
[3] The following entries are written in the left-hand half of the folio.
[4] This is the last entry in the left-hand half of the folio.
[5] The two following entries are written in the right-hand half of the folio.
[6] The three following entries are written in the left-hand half of the folio.
[7] The three following entries are written in the right-hand half of the folio.

| William Skyrme | iij gaddes |
| Richard Maldson | vj gaddes |

[473.XI.2]					180

Item that [the]r[1] ar certeyne places in a banke called Claydicke [ar][1] in decay and ought to be repared and amended by the partes and lotes of thes persons following that is to say

[2]Mr Hunston esquier	one gadd
Richard Jeator	iiij gaddes
Thomas Grebby	one gadd
John Shepperd	viij foote di. qr.
Henrie Hoppkinson	viij foote di. qr.
John Dickonson	viij foote di. qr.
John Burton	one gadd ix foot di.
John Dickonson	ij foote qr.
the little chauntrie	iij gaddes
the great chauntrie	xx[ti] gaddes
Mr Hanby	v gaddes
Mr Dymock	xx[ti] gaddes
the heires of John Lownde	ij gaddes
the heires of Thomas Allinson	iiij gaddes
Leonard Castle	xij gaddes
John Burton	viij foote
Peter Margerie	one gadd
William Quadring	one gadd
lord Sheffeld	one gadd
Barnard Julion	iiij gaddes iij foot qr.
John Grene	iij gaddes
Christofer Pickering	one gadd j foot
Martin Julion	v gaddes ix foot
Richard Wastler	one gadd ix foot di.
John Westland	one gadd
Richard Munck	one gadd j foot
Robert Gannock	xvj gaddes v foot di.
Fraunces Browne	vj gaddes ij foot qr.
Thomas Knight	iij foot di. qr.
John Randall	one gadd one foot qr.
Richard Larkes ⎱ [3]Thomas Larkes ⎰	iij gaddes
[4]Nunes of Leggeborn	j gadd di.
William Fendick	di. gadd
John Grebby	j gadd di.
John Fletcher	j gadd
William Scot	vj gaddes
theires of John Munck	iiij gad

---

[1] There is a small hole in the folio here.
[2] The following entries are written in the left-hand half of the folio.
[3] This is the last entry in the left-hand half of the folio.
[4] The following entries are written in the right-hand half of the folio.

Roger Pinchebeck	viij foot di.
heredes William Howson	j gad ix foot
William Fell	ix foot qr.
Thomas Paynson	vj gad
William Grescroft	iij gad
Rankine Allinson	one gad
[1]William Fynne	vj gaddes

[473.XI.2d]   181

Item they saye that cert[ain]e places in a banke called the Mere Endes ar in decay and must be repared by the fruntagers of the same that is to say

[2]Ralph Grebby	vj gaddes
The great chauntrie	lxx gaddes
Mr Hunston	ij gaddes
William Grescroft	ij gaddes
Richard Larkes	iiij gaddes
Thomas Grebby	iij gaddes
William Skerme	iij gaddes di.
Mr Dymock	vij gaddes
William Grescroft	vj gaddes
Mr Hunston	v gaddes
Parson Stevenson	iiij gaddes
The great chauntrie	xliij gaddes
The great chauntrie	ij gaddes
John Bawdrie	j gadd v foot
John Merreld Adlard Merreld	ij gaddes j foot
Alexander Harnes	j gadd j foot
Mr Irby	j gadd ij foot di.
John Dickonson	ij gaddes
Henry Hopkinson	i gadd viij foot iij qr.
Mr Irby	j gadd
Thomas Grebby	iij gaddes
John Bell	ix foot
Thomas Paynson	i gadd j foot
Mr Dymock	j gadd ij foot di.
[3]Thomas Bawdrie	ix foot qr.
[4]Thomas Paynson	ix foot qr.
Thomas Larkes	ix foot qr.
Simon Magnes	v foot di.
Ralfe Greby	j gadd iiij foot
Simon Magnes	ix foot
William Cutbert	viij gaddes

[1] This is the last entry in the right-hand half of the folio.
[2] The following entries are written in the left-hand half of the folio.
[3] This is the last entry in the left-hand half of the folio
[4] The following entries are written in the right-hand half of the folio

Mr Dymock   viij foot di.
¹Thomas Knight   iiij gaddes

Item they say that theyr is a certey [sic] pece in the South Dyk conteyning iiij gaddes defective and ought to be repared by the heires of Sir Thomas Allinson clark.

Item that certeine places in the Ape Dyk ar in decay and ought to be repared and amended by the fruntagers ther that is to say

²[473.XI.3]   182

(*Butterwicke*) Nichill ad presentandum sed alia bene nisi that the inhabitauntes of Butterwicke & Freston within that hundreth shall make and repare the dreane runyng over Market Gat ther with a carte bridge over the same and to dyke the same dreane frome that bridg to Hall Howse Nowke and frome Overgot Hilles unto Butterwike Gote.

(*Freston*)³ Item they say that yt is nessessarie that the towneshippe and inhabitantes of Freston make a sufficient cart bridge over a sewer in a heighway lyeng nere Richard Clayes howse in Freston.

(*Toft*) Item thay say that ther is a comon sewer in Toft called the Graft is in decay in dyking and ought to be dyked and amended by the owners of the landes ther.

Item that the sea gote is in decay uppon the seae syd and ought to be repared by the owners of the landes ther.

Item that ther is one petie dreane ther betwixt Freston west feld and the north feld of Toft defective and in decay and ought to be repared and dyked frome Stevenson Crosse unto a closse called Carter Grene by the frontagers of the same as well Freston as Toft.

Item that one Wardick Banke and Indick Bank is ther defective and ought to be repared by the inhabitaunce of Toft that is every man his lote and parte as appeareth by a book of the same lotes.

²[473.XI.3*d*]   183

⁴Mr Castle   ij gaddes
The heires of John Magnes   iij gaddes
William Bawdrie   iij gaddes
Mr Hunston   vij gaddes
Richard Larkes   j gadd
John Bawdrie   iiij gaddes
theires of Robert Kydd   iiij gaddes
Mr Castle   iiij gaddes
Alen Munke   x gaddes
⁵Mr Castle   viij gaddes

---

¹ This is the last entry in the right-hand half of the folio.
² Front and dorse of this folio have been reversed: the true order of sections is therefore 181, 183, 182.
³ An illegible marginal note follows.
⁴ The following entries continue from 181 (cf. 187, where the particulars are repeated). The first nine entries are written in the left-hand half of the folio.
⁵ The following entries are written in the right-hand half of the folio.

John Burton	iiij gaddes
John Busshe	vj gaddes
Fraunces Browne	xix gaddes
Mr Hunston	xvij gaddes
theires of John Munke	x gaddes
[1]the great chauntrie	vj gaddes

(*Leverton*)   Item they say that ther ar tenn gaddes on the Indick next to Leake Banke at a place called Gryde ar in decay and ought to be repared and amended by [*blank*]

Item other iij gaddes in the same Ingdick at the Ingdicke gappe ar lykewise in decay and ought to be repared and amended by [*blank*]

(*Benington*)   Nichil ad presentandum sed omnia bene.

[473.XI.4]   184

(*Skirbeck*)   Item they say that ther is certeyne places in the seadicke of Skerbecke in decay and ought to be repared and amended by theis parsons following every man his lote that is to say

[2]First the lord of Molton for Ringle Horne	xlv foot
theires of Richard Goodine	ix foote
Mr Anthony Clamond	xv foote
theires of Richard Goodin	xij foote
Thomas Southen	xij foote
Mr Carre	ix foote
the lord of Saint Johns	xij foote
[3]the towne of Boston	xij foote
[4]the heires of Mr Nicholas Robertson	xviij foote
theires of Alece Mote	xxx fote
the parson of Skerbecke	xviij foote
the lorde Barnes	xxvij foote
the abbot of Kirkestead	vj foote
[1]the heires of Richard Goodwine	xix foote

[5]Item they say that a sewer betwene Boston and Skerbeck frome the foote bridge at the lowe end of Bargat in Boston to the sea gote is defective and in decay in dyking and scowering and hath accustomablie bene used to be dyked by the fruntagers ther.

Item they say that Skerbeck Gote is defective.

(*Seebankes warr' inde landlawer*)   Item they say that whear the defaltes in the sea bankes in Skyrbeck ar presented to be repared by lotes whearin some ar muche more charged then others contrarie to equitie, that yt is most nessarie that the same seabankes be hearafter amended and repared by landlawer whearby the same bankes may be better kept for the safegarde of the cuntrie.

---

[1] This is the last entry in the right-hand half of the folio.
[2] The following entries are written in the left-hand half of the folio.
[3] This is the last entry in the left-hand half of the folio.
[4] The following entries are written in the right-hand half of the folio.
[5] A roughly drawn hand in the margin points to this paragraph.

[473.XI.5] 185

The verdict of the dickegraves of the wapentacke of Skyrbecke in the parties of Holland before the quenes maiesties justices of sewers in the same partes the last day of June in the tenth yeare of the reing of our sovereing ladie quene Elizabeth

(*Skirbecke*) Which say uppon ther othes that the seadickes in Skerbecke ar in decay in certeyne places and ought to be amended by the lotes and charges of theis persons following.

[1]First the lord of Saint Johns	xxx foote
the lord of Molton in Ringle Horne	xlv foote
the heires of Richard Goodine	ix foot
Mr Anthony Clamond	xv foote
theires of Richard Goodine	xij foote
Mr Sowthen	xij foote
Mr Carr	ix foote
the lord of Sainct Johns	xij foote
[2]the towne of Boston	xij foote
[3]the heires of Mr Nicholes Robertson	xviij foote
the heires of Allece Mote	xxx foote
the parson of Skerbeck	xviij foot
the lord Barnes	xviij foote
in Rigdick the abbot of Kirkestead	vj foote
[4]the heires of Richard Goodine	xix foote

Item they say that the gote called Skirbecke Gote is defective and must be repared.

Item that the comon sewer betwixt Boston and Skerbecke is defective frome the foot bridge in Bargat unto the sea gote & must be repared and diked by the fruntagers of Boston and Skerbecke.

(*Seabankes warr' inde landlawer*) Item they say that wheare the seabankes in Skerbecke ar presented to be repared by . . . [5]and partes that it is more nessessarie to repare and amend the same hearafter . . . landlawer wheareby the bankes may the better be amended for the safegard . . . cuntrie.

(*Toft*) Item they say that one common sewer ther called the Graft is defective and ought to be re[pared] by the owners and inhabitors ther.

Item that the sea gote ther is defective on the sea syd and is to be repared by the owneres . . .

Item that one petie dreane betwixt the west feld of Freston and the north feld of [Toft][6] . . . and must be repared by the frontagers of both townes.

[Item] that one Wardick and Indick is defective and must be amended by lot as appea[reth] . . .

[1] The following entries are written in the left-hand half of the folio.
[2] This is the last entry in the left-hand half of the folio.
[3] The following entries are written in the right-hand half of the folio.
[4] This is the last entry in the right-hand half of the folio.
[5] A piece of the right-hand side of this folio is missing.
[6] See p. 28.

Fres[ton] Item that it is nessarie that the inhabitaunts of Freston shall make one cart bridg over a sew[er] . . . Richard Clay howse.

(Wrangle) Item that the gote and comon sewer is defective [and] must hedged and . . . Parker howse unto the out end of the hedging . . . the sea and . . .

Item they say that one clowe called Bellerettie . . . thre other clowes at the gowle ar defective and . . .

Item that ther ar certeyne places in Damenfendick . . . and amended by the lotes and charges of theis parsons . . .

[1]First Osias Benne	one gadd
Gild of Boston	one gadd
Mr Fraunces Read	one gadd
Osias Benne	iiij gaddes
Mr Fraunces Read	ij gaddes
the same	vj gaddes
Salomon Clarkson	one gadd
Osyas Bennie & John Watson	ij gaddes
Mr Bartie for Willoby	iiij gaddes
lord Sheffeld	iiij gaddes di
[2] . . .	ij gadd
[3]Thomas Hynd & Osyas Benne	ij g[addes]
Prior of Sempringham	one gadd
Walter Hopester	iiij gaddes
Mr Bartie	ij gaddes
lord Sheffeld	. . .
Mr Fraunces Read	. . .
theires of Mr Dymock	. . .
Walter Hoppester	x . . .
[4]Mr Hanby	xvj . . .

[373.XI.6]   186

(Wrangle) Item they say that ther ar certeyne places in the Infendick defective and ar to be repared and amended by the lotes and charges of theis persons following.

[5]First Mr Hanby	xix perches
Mr Fraunces Read	v perches
Mr William Read	iiij perches
[6]the lord Sheffeld	x perches
John Cutt	ij perches

the quene for landes late belonging to Freston Abbey one gadd

(Leake) Item they say that the north syd of Leake sea gote head is with the crike to the same belonging is in decay and ought to be repared and amended by landlower.

---

[1] The following entries are written in the left-hand side of the folio.
[2] The remaining entries in the left-hand side of the folio are illegible.
[3] The following entries are written in the middle of the folio.
[4] This is the last entry in the middle of the folio. There may have been entries in the right-hand part, but that is missing.
[5] The three following entries are written in the left-hand half of the folio.
[6] The three following entries are written in the right-hand half of the folio.

[Item] they say that lv gaddes in a banke called Wickehering Bank ar defective and ar [to be] repared by the landes lyeng without Cockesteight.

Item that thar ar certeyne places in the same bank defective and ought to be repared by the lotes and charges of theis persons following.

[1]First Robert Turpine	viij gaddes
Richard Jeator	ij gaddes
John Anthony	iij gaddes
William Fynne	iiij gaddes
William Skrime	iiij gaddes
Richard Maldson	vj gaddes[2]
John Sheppard	viij foot di. qr.
Henry Hoppkinson	viij foot di. qr.
Fraunces Read	viij foot di. qr.
[3]. . . ton ⎫ . . . bby ⎬	j gadd ix foot di.
. . .	ij foot qr.
. . . rie	iij gaddes
. . . trie	xx gaddes
Mr Hanby	v gaddes
Mr Dymock	xx gaddes
theires of John Lownd	ij gaddes
theires of Thomas Allenson clar'	iiij gaddes
Mr Castle	xij gaddes
John Burton	viij foote
Peter Margerie	one gadd
William Quadring	one gadd
the lord Sheffeld	one gadd
Barnard Julion	iiij gaddes iij foot qr.
John Grene	iij gaddes
Christofer Pickering	one gadd j foot
Martine Julion	v gaddes ix foot
[4]Richard Wastler	j gadd ix foot di.

[5] Defaltes in the Clay Dyk

First Mr Hunston	one gadd
Richard Jeatore	iiij gaddes
Thomas Grebby	one gadd
John Westland	one gadd
theires of Muncke	j gad j foot
Robert Gannock	xvj gaddes v foot di.
Fraunces Browne	vj gaddes ij foot qr.
Thomas Knight	iij foot di. qr.
John Randall	j gadd vj foot qr.

[1] The following entries are written in the left-hand half of the folio.
[2] A line is drawn below this entry.
[3] A piece of this folio is missing.
[4] This is the last entry in the left-hand half of the folio.
[5] The following entries are written in the right-hand half of the folio.

Richard Larkes and Thomas Larkes	iij gaddes
the nuns of Legborne	j gadd di.
William Fendick	di. gadd
John Grebby	j gadd di.
John Fletcher	j gadd
William Scott	vj foot
theires of John Munck	iiij gaddes
Roger Pinchebek	vij foot di.
theires of William Howeson	j gadd ix foot
William Fell	ix foot qr.
Thomas Payson	vj gaddes
William Grescroft	iij gaddes
Rankin Alinson	j gadd
[1]William Finn	sex gaddes

Adhuc Leake

[473.XI.7]   187

(*Leake*) Item they say that ther ar certeyne places in the Meare End defective and ought to be repared by the lotes of theis men following.

[2]First Ralf Grebby	vj gaddes
the gret chauntrie	lxx gaddes
Mr Hunston	ij gaddes
William Grescroft	ij gaddes
Richard Larkes	iiij gaddes
Thomas Grebby	iij gaddes
William Skreme	iij gaddes di.
Mr Dymock	vij gaddes
William Grescroft	vj gaddes
Mr Hunston	v gaddes
Parson Stevenson	iiij gaddes
the great chauntrie	xliij gaddes
the same	ij gaddes
John Bawdrie	j gadd v foot
John Merreld and Adlard Merreld	ij gaddes j foot
[3]Alexander Harnes	j gadd j foot
[4]Mr Irby	j gadd tow foot di.
John Dickonson	ij gaddes
Henrie Hopkinson	j gadd viij foot iij qr.
Mr Ireby	j gadd
Thomas Grebby	iij gaddes
John Bell	ix foot qr.
Thomas Paynson	j gadd j foot
Mr Dymock	j gad ij foot

[1] This is the last entry in the right-hand half of the folio.
[2] The following entries are written in the left-hand half of the folio.
[3] This is the last entry in the left-hand half of the folio.
[4] The following entries are written in the right-hand half of the folio.

Thomas Bawdrie	ix foot qr.
Thomas Paynson	ix foot qr.
Thomas Larkes	ix foot qr.
Simon Magnes	v foot di.
Ralf Grebby	j gad iiij foot
Simon Magnes	ix foot
William Cuttberd	viij gaddes
Mr Dymock	viij foot di.
Thomas Knight	iiij gaddes

Defaltes in the South Dyke

First the heires of Sir Thomas Alleinson clark hath the iiij gaddes defec'.

Defaltes in the Ape Dick

[1]First Mr Castle	ij gaddes
the heires of John Magnes	iij gaddes
William B[a]wdrie	iij gaddes
Mr Hun[ston]	vij gaddes
Richard Larkes	one gadd
John Bawdrie	iiij gaddes
theires of Robert Kydd	iiij gaddes
Mr Castle	iiij gaddes
Allen Munke	x gaddes
[2]Mr Castle	viij gaddes
[3]John Burton	iiij gaddes
John Busshie	vj gaddes
Mr Browne	xix gaddes
Mr Hunston	xvij gaddes
Thomas Bawdrie	xviij ga[ddes][4]
the heires of Munck	x g[addes]
[5]the great ch[a]ntrie	vj g[addes]

(*Benington*) Nichill habent ad presentandum sed omnia bene.

(*Butterwick*) Item they say that the inhabitaunts of Butterwick and Fresto[n] within Butterwick [hun]dreth shall make and repare a bridge in Market Gat and dyk the dre[an f]rom the same gote unto Hall Howse End and from the Overgot Hilles Butter[wick] . . . so muche as is defective.

[6]Item they say that ther ar x gaddes at Ing Dyk in a place ther called the . . . ar faltie & ar met to be amended by landlawer.

[6]Item iij gades ther at the Ingdick gappe ar defective and ar to be amended as is afore said.

[473.XI.8]   188

The verdict of the dike[reeves' in]quest for Leverton

(*Leverton*) Item the mayn dreyne . . . goyng a gret compas abowt

---

[1] The following entries are written in the left-hand half of the folio.
[2] This is the last entry in the left-hand half of the folio.
[3] The following entries are written in the right-hand half of the folio.
[4] The right-hand lower edge of this folio is defective.
[5] This is the last entry in the right-hand half of the folio.
[6] These entries refer to Leverton: cf. pages 29, 36.

is necessary to be reformed, & new diked more directly, that is to say from the old dreyne at the long kirke stight unto the new sea gote with iij new bridges to be made that is one over the hye gate & a nother over the owt gate & the thirde bridge to be made over Havernewlandgate & all this . . . to be done by acar money.

First the seid new dreyne to begyn at the long kirke stight to turne from the old dreyne into a old dike betwix the pastur of Richard Wastler beyng under full age on the sowthe parte, & the pastur of Richard Fendike beyng also under full age on the northe parte, contenyng in lengthe [blank] falles, & beyng all redye a old dike abowt viij footes wide it may be diked & made wydder by ij footes that is on eyther side a foote payng nothyng therfore to the owners of the growndes for because theire fense shalbe the better, & maynteyned herafter withowt any charge of the said owners hereafter, but onely for the mayntenance of the seid dreyne for theire number of acres like to all other acres within the seid towne of Leverton.

And to pay nothyng for the rowme of the bankes to be casted upon theire growndes.

Item to go further in a like old dike betwix the said pastur of the said Richard Wastler on the southe parte, & the pastur of John Westland of Benyngton senior on the northe parte, contenyng in lengthe [blank] falles & it may be maid widder as the other before is said in all thynges.

And to pay nothyng for the rowme of the bankes as before is said.

Item to go further turnyng at the end of John Westlandes seid pastur next the hye gate, conteynyng in length [blank] falls, to be made as is before said.

And their a bridge through the hye gate.

Item to go further in a old dike or a flat or Howle Marebank betwix the arr' land of the seid Richard Wastler on the sowthe parte, & the arr' land of Francis Reade gent. on the northe parte, conteynyng in lengthe [blank] falles & to be diked & made x footes wide payng therfore to the seid owners of the seid growndes after [blank] the acre for the parchas of the growndes.

& to pay nothyng for the rowme of the bankes to be casted upon theire groundes.

Item to go further betwix the said arr' land of the seid Richard Wastler on the sowthe parte, & the arr' land of William Busshey of Benyngton on the northe parte, conteynyng in lengthe [blank] falles & to be dyked & made xj footes wide, payng therfore to the owners of the seid growndes after [blank] the acre, for the parchas of the seid growndes.

& to pay nothyng for the rowme of the bankes, as before seid & then a bridge through the owt gate.

Item to go further in a old pety dreyne betwix the arr' land of William Wastler beyng under full age on the sowthe parte, & the arr' land of William Lym on the northe, beyng in lengthe [blank]

falles & beyng all redye a old pety dreyne abowt iiij footes wide it
may be dyked & made widder by viij footes, to be in all xij footes
wide, payng therfore to the seid owners of the seid growndes after
[*blank*] the acre for the parchas of the seid growndes.

& to pay nothyng for rowme of the bankes, as before said.

& then a bridge through Havernewlandgate.

Verte

[**473.XI.8***d*]   189

Item to go further all upon the northe side of the arr' land of
Roger Grene next the arr' land of John Westland on the northe,
conteynyng in lengthe unto the Quales [*blank*] falles, & to be diked
& made xij footes wide payng therfore to the owner of the said
grownde after [*blank*] the acre for the parchas of the said grownde.

& to pay nothyng for the rowme of the bankes to be casted upon
theire seid growndes.

Item then to enter & dike through the old graft at the Quales
unto the new gote there.

Item x gaddes at the Eyng Dike next Leeke Bang at a place there
called Gride ar fawtie & ar mete to be amended by acre money
because there is no sufficient booke to mesure by.

Item iij gaddes there at the Eyng Dike gap ar fawtie in like maner
. . . to be amended as the other before is said.

[**473.XI.9**]   190

(*Gosberton and Surflet*] Item the seyd jurey say that ther ys a
drene called Rusgate Ey belongyng to Gosberton & Surflet wyche ys
defectyve for lack of dyking from a place nye Fen End Bryg unto
the lymyttes of Surfte under the sedyck in the same drene & the one
part of the seyd drene ys to be dyked by the lordes & fre holders
of Surflet as yt hathe ben used to be done, & thother part therof to
be dyked clensed & scoured by the lordes & freholders of Gosberton
as ytt hathe ben lyke wyse used to be don & the bangkes of the same
drene bothe within Surflet shyft & Gosberton shyft ar defectyve in
dyvers places for lack of hyght & breade & ought to be amended by
the lordes & freholders of the seyd townes as joyse bokes of the
same do apoynt the same to be don.

Item the seyd jurey say that ther ys a drene called Lee Beache
tendyng from the fens att Wryghtbold unto the see goote att Surflet
of the wyche part was dyked thys last yere past & some of the same
drene betwene Gosberton & Pynchebek ys not yet dykyd & owght to
be dyked by the lordes & owners of landes or groundes next adionyng
to the same drene.

Item the seyd jurey say that wher as ther ys a pare of clous
erected in the seyd drene att Wryghtbold aforeseyd by the lordes
Burne & other tounes ther about wherby the fen waters owght to
have passage to the sea att serten tymes of the yere as ys apoynted by
laus for the same wyche clous hathe not thys yere ben used accordyng
to the laws & ordinances therof heretofore made, wherby the tounes

of Gosberton & Surflet hathe ben greuously noyed & damnyfyed by the gret [473.XI.10] abundance of water cumyng in att the sayd clous contrary to the laus therof.

Item the seyd jurey say that the bankes of the seyd ar defectyve for lack of hyght & breade & owght to be amended by the lordes & owners of the groundes next adionyng to the same.

Item the seyd jurey say that ther ys a pare of clous standyng in the seyd drene called the Beeche att Surflet wyche of old tyme by laus have ben ordeyned to stand ther to strey the owt rages waters dessendyng in the same drene for a tyme for the savyng of all the landes & pastures bothe within Gosberton & Surflet wyche seyd clous ar in dekey & owght to be neu made by the lordes fre holders & owners of Gosberton & Surflet aforeseyd by acre sylver.

Item the seyd jurey say that Gosberton Nudyck ys defectyve for lack of dykyng in dyvers places & owghto [sic] have ben dyked the one by Laurens Baker for Wryghtbold & the other by the commons of the inhabytans of Gosberton aforeseyd.

Item the seyd jurey say that ther ys ij bryges over Gosberton Ey ar in dekey & owght to be amended by the inhabytans of Gosberton aforeseyd.

[473.XI.11]   Byker   191

Also the sayd jury saythe that ther ys one dyke callyd the New Dyke extendyng from the est end of Hellpryngham Beck to a plasce callyd Byker Cranmer Hoorn betwyx the common fen of Byker & [Don]yngton wyche ys defectyve for lacke of bankkyng dykyng rodyng hookyng scowryng & clenseyng wyche owgth to be doon suffycently so oft as nede dothe requer by the in habyteres of Donyngton & Byker.

Item the sayd jury saythe that Haman Becke from Cranmer Hoorn to Swan Wathe in scerten places ys defectyve for lacke of banckkyng dykyng rodyng hookyng scowryng & clensyng wyche owgth suffycyently to be doone so oft as nede doth requeyre by the lordes & fre howlderes of Byker aforsayd from tym to tym. And also the sayd Hamand Bek from Swan Wath to the northe end of Canttlatt Rowgth to be doon & kep as ys aforsayd by the in habyteres of Byker by commons so oft as ned requyryth.

Item the sayd jury sayeth that Mr Holland Rowgth ys in grett rewyn & decay to the grett hyndrans of the holle contre by cause the water can have no passage for the defautt of bankkyng dykyng rodyng hookyng scowryng & clensyng wyche owgth suffycyently to be done & kep so oft as nede doth requere by the inhabyteres of Swynshed & Wygtoft.

[473.XI.12]   192

(Swyneshed & Wigtoft) John Wolmer & his felowes say the est mere of Sw[yneshed] & Wigtoft frome Gunflete to Categate Brige is defective and owght to be diked so ofte as nede shall require by the land holders of Swinshed & Wigtoft by acre sylver.

D

[Item] they say that thest mere of Swineshed & Wigtoft frome Fishemerend unto Kitgate Brige is defective & owght [to be] likewise diked by the land holders of Swinshed & Wigtoft by acre sylver.

[Item] they say that the said meres frome Kitgate Brige unto the gate is sufficientely diked by the land holders of [Swinsh]ed & Wigtoft by acre sylver.

Item they say that the sey gote belongynge to Swineshed & Wigtoft is sufficiently made by the land holders of Swineshed & Wigtoft.

Item thei say ther is a paire of clowes standing at Symonwer is sufficiently made by the inhabitantes of Swineshed & Wigtoft.

Item they say ther is a dike goyng frome the clowes to Hamon Becke is defective & owght to be diked by the inhabitants of Swinshed & Wigtoft.

Item they say a stowe callid Acreland Stowe at Fishemerend owght to be cute open frome mydmarche unto mydaprill for the convaiance of the water of Swineshed & Wigtoft to the draines of Sutterton Algarkirke & Fosdike according to the old custome.

Item they say that ther is iiij⁰ʳ brigges that is to say the Stone Brige Butler Brige Kitgate Brige & Spittillcrose is defective & awght to be made by the inhabitants of Swineshed.

Item they say ther is towe briges callid Liman Brige & Mussildike Brige is defective & awght to be made by the inhabitants of Wigtoft.

Item they say that the skirthe belongyng to Swineshed & Wigtoft is sufficientlie diked by the inhabitants of Swineshed & Wigtoft.

Item they say that ther is a drayne callid Hamon Becke goyng frome Bronde Dike unto Litill Hamon Becke at Kirton Holme is sufficienly diked the one halfe by Swineshed & Wigtoft the other halfe by Sutterton Algarkirke & Fosdike excepte certyn rodes belongyng to Sutterton Algarkyrke & Fosdike.

Item they say ther is a banke callid the West Banke goyng frome Willowe Bothe unto Flete End is defective in dyvers places & owght to be made & repayred as oft & [sic] nede shall require by the inhabytans of Swineshed. And frome Fletend unto . . . gowle owght to be made as ofte as nede shall require by the inhabytans of Wigtoft.

[Item] they say ther is a brige lieng at the Abby gates is in decay & owght to be made by the landes belongyng to the said . . . of Swineshed.

[Ite]m they say that every person havyng paster grownd on (theste)² syde of the West Mere owght to kepe his heding sufficienly frome tyme to tyme for the keping of the water in the seid West Mere upon payne for every heding iij s. iiij d.

---

¹ The left edge of this folio is defective, and if there were ever marginal headings they are now illegible.

² " theste " has been scored through and " the west " written above and in turn scored through.

[473.XI.13]   193
                        Donyngton vardytt
(*Donyngton vardytt* 10 *Eliz.* B. 15)   First the said jury sayth that
wher ther was a verdytt & inquessysson founde at Boston in the
parties of Holland in the county of Lyncoln the Monday next after
the feast of Santt Peter the Adwynculay called Lamas day that ys
to say the iiij day of Awgust in the xxxvj^th yer of our soveringe lord
kinge Henry the viij^th by the grace of God of England Fraunce &
Ierland king defendore of the fayth & in erth of the church of England & Ierland supprym hedd, befor Sir John Coppelldyck knyght
John Wyngfelld esquyar   George Semppoll esquyar   Thomas
Holland esquyar   Nychollis Roberttson   Antony Irby   Richard
Ogell   Thomas Brown   Blasse Holland & John Bolls comyssyonars
& Justes of our soveringe lord the kinge, to & att all & syngeller
sewers bryggs stremes callsayes & trenches of freshe waters in the
county aforsaid & to surway her & termen etc., by the othe of
Thomas Conny the younger of Kerton & his fellowes chargedd &
swarn, ytt ys fowndd & presentedd, that ytt ys nessesary for the
comon welth comodyte profett & savgardd as well for partt of the
partys of Holland that ys to say Quatheringe Donyngton & Beker
as for the partt of the partyes of Kesten that ys to say Helppering-
ham Swaton Byllingborwgh Horbblyng Lyttell Holl & dyvers other
townes of the said partyes to have a newe drean & sewer maid &
dyckedd for the convaiunce of the water dessending owtt of the
said parties of Kesten owt of Helpering' Bek & in to the fenes of the
said partyes of Kesten & Holland, & the Eyght Hundryth Fene
from a place calledd the Greft at Helperingham Bek End aforsaid
& from the said Bek Endd next unto the said place in Helperingham
aforsaid in the said county of Lyncoln over the fenes of Lyttell Holl
& Beker aforsaid unto a place called Wragmanstak in Beker aforsaid,
in the said county of Lyncoln & from the said [place] calledd
Wragmanstak by the lemetts of Holl Dyck unto a sewer called
South Ee in the Eyght Hundryth Fen in the said partyes of Holland
& county aforsaid & by the said South Ee unto a place called
Gellsyke in the said Eyght Hundryth Fen & from Gelsyk aforsaid
unto the gotts lyinge & yssuyng in to the haven at Langrake owtt
of the said Eyght Hundryth Fen in the county aforsaid & the same
sewer to be dyckedd maid & bankedd from Helperingham Bek End,
& from . . . ¹place called the Greft unto Gell Syk aforsaid the half
parte therof that ys . . . the west part of the same by the lords
frehollders tenantts & inhabytauntes of
[*Endorsed:*]B 10 Eliz. 2

[473.XI.14]   Donyngton vardytt   194
(*Donyngton vardytt.* 19)   Swaton Helperingham Lyttell Holl
aforsaid & the other half parte therof that ys to say the est parte of
the same by the lords freholders tenantts & inhabytants of Donyng-

¹ The bottom left-hand corner of this folio is missing.

ton Quathering & Beker aforsaid & from the mouth of Gyllsyk aforsaid to the gotts by the tenantts of the Eyght Hundryth Fen, & ytt was then also presenttedd that ytt was nessassery that the same showld be maid dyckedd & clenssedd in manner & furm as ys aforsaid befor the feast of Santt Marten in wenter then next comyng apon a payn of the lords freholders & inhabytantes of every towne aforsaid to forfett xl s. also ytt was then & ther said & presenttedd by the said jury that ytt was lykwysse nessasery for the comon welth & savgarde aforsaid that ther shalbe maid & laydd eyght small gotts called pysse goots apon the banke of the haven at Langrak aforsaid in the syke end essuynge of the Lowe Fen & Hyghe Fen called the Eyght Hundryth Fen into the said haven at Langrake aforsaid & Brothertoft & every on of the said gotts to conteyn in lynghe xx^{ti} foytt & bredd & deppnes every way two foytt at the least & foure of the same to be maid & keppt by the inhabytauntes & tenantts of the Eyght Hundryth & two of the same to be maid keppt & layd by the inhabytauntes of Donyngton Quathering & Beker & the other two of the said gotts to be maid laid & keppt by the inhabytauntes of Swaton Hellperingham Lyttell Holl Greatt Holl Hekington Byllingborowgh & Horblyng & four of the same gotts to be laydd at the heyght of the watter & other four of the same to be laid at the lowest of the watter & lykwysse the said gotts to be maid & laydd in maner & furm aforsaid befor the feast of Santt Marten apon the payn of every townshipp to forfett xl s.

Item the said Humfrey Grandorge & other his fellowes nowe sayth apon ther othes that the said drayn ys nott maid nor dyckedd in maner & furm as ys aforsaid to the greatt hynderaunce of the countre, & the said jury sayth furder that they thynk apon ther conssyaunces that ytt ys mett convenentt & nessaserye that the same drean be maid dyckedd for the advauncementt of the comon wellthes in maner & furm as ys aforsaid.
[*Endorsed*:] 10 Eliz. B

[473.XI.15]   195
The vardytt of Donyngton maid this ij day of Septem[ber]
anno domini 1562

(*Donyngton vardytt.* 13)   Item ther ys on comon sewer in Donyngton called Golldyck extending from a place called Marloydd to a place calledd Donyngton Hye Bryge of Brygdyck, which is fawty & ys nott suffycentt in bredd & deppnes & the banks ther of laks boyth heyght & bredd, & owght to be dyckedd skoweredd & bankedd by the land holders in Donyngton as aperyth by a joste bowke.

Item ther ys on other comon sewer in Donyngton aforsaid called the Newdyck extendinge from the said Hye Bryge of Brygdyck, to a place called Beker Newdyck or Helperingham Bek which ys nott suffycentt in bredd & deppnes, & the banks therof lakes boyth heyght & bredd & owght to be dyckedd skoweredd & bankedd, by the lords & landholders in Donyngton as aperyth by a jost bowke.

Item ther ys on bryge in Donyngton calledd the Hye Bryge of Brygdyck, or Holland Bryge which ys in rewen & decay & owght to be reparydd & amended by the inhabytauntes of Donyngton.

Item ther ys on brygge in Donyngton markythe place called the Lords Bryge whiche ys in rewen & decay & owght to be maid reparydd & amended by the lord of the manor of Wyks in Donyngton.

Item ther ys on brygge in Donyngton, aganst Rychard Loves howsse in Brownyngwak which ys in rewen & decay & owght to be reparydd & mended by the inhabytauntes of Donyngton.

Item ther ys on bryge in Donyngton calledd the Cowebryge aganst Meddylfen which ys in rewen & decay, & owght to be maid reparedd & mended by the inhabytauntes of Donyngton.

Item ther ys on hye way called Brygdyck within the partys of Kesten & Holland, extending from the howsse of Santt Savyors at Brygend in the parties of Kesten unto a place calledd Holland Brygg or Donyngton Hye Brygge of Brygdyck, whiche ys in great rewen & decay, & dyvers & sondry brygges in the said way ys utterly decaydd & gon, & the same owght to be reparydd & amended, by the howsse & landes of Santt Savyors at Brygend aforsaid.

[473.XI.16]   196

(12 *Byker Almondbycke*) Item the sayd jury saythe apon ther othes that a comonde drene or sewer called Almondbecke is defyctyve & in decay in maney & deveres places which oughte to be dekyd & kypete in suffecient repare with dekyng & rodyng & banckyng so ofte as nede shall reuere by the lordes & tenintes fryholderes & copyholders belonggyn unto the saym towne of Byker aforsayd.

(*The Newdyke*) Item the sayd jury saythe that the Newdyke betwyn Donyngton Fyne & Byker Fyne is in rewyng & decay in maney & dyveres places wich owght to be dycked banckyd & hoked by the inhabitauntes of Bycker aforesaid as often as nede shall requyre by comman meynworke.

(*Bycker Dyke*) Item the said jurye sayth that ther is one comman dycke called Bycker dyke wich ys in ruyng & decay & howght to be dycked royded & bancked by the habitayres of Byker afforesaid by comman menworke.

(*Ee of Bicker*) Item the said jury sayth that the comman ee in Bycker afforesaid is in ruyng & decay in many & dyvers places & howght to be dycked roded & clenssed by the inhabiteres of Bycker afforesaid.

(*Feyld dreyne*) Item the said jurye sayth that the feylld dreyne runnyth into the common ee of Bycker & neyded none other conveances of the water.

(*Rowght Haymon Becke*) Item the said jurye sayth that one rowght that of Haymon Becke called Mr Holland Rowght is defectyve boyth for dyken rodyng & banckyn & howght to be dycked roded & bancked by Quaterryng Donyngton Bycker Horblyng & Byllyngborow.

(. . . *ead*)   Item the sayd jurye sayth upon ther othes that at the said Haymon Becke ther ys a weresteyde called the Barre which is defectyve & to narow in br[eadth] & also to sholld.

(. . . *called* . . . *Becke*)   Item the said jurye upon ther othes say from Brond Dyke unto a place called Skyrbycke which is called Haman Becke is defectyve in dyveres & sundrye places from an serteyne place called the Forthend is defectyve for defalt of dyke[ng] rodyng & clensyng to Skyrbycke Goyte which [ought] to be dycked by the habitauntes of Framton Wyberton & Skyrbecke . . . to the utter undoyng unto the said towneshyp of Bycker.

[473.XI.17]   197

(*Surflett & Gosberkyrk seebank*)   Item the seyd jur' say that there ys two places in the see bank where of old tyme a gote hath lyeng, that ys not of suffycyent height or bred, and ought to be repayred exalted & amended by the inhabitans of Surflett & Gosberkyrk.

([*Bu*]*rn Ee*)   Item the seyd jur' say that the bankes of the great drean & ryver in Surflett called Burne Ee ys defectyve in certeyn places that ys to say, at Newbery sewer which ought to be made repared & amended by the landholders of Sir Thomas Dalaland knyght, and at Richerd Burton house . . . which owght to be made repared & amended by the landholders of the late dyssolved monastery of Swynneshed and at Gilbert Durbagg wateryng whiche ought to be made repared & amended by Thomas Fysher & Gilbert Durbagg.

(*Clowes in the Beache*)   Item the seyd jur' say further that the clowes in the Beche at Surflet standyng at Lowegate End ys utterly decayed & broken, whiche shuld be made & repayred by the lordes & landholders of Surflett & Gosberkyrk by acre sylver.   And they say further that yt ys mete necessary & convenyent that the seyd clowes shulbe made & repayred for the savegard of the landes of the lordes & landholders of Surflett & Gosberkyrk aforeseyd that the seyd landes lyeng within the seyd paryshes of Surflett & Gosberkyrk myght by ther petty drayns, drean ther landes adioynyng by the same, whiche yf the seyd clowes be not made for the reasonable stay of the fen water, the landes pastures & medowes all from the hye way of Surflett west ward towardes Barrope Chele & Rusgate wolbe utterly surrounded and drowned to the great inestymable hyndrans of the lordes & landholders of Surflett & Gosberkyrk aforeseyd.

(*A brygg at Hawkyns*)   Item the seyd jur' say that ther ys one brygg over the seyd ryver called the Beche at a place called Hawkyns whiche ys utterly decayed so that the quenes subiectes can not passe with owte danger and ought to be made & repayred by the inhabitans of Surflett & Gosberkyrk.

([*S*]*urflett Newdyk*)   Item the seyd jur' say that the fen bank of Surflett called the Newdyk of Surflett ys in ruen & decay in certeyn places and ought to be made repared & amended by the lordes &

landholders of Surflett aforeseyd accordyng to a joyce boke therof, of auncy[n]te accustomed & used.

(*North bank of [Par]kes*) Item the seyd jur' say that ther ys an other bank ther of the north syde of the Parkes whiche ys in decay in many & sundrye places and ought to be made repayred exalted & amended by the landes adioyning & boundyng uppon the seyd bank.

(. . .) Item the seyd jure say that ther ys an other bank extendyng from Quadryng Upp Fen barr[1] . . . strop Crosse in great decay whiche ought to be made & repayred by the inhabitans . . . & Quadryng Hundreth.

[473.XI.18] 198

(*Clowes at Wryghtbold*) Item the seyd jure further say that their arr a payer of clowes erected & sett at Wryghtbold[2] . . . whiche ys in great decay & not worthy to be suffered to stand & to run excepte . . . substancyall & suffycyent then they heretofore have bene, whyche ought to be . . . kepte suffycyently by the lordes & landholders of the lordshyp of Burn & other tow[n]es in . . . Kesten. And that they ought not to run butt of suche reasonable gage as the bankes . . . ber yt and that the waters of the groundes within Surflett & Gosberkyrk myght run & drean . . . And that ther shuld be two lokes & kees ordeyned for the same the one to be in the kep . . . [of the] dykereves of Gosberkyrk & Surflett and the other to be kept by the inhabitans of Burn.

(*Beache Bank*) Item the seyd jur' say that the bank of the seyd ryver called the Beache of the north syde extendyng from Wrightbold to Pawles Stowe, ys in many & sundrye places defectyve & ought to be . . . exalted & repayred & amended by the lordes & landholders of Gosberkyrk boundyng & adioynyng uppon the seyd ryver & bank.

(*The Old Fendyk in Gosberkyrk*) Item the seyd jure say that ther ys one bank in Gosberkyrk called the Old Fendyk whiche ys in great ruen & decay & ought to be made repayred & amended by the lordes & landholders of Gosberkyrk accordyng to ther joyce boke therof whiche yf yt be not substancyally made & repayred in hast wyll surround the angle and quarter of Chele in Gosberkyrk & Surflett aforeseyd.

(*A gole in Rusgate Ee of the south syde*) Item the seyd jure say that ther ys one great gytt or goole runnyng owte of the great ryver of Gosberkyrk & Surflett called Rusgate Ee nygh unto the clowes of the south syde of the seyd ryver whiche ought to be made & repayred by the inhabitans of Gosberkyrk by comon mynwerk.

(*Rusgate Ee bankes in Surflett shyft*) Item the seyd jure further say that the banke of the seyd ryver called Rusgate Ee within the shyft of Surflett from the fen end of Rusgate to Nutkyn Brygg ys

---

[1] The bottom left-hand corner of this folio is missing.
[2] The top right-hand edge of this folio is defective.

defectyve in dyverse places & ought to be made & repayred by the
lordes & landholders of Surflett aforeseyd accordyng to a joyce
boke therof.

(*A were in the same ryver*)   Item the seyd jure say that ther ys
one were in the seyd great ryver nygh to the Stone Brygg in Gosberkyrk so narrowe & so strate that the water in the seyd ryver cannot
have hys ryght course & reddy pasage to the see.

(*The bank in the same*[1] . . . *in Gosberkyrk shyft*)   Item the seyd
jure say that the banke of the seyd ryver within the paryshe & shyft
of Gosberkyrk ys in great decay for lak of hyght from Stone Brygg
to Cokerell Hough and ought to be repared exa[lted] and amended
by the landholders of Gosberkyrk accordyng to the joyce boke ther.

(. . . *kepyng owte* . . . *ryng owte*)   Item the seyd jure say that the
wynter last past ther was a gytt or gole brake over the bank of the
seyd ryver of the north syde nyghe to Party Brygg by reason wherof
the waters of Quadryng dyd overflowe the seyd bank & run into
the seyd great

Plus in folio sequenti

[473.XI.19]   199
(8) ryver of Gosberkyrk & Surflett aforeseyd called Rusgate Ee by
reason of the rage & great[2] . . . that the seyd waters of Quadryng
hadd into the seyd ryver, overcharged the seyd ryve[r] & so greatly
that at the meatyng of the seyd ryver with the great ryver called the
Be[ache] caused the water therin, whyche shuld run with the seyd
ryver of Rusgate Ee to the see gote to ret[urn to] the hede & course
of the seyd ryver called the Beache bak ageyn & returned the water
into the petty d[rain] called the Tundam & the Ley Fen Lode by
reason wherof the landes medowes & pastures to . . . Rusgate &
Chele were greatly overflowen surrounded & drowned to the great
enesty . . . hyndrans of the lordes landholders & occupyers of the
groundes towardes Rusgate & Chele, w[hich] forseyd bank of Gosbertown Ee yf yt shuld not be suffycyently & substancyally
amen[ded] repayred exalted & amended to kepe the seyd waters
owte of the seyd ryver shuld not only be an utter surroundyng &
drownyng of suche townes within the partyes of Kesten . . . of ryght
drean by the seyd ryver of Rusgate Ee but also shall surround &
drown the . . . quarters & angles of Gosberkyrk & Surflett towardes
Rusgate & Chele aforeseyd.

(*Defaltes in the drean under the sedyk in Surflett shyft*)   Item the
seyd jur' say that the seyd ryver within the shyft of Surflett whic[h
is] called the drean under the sedyk ys defectyve for lak of dykyng
and scowryng . . . places and ought to be dyked scowred & clensed
as folowyth at the places herea[fter] . . . lymyted that ys to say at
Peter Sedyk End by the land holders of Hardgrave, at . . . by Sir
John Tempest knyght & the landholders of Mr Pagenham, and nygh
unto the . . . fale at the gote by Mr Robert Markham esquyer.

---

[1] The bottom left-hand margin of this folio is defective.
[2] The right-hand edge of this folio is defective.

(*The Newfendyk in Gosberkyrk*) Item the seyd jure say that ther ys a bank in Gosberkyrk called the Newfendyk whiche . . . in certeyn places & ought to be repayred exalted & amended by the lordes & landholders of Gosberkyrk accordyng to the joyce boke therof made. And also the ryver under . . . for lak [of] rodyng & clensyng and ought to be roded & clensed by the . . . lordes accordyng to ther seyd joyce bok.

(*Leyfenlod & Tundam Lode*) ¹Item the seyd jur' say that ther ys a certeyn petty dreyn in Gosberkyrk . . . lode whyche ys in ruen & decay for lak of dykyng rodyng and [clensyng] and ought to be dyked roded & clensed by all those that doo adioyne unto . . . lye uppon the same, and they say further that ther ys another . . . the Tundam Lode extendyng from the Myddelfeld of the . . . unto a place called Swyncote Pyngle at Cresyhall and . . . Rusgate Ee to Hedeland Rygg and so to the Grayns in Henry . . . petty drean called Leyfenlode & yt doth mete, and so run together to Hye . . .
[*Endorsed*:]Surflett

[473.XI.20]   200
(*Sutterton. . . . Hundrethe. Alger Hundreth*) Also the sayd jure saythe that ther is a certen drow waye in Wigtofte and Sutterton begynninge att Struges and from Struges to a lane called Squyer Lane and from Squyer Lane to a stone brige in Fyschermer End in Sutterton aforsayde called Wasse Brige & from thens to a place called Symon Wer the which drowe way is in ruin and decay for lacke of exaltinge reparinge and amendinge in serten placis by the space of xxx roodes at the leaste from Symon Wer to Acreland Stowe and ought to be repared exalted and amended now and from tym to tym and as ned shall requer by the inhabitantes of Sutterton Algerkerke and Fosdycke by commen menwarkes as is aforsayd accordynge to ther oulld custum.

²Also the sayd jure saythe that the parte of Brand Dyke of Kym Dyke and of the [Sc]ottpittes belonginge to Sutterton Algerkyrke and Fosdycke ought to be dycked clensed and scowred from tym to tym so oft as ned shall requer by the inhabitantes of Sutterton Algerkyrke and Fosdycke accordynge to ther oulld coustum and the Scottpites belonginge to Sutterton Algerkyrke and Fosdycke is begininge a[t] a certen rondell at the west end of a oulld wathe called the Fenhouse Wathe and from thens to a cutter or dreane at Kyrton Hom goynge toward Simon Wer the whiche Scottpites ought to be dycked from tym to tym so oft as ned shall requer by the inhabytantes of Sutterton Algerkerke and Fosdycke accordynge to ther oulld coustum ³exceptt serten rodes belonginge to Swinsted⁴ & Wigtofte.³

Also the sayd jure saythe that the parte of the Weste Causey

¹ A hand drawn in the margin points to this entry.
² The left-hand margin of the folio is missing, from this point on.
³ Words " exceptt-Wigtofte " added in a different hand.
⁴ *Sic.*

ledynge from Swinshed belonginge to Sutterton Allgerkerke and Fosdycke and one banke called the Weste Banke from the medes of the Mydelle Dycke of Willow Bothe to the Horne and ougthe to be exalted repared and amended from tym to tym as ofte as ned shall requer by the inhabitantes of Sutterton Algerkerke and Fosdycke by comen menwarke as is aforsayd accordynge to ther oulld coustum.

[1]Also the sayd jure saythe that the dreane of Algerkerke and Fosdycke is in ruin and decay for wantt of dyckeing in serten pallces as well in bred and in dypnis by the space of ij C. roodes & ought to be dycked in bread x fott & in dypnis ij fott mor then itt is now.

[2]Also the sayd jure saythe that Kirton ought to make or manten one gatte wher they have stopte owr drove waye att Swymonwer by beryeres and itt hathe bene accustomed to the inhabitantes of Sutterton Algerkerke Fosdycke for to have owr drove way upon the comon[2]

Also the sayd jure saythe thatt Wigtofte & Swinsted[3] ought to have a deane[3] from Symonwer to the west syd of a gatt called Mores Gatt to a place caled Acerland and from thence to ther se goott.

[4]Also the sayd jure sayth that the se banke of Fosdycke aforeseyd for the . . . in dekay for wantt of amendynge . . .

[473.XI.21]   201

Item that the common sewer in Kyrton called Kyrton Ee is defective in certene places & ought to be dycked roded & scowred as ofte as nede shall require by perticuler house rodes & acre sylver of the lords & land holders of Kyrton as haith bene acostomed.

Item that the brydges within Kyrton called Blome Brydge & Meres Brydge ar defective & owght to be repared by the lordes & landholders within Kyrton aforesaid.

Item that the sedycke bankes & Golle Cryke within Kyrton ought to be repared as ofte as nede shall requyer one menwarke day yerly by fermors being landholders & the rest by the inhabitance of the same towne of Kyrton by common menwarkes as haith bene acostomed.

[473.XI.22]   202

F° 10

[5](*Sutterton . . . Hundrethe . . . ndrethe*) The sayd jure saythe that a drean or commen sewer begynes att a place called Symmonwer and from thens by the este syde of a gatt called Mores Gate to a

---

[1] The remainder of the folio is written in a different hand.
[2] This paragraph is cancelled, by the deletion of the first two or three words in each line.
[3] *Sic.*
[4] This paragraph is almost illegible because the bottom of the folio is in bad repair.
[5] The left-hand margin and bottom left-hand corner of this folio are defective, and what remains of the bottom of the folio is in bad repair.

place called Acerland Stowe in Sutterton and from thens to a place
in Fyshmerend called Wasse Brige in Sutterton aforsayd and from
thens to a place called Jhon Dycconson house now Thomas Yorkes
house and from thens to the south end of a pastur in Sutterton
aforsayd the whiche pastur is called Squyretofte & buttes of a waye
called Boston Waye or Strugges Waye & from the sayd Strugges
Waye to the gotte of Algerkerke & Fosdycke the whiche suer oughte
to be dycked clensed & scowred so oft as ned shall requer from Symonwer to a brige called Wasse Brige, by the inhabitauntes of Sutterton
Algerkerke and Fosdycke by commen menworke accordynge to ther
oulld coustom that is to say Algerkerke & Fosdycke ij pence or ij
roodes or ij spaydes . . . ne j spad or j rood and from the sayd brige in
Fysh[m]erend called Wasse Brige to a house called Jhon Dycconson
house ought to be dycked from tym to tym by the inhabitauntes of
Algerkyrke and Fosdycke by commen menworke. And from the
sayd house called Jhon Dicconson house to the southe end of a
pastur called Squyer tofte ought to be dycked clensed and scowred
from tym to tym & as ofte as ned shall requer by the inhabitantes of
Sutterton aforsayd by commen menworke. And from the sayd
southe end of Squyer tofte to the gootte of Algerkyrke and Fosdycke
ought to be . . . ed roded scowred & clensed by the inhabitantes of
Algerkerke and Fosdycke now & from [tym] to tym and as ofte as
ned shall requer.
 . . . Jhon Dycconson house aforsayd to the goott of Sutterton is in
ruin and decay in . . . [pl]aces that is to saye betwen the personage of
Algerkerke and a place called Bransforthe . . . C. roodes and betwen
Bransforthe Brige and the goot one C. roodes and ought to . . . in
bread x fott and in depnis ij fotte mor then itt is now . . . lordes and
freholders and copiholders of Sutterton aforsayd by acerselver.
 . . . jure saythe that ther is a certen ston brige in Fyshmerend in
Sutterton aforsayd . . . brige over the common suer of Sutterton
Algarkyrke & Fosdycke is in ruin and decay . . . endynge of the
stone warke and ought to be . . . tym to tym by the inhabitantes of
Sutterton Algerkerke and Fosdycke . . . ould coustom as is aforsayd.
 . . . that ther is on lane called Gokeshorne Lane comynge from
Symmon Were . . . [h]orne to a house of on William Houson of
Wigtofte & is in ruin . . . reparinge and amendynge in sertyn placis
by the space . . . for sayde house of William Houson of Wigtofte
. . . [p]lace called Fyshmerend and ought to be . . . tym to tym and
as ned shall requer . . . by commen menworke as is aforsayd.
 . . . begyne . . . att . . .

[473.XI.23]   203
 (7) A place called Tathes Corner where they fall all together into
the great ryver called the Beache and so to the see, whiche forseyd
Tundam Lode ys in great ruen & decay for lak of dykyng rodyng
scowryng & clensyng and ought to be made dyked roded scowred
& clensed as hereafter folowyth accordyng to an old verdyt therof

found & presented that ys to say to be dyked scowred & clensed from the seyd Myddelfeld to a place called Swyncote Pyngle and so to a place called the Grayns by all suche landes medowes & pastures as drayneth by the same, and from the seyd place called the Grayns to Tathes Corner to be dyked roded scowred & clensed by the inhabitance of Rusgate Wardegate & Belnes in the paryshe of Gosberkyrk that have ther landes drayned by the same.

(*Fen End Brygg in Gosberkyrk*) Item the seyd jure say that ther ys a brygg over the great ryver called Rusgate Ee at the fen end in Rusgate whiche ys defecty[v]e and ought to be made repayred & amended by the inhabitans of Gosberkyrk.

[473.XI.24]   204
[1]Item the jury sayth that the Newdyke in sarten places frome Marlode to Westrope Stylle is defyctyve in devers places & ought to be repared & amended frome tyme to tyme so ofte as nede shall requere be the lordes & frye holderes of Quaderyng & Quaderyng hundrythe.

(. . . *gote*) Item the sayd jury saythe that there is a sertene fylde dreane leynge at Angte which is in rewyn & decay & ought to be amended from tyme to tym for the convaance of the water to the sey so ofte as ned shall requere by the lordes & fryholderes & the inhabetance of Quaderyng & Quaderyng hunderythe aforesayd.

(. . .) Item a dyke called the Syde Dyke betwyxte the Strope Horne & Marlode is defyctyve [in] sartayn places of the saym banke which owght to be mayd & reparred from tyme to tyme so ofte as nede shall requer be the lordes & fryholderes & inhabeteres of the sayme towne.

(. . .) Item the sayd jury saythe that a banke called the Upfyne Banke from Westrope Bares to the Strope Hyrne is defyctyve in sartayn places which oughte to be amended from tyme to tym so ofte as nede shall requer be the bownderes & owneres of . . . banke as it haith acostimable be done.

(. . .) Item the sayd jury saythe that ther fyne drene frome Dowe Howrne to Boston we beynge charged from a style called Quaderyng Stylle betwyn Surflyte Fyne & Quaderyng to a place called Marlode betwyn Donyngton & Quaderyng whiche oughte to be dekyd houcked roded as ofte as nede shall reqere [by] the lordes fry holders & inhabeteres of Quaderyng & Quaderyng hundrythe.

Item the sayd jury saythe that the commond sewere called Hamonde Becke extendyng from Marlode unto Mr Holand Rowghte outhte[2] to be deked scowered & rod[ed] be Donyngton to Byker lande & from Byker land to Mr Holandes Roughte be Beker & Mr Holand Rowghte oughte to be deked roded & hokyd unto a place called Bronde Dyke End be Donyngton Quaderyng & Byker &

---

[1] Both the left and right margins of this folio are defective and the marginal headings are largely illegible.
[2] *Sic.*

Byllyngbrow & Horblyng & from Bronde Dyke End to Sterbyke Gote ought to be deked be the inhabetance of the Eyghte Hundrythe.

Item the jury saythe that Hamond Beck is defyctyve at one place called the Barle . . . that ys to narow & to sheld.

Item the sayd jury sayth that Hamond Becke is defyctyve agyeynste Framton forthe . . . not of brede & depnes as it owghte to be.

[473.XI.25] 205

[1](*The Slakers* 33) Item the sade jurie saethe that for as muche as upon the grete risse of the freshe wateres floudes issuynge owt of the partes of Kesten from Cate Bridge into the rever of Glene & also the waters dessendinge from Burn into the sade rever of Glene & so dessendinge to Pinchebeck from thens to Surflett and so from thens to the sey cannott be kept in the chanell & within the bankes but bursteth & breketh over the same bankes as well into the fennes of bothe sides the sade rever as into the sade town whereby not only the same be yerly in greate daynger to be surrounded by the rage of the sade freshe waters but it dothe also bown and swell over the bankes in dyveres & sondrye places ; the sade jure therefore thynks it mete & necessarye that ther be made slakers for the abattynge of the rage of the same waters the one of the same slakers . . . lade upon the bankes called the Commoned Bank at Dove Hurn over the southe side and the other to be lade over the common banke at Dove Hurn over the northe side.

(. . . *partialiter Brigges resp'*) Item thay say that ther is a certane brigge in Pinchebeck called Heringe Bridge in ruyng and decay and ought to be repared made and amended by the quenes maiestie lordes & freholders off Pinchebeck by acre sylver.

(*Brigges*) Item they say that ther is one other bridge lyeng over Sterfen Graft adionynge upon the groundes of Thomas Harlwyne in Mylner Grene ys in ruing & decay and one other brydge called Whaplode Brigge and ought to be made & repared as hathe bene accustomed.

(*A gote betwixt Burn Eye & the Graft*) Item the sade jurie thynkes yt very mete & necessarye that a certaine hollowe trey or . . . betwixte Burn Eye & the Graft called Northegate Graft be ordened & decreed by la[w] . . . suewers to lye to take in water as well for the grete daunger of [yer as for . . . drynke for suche thynhabetantes of Pinchebek as dwell farre from the seye & to . . . in suche order as by the former lawes ys decreed.

(*Surflet must bestowe two menwarkes days*) Item the sade jurie thynkes yt very necessarye that the inhabetauntes of Surflett shall bestowe two menwarkes days in the monthe of October & November in the outfall of Burn Eye nowe called Glene yerly for kepinge the owtfall perfet & c . . . from sandde beddes & sylke as in a fermer verdit geven up at Boston heretofore dothe appere & this to be down

[1] The right-hand edge of this folio is defective.

yerly & effectually upon pane of x li.

(*The lawe for Catebridge*) Item the sade jure saethe that wheras ther was a lawe made for . . . [Cate]bridge at bothe endes of suche heyght & bredthe . . . floude myght passe throughe the arches of the same bridge withe . . . made in suche order as the same may . . . at every fresh water floude dothe so rage that the bankes of bothe sid[es] . . . and Burne Eye ar not able to kepe the violens of the same . . . and brekethe out to the grete losse & hyndraunc[e] as well of . . . of Kesten as Holland : the sade jurie therefore thynkes it very mete & . . . that the bankes at the sade bridge end be sufficiently made of suche heigh[t] . . . as the waters may passe orderly by the arches of the sade bridge an[d] . . . otherwyes.

xxxij folia

Spaldyng de 29 . . .

[*Endorsed*:] Anno decimo Elizabethe 1568 North Slaker for Gleyne. Ro. Pulvertoft gent. forman.

[473.XI.26]

[1](*Gednye*) The verdyt of Roger Morrowe of Sutton yoman & his fellowes of the degrewes queste

Item the sayde jurye sayethe upon there othes that all the hedynges from Weste Plowe Landes hedynges to Gednye sedycke beynge the west hedynges & the out rynge of our towne is in decaye & for lacke of height & brethe & ought to be mayde kept & exalted from tym to tym as well by our sovereinge laydye quen as lorde & ther tenantes.

Item the sayed jurye saythe that the quens maiestye hathe xv^{ti} rodes in defaute of the Pollete fee in Gednye hedynges and ought to be repared and exalted from tym to tym by her or by her tenantes.

Item the sayde jurye sayethe that Peter Trotte hathe x rodes in the sam defaute of my lordes Wentworthes hedynges & ought to be repared & exalted from tym to tym by the forsayde Peter Trotte.

Item the sayde jurye saythe that my lorde Wentworthe hathe x rodes in the same defaute and ought to be repare by hym selfe or by his tenantes.

Item they saye that our sovereinge laydye the quens maiestye hathe x rodes in the same defaut of the monestrye of Crowlande & ought to be repared from tym to tym by her or by her tenantes.

Item Wylliam Cokere of Flete Feenn hathe xx^{ti} rodes in the sam defaute & ought to be repared from from [*sic*] tym to tym by the forsayd Wylliam Cookere.

Item theye saye that Thomas Fysshere of Gednye Feenn hathe x^{ti} rodes in the same defaute & ought to be repared from tym to tym by the forsayd Thomas Fysshere.

Item theye saye that the lorde Wentworthe hathe xx^{ti} rodes in the sam defaute & ought to be repared from tym to tym by hym selfe or by his tenantes.

---

[1] A small part of the lower right-hand margin of this folio is missing.

Item they saye that John Rodgman hathe x^{ti} rodes in the same defaute of the quens fee late the Paulete that he hethe be leese.

Item theye saye that our sovereinge laydye the quens maiestye hathe for the monestrye of Crowlande xv^{ti} rodes in the same defaute & ought to be repared from tym to tym by her or by her tenantes.

Item theye saye that our sovereinge laydye the quens maiestye hathe for the monestrye of Crowland . . . rodes in the sam defaut & ought to be repared from tym to tym by her or by her tenantes.

Item theye saye that the lorde Wentworthe hathe lxxx rodes of Rousdooll hedynges in the sam defaute & ought to be repared from tym to tym by hym selfe or byis[1] tenantes.

Item theye saye that John Man esquyere hathe for Dentons landes xv^{ti} rodes in the sam d[efault] and ought to be repared from tym to tym by the forsayd John Man esquyere.

Item theye saye that the feffours of Gednye Fenn hathe xxx^{ti} rodes in the sam defaute & ought to [be] repared & kept from tym to tym by the forsade feffours.

Item theye saye that our sovereinge laydye the quens maiestye hathe for the Pawllet fee vj rodes in the sam defaute and ought to be repared from tym to tym by her or by her tenantes.

[473.XI.27]   206

Item theye saye that Robert Rodgman hathe of West Plowe Land hedynges xx^{ti} rodes in the sam defaut and ought to be reparede from tym to tym by the forsayde Robert Rodgeman.

Item theye saye that from Sowthe Ee Bancke to a place called Fysshers Crosse in the West Drowe his in defaute for lacke of height & ought to be reparede in suffycyente height & bretes by acer sylver, for thys tym and afterward to be mayd by the lande holdders of the est syed.

Item theye saye that our sovereinge laydye the quens maiestye hathe for Parcke Dooll x^{ti} rodes in the sam defaut & ought to be repared from tym to tym by herselfe or by her tenantes.

Item theye saye that John Rodgeman hathe fror[1] Thyssyll Dooll x^{ti} roodes in the sam defaute & ought to be repared from tym to tym by the forsayd John Rodgman.

Item theye saye that there is a hedynge betwen John Rodgman & the quens dealfe about iij rodes in the same defaute & ought to be mayd by the townshype of Gednye from tym to tym by commonde menworkes.

Item theye saye that John Rolde the sonn of Rychard hath xij rodes at Showthell Cloute is in defaute for lacke of height & ought to be kept & repared from tym to tym by the forsayd John Rolde.

Item theye saye that John Burton hathe vj rodes of the west hedynges in the sam defaut for lacke of height & ought to be kept & repared from tym to tym by the forsayd John Burton.

Item theye saye that Isbell Burton of Lutton wydowe hathe xx^{ti}

[1] *Sic.*

rodes in defaute for lacke of height & ought to be kept & repared from tym to tym by the forsayd Isbell Burton.

Item theye saye that Robert Rodgman hathe of the weste hedynges iij rodes at Homs Crose in the same defaut for lacke of height & ought to be kept & repared from tym to tym by the forsayd Robert Rodgman.

Item theye saye that Jonn Kydde hathe a hedynge betwen John Rolde the son of Rychard and her selfe is in defaut for lacke of height & brethe & ought to be kept & repared from tym to tym by the forsayd Jonne Kydde.

Item theye saye that John Rolde the sonn of Rychard hathe a hedynge betwen John Knapton & hymselfe is in defaut for lacke of height & brethe & ought to be repared & kept from tym to tym by the forsayd John Rolde.

Item theye saye that John Burton hathe a hedynge betwen the iij acres of the quens maiestye & hymse[lf] is in defaut of breth & ought to be repared from tym to tym by the forsayde John Burtun.

Item theye saye that John Callowe hath iij rodes in defaut for lacke of height & ought to be kept & repared from tym to tym by the forsayd John Callowe of Lutton.

Item theye saye that Sir Wylliam Howell clarke hathe ij rodes in defaut for lacke of height & ought to be kept & repared from tym to tym by the forsayd Sir Wylliam Howell clarke.

Item theye saye that Rychard Welbye gent. hathe of the west hedynges iij rodes in defaut for lacke of height & ought to be kept & repared from tym to tym by the forsayd Rychard Welbye gent.

[473.XI.28]

Item theye saye that Robert Oterbye hathe a hedynge betwen Rychard Welbye gent. & hym selfe in defaute for lacke of height & ought to be kept from tym to tym by the forsayd Robert Oterbye.

Item theye saye that the parson of Gednye hathe in Preast Fealdes lxxx rodes in defaud for lacke of height & brethe & ought to be kept & repared from tym to tym by the forsayd parson of Gednye.

Item theye saye that all the hedynges from Towgoutes to Clapooll ought to be mayd as theye have benn from tym to tym accostomed by the townshype of Gednye by common menworkes.

Item theye saye that Adlerd Welbye esquyer hathe iij rodes in is doll[1] in Heenopes Drowe is in defaut for lacke of height & ought to be kept & repared from tym to tym by the forsayd Adlerd Welbye esquyere. Also theye saye that the townshype of Gednye ought to mayke on rode agaynste his stowe from tym to tym by commond menworkes.

Item theye saye that there is betwen Towgottes & Gednye Crosse xij rodes in dedfaute for lacke of height & ought to be repared & kept from tym to tym by the townshype of Gednye by commonde men-workes. Also theye saye that there is iij rodes at Towgottes betwen

---

[1] *Sic.*

John Callowes stowe & Towgottes Bridge is in defaute for lacke of height & ought to be kept & repared from tym to tym by the townshype of Gednye by comonde menworkes.

Item theye saye that Rycharde Putterell hathe iij rodes agaynste the Ee for lacke of height & ought to be kept and repared from tym to tym by the forsayde Rychard Putterell.

Item theye saye that there is a place called Pynne Stoocke about iij rodes in defaut for lacke of height & ought to be repared & kept from tym to tym by the townshype of Gednye by comond menworkes as it hathe benn accoustomed.

Item theye saye that the ayres of John Batman ought to mayke a lawfull stowe at Homs Crosse wherbye that the water ought not come[1] into the height[1] waye & ought to kepe the same in suffycyente height & brethe all all[1] tyms when nede shall requyere. Allso theye saye that the comond waye is from Lease Yeattes to Sedycke Bridge ought to be mayd from tym to tym by the inhabytours of Gednye by commonde menworkes.

Item theye saye that Youldycke to Goddessmond Gettes is in decaye for lacke of height & brethe & ought to be mayde by the lande holders of bothe sydes of the sayd dycke. Allso theye saye that the water from Joull Dycke to Ravenes Dycke ought to fall owt of Mappes Gette & so to fall into the Olde Ee at Mappes Gette & so to ha[ve] his full course accordynge to the olde custom etc. Allso theye saye that Ryefelde water ought to fall in on the northe syde of the clowes betwen John Johnsons lande & the clowes etc. Allso they saye that the pete dreanne from Stanegatte Bridge to Burman Bridge is in decaye for lacke of dyckynge & rodynge wherbye the Weste Water is stopped of his course & ought to be dycked scowred by the lande holders of both sydes of the same. Allso theye saye from Burman Bridge to the commonde suers in lycke defaute & ought to be dycked [&] scowred by the lande holders of bothe sydes of the same etc.

[473.XI.29] 207

Item theye saye that ther is a petye dreanne runnynge from Couslape Bridge to a bridge called Blasgatte is in decaye for lacke of dyckynge & rodynge wherbye the water is stopped of his derecte cous & ought to be dycked scowred & clensed by the land holders adyonynge of bothe sydes of the sam etc.

Item theye saye that the comond suers from Southe Ee to Hodge Hell ought to be dycked scourde & clensed contynuallye from tym to tym by the tenantes by acre sylver. Allso theye saye that from Hodge Hell to Brodegatte Bridge ought to be dycked scowred & clensede by the parson of Gednye. Allso theye saye that the quens hundrethe is from Brodgatte Bridge to a bridge callede Clapoll Bridge & ought to be dyked & roded when ned shall requyere by the quens maiestye of the manor called Pawllett etc. Allso theye saye

[1] *Sic.*

E

that the lord Wentworth hundrethe is from Clapoll Bridge to the Ambyll Tree ought to be dycked scowred so often as nede shall requyer by the forsayd lorde Wentworthe of the manor of Gednye.

Item theye saye that the quens maiestye hundrethe is from the Ambell Tree to the Comente before the gottes mouthe ought to be dyked scoured & clensed by the quens maiestye of the dyssolved monestrye of Crowlande etc. Allso theye saye that there ought ij menworkes days to be mayde by the yeare to the maytaunces of Lutton dames & the Flete.

Item theye saye that there is a petye dreane in Chappell Gatte & ought to ronne owt of the pette in Chappell Gatte betwen George Partryge & Lettus Clarkson & ought to be dyked scowred & clensede from tym to tym by the sayd George Partryche. Allso theye saye that there is a hedynge ledynge from Gednye Crosse to a pasture of Robert Hylls & ought to be mendyd & exalted from tym to tym by the inhabytours of Gednye accordynge to the olde coustom. Allso theye saye there is an other hedynge ledynge from Robert Hylls pasture to Clapowll & ought to be kepte accordynge to the olde coustome.

Item theye saye that the lorde Wentworthe ought to mayke a bridge at Ravens Dyke which is in defaut & ought to be mayd & kept up wherby the comonde pepeoll maye have passayge. Allso theye saye that the quens maiestye ought to mend a sertyn brydge called Brodgatte Bridge so often as ned shall requyer & ought to be donne by our sovereinge laydye the quen of her manor called Pawllette.

Item theye saye that there is anothere bridge caulled Pexton Bridge & ought to be mended from tym to tym so often as nede shall reqyere by our sovereinge laydye the quen of her manor of Crowland.

Item theye saye that there is a bridge called Sedyke Bridge which ought to be mayd & kept from tym to tym by acre sylver. Allso theye saye that there is anothere bridge callede Pyesgatte Bridge & ought to be mayd kept from tym to tym by acre sylver as welbye our sovereinge laydye the quen as lorde & there tenantes. Allso theye saye that th[ere] is another brydge callede Noddes Bridge & ought to be mayde & kept by our sovereinge laydye the quen of the manor of Crowland.

Item theye saye that there is a sertayn bridge callede Couslape Bridge which is in rewe[1] & decaye & ought to be exalted & mended by our sovereinge laydye the quen of the manor of Crowland. Allso they saye that there is anothere bridge called Flaxma[ns] Bridge & ought to be mended from tym to tym by the sayde lorde Went-worthe. Item thei saye that John Blancke doth permit is[1] hedynge lyenge of the west parte of Gednye Ee to be so lowe for lacke of height & brethe that the water overflowethe the landes adyonynge to the sayde Ee. Allso thei saye that John Callowe of Lutton

[1] *Sic.*

yoman ought to kepe repare & mayke iij hedynges next the hedynges of John Blancke which nowe is in defaut for lacke of brethe & height & ought to be mayd kept from tym to tym by the sayd John Callowe.

[473.XI.30]

Item thei saye that ther is a hedynge ledynge from Youldycke to the forsayde John Blancke lande is in defaut for lacke of heighte & brethe & ought to be mended from tym to tym by the forsayde John Blancke. Allso thei saye that there is another hedynge ledynge from John Blancke to Thomas Allsons is in defaute for lacke of height & breth & ought to be exalted & kept by the forsayde Thomas Allson.

Item theye saye that ther is a hedynge ledynge from Thomas Allson to Thomas Batman which is in defaut for lacke of heighte & brethe & ought to be amended from tym to tym by the forsayd Thomas Bateman. Allso theye saye that John Cowper ought to kepe a daenn[1] which is in defaute for lacke of height & brethe & ought to be kept up from tym to tym in suffysyent heighte by the forsayd John Cowpere.

Item theye saye that John Callowe of Lutton yoman haithe an hedynge lyinge in Swanpytt Dooll & Symon Malles Felde to the number of xx[ti] rodes which is in defaut for lacke of heighte & brethe & ought to be mayd from tym to tym by the forsayd John Callowe.

Item thei saye that there shall no man laye any leape nor nett to be sett at Towgottes wherby that Ryefelde water have anye henderaunce upon payne as it shall be thought mett by the comyssyoners.

Item thei saye that Gednye Gatte from Sowethe Ee to Leasse Yates ought to be mayd & kepte contynewallye from tym to tym by comonde menworkes by the inhabytours of Gednye in suffycyent height & brethe.

Item thei saye that it is mette & conveniaunte that a sertyn clowe ought to be mayd & kept at a place there called Dame Land in the Weste Ee & ought to be mayd & kept there by acrer sylver as well by the quens maiestye as lorde & ther tenantes within the townshype of Gednye.

Item thei saye that there is a sertyn drowe called Mouldrowe which is in rewe[1] & decaye & ought to be exalted & amended from tym to tym by comonde menworkes of the Feenne End. Allso thei saye that the delfe called the Abbottes is in defaute in sertyn places & ought to be mendyd from tym to tym by our sovereinge laydye the quen of her manor of Crowland. Allso thei saye that my lord Wentworth delfe from Ravens Dycke to the on[1] parte of the quens delfe. Allso the quens delfe to a sertayn stoocke called Peynns Stocke is in decaye in sertyn places & ought to be mayd by the sayd lord Wentworthe & the quens maiestye for her manor of Pawlette fee. Allso thei saye that there is a sertyn yousse bancke called

[1] *Sic.*

Southe Ee Bancke ledynge from Flete hedynge to Sutton hedynges is in rewe & decaye in sertyn places & ought to be mayd in suffycyent height & brethe by the quens maiestye the lord & all other landeholders within the towne of Gednye as by a sertayn yousse booke therof mayde.

Item thei saye that Gednye hedynges ledynge from Southe Ee to the Comentye is in decaye in sertyn places for lacke of height & brethe & ought to be mayd from tym to tym by the landholders adioyninge thereupon one the este syde as well by the quens maiestye as lord & all other tenantes.

Item thei saye that there is a sertayne petye draene on the west syde of Gednye Gatte & ought to rune over a sertyn laynne at Fyshers Corner & ther to have his passhayge throughe an holl tree in to the West Ee & ought to be kept there by the comentye.

[473.XI.31]   208

Item theye saye that ther is sertayne laynes ledynge from Sturtun Cloute to a place called Fletstocke is in decaye for lacke of height & brethe & ought to be mended & exalted from tym to tym by the inhabytours of Gednye End by comone menworkes. Allso theye saye that ther is a sertyne petye drean ledynge from Sowthe Ee to Lease Yattes called the West Ee & ought to be dycked scoured & clensyd from tym to tym by the sayd landholders on the west syde as well our sovereinge laydye the quen as lord & there tenantes.

Item theye saye that ther is a sertyn hedyn ledynge from Gednye hedynges to Sutton hedynge & ought to be exalted & kepte from tym to tym by comende menworkes at a place ther callede Olders Tree etc.

Item theye saye that it is mette that a payre of clowes be mayde at Ravens Dycke in the comone ee by acrer sylver as well by our sovereinge laydye the quen as lord & all other there tenantes. Allso thei saye that Rayvens Dycke is in decaye for lacke of height & brethe & ought to be mayde in suffycyent height & brethe from a place called my lord Wentworthe delfe to Sutton hedynge by the townshepe of Gednye by comone menworkes.

Item theye saye that ther is a drowe caulled Ravens Drowe to a place callede Hous Crosse & ought to be mendyd & kepte by the inhabytours of Gednye by comone menworkes. Allso theye saye that ther is a sertyn lanne caulled Cokborne Fendycke which is in lycke defaute to a place called Towgottes & ought to be mayd & kept by the inhabetours of Gednye by comonde menworkes.

[1]Item the sayd jurye saye that Flette Landmere ys defectyve and in grete rewen & dekaye for lacke of heyghth and bredde frome Sowght Ee Bangke to Spaldyng Gayte.

[473.XI.32]

Item the sayd jury saythe uppone ther othes that ther is one other dycke or banke called the Cawsse is defectyv for lack hayght

---

[1] This sentence has been added in a different hand.

& bredth & owght to be repared & mayd by the inabytans of Moltone
by comon menework.

Item the sayd jury sayth that ther ys one pette seware or drene
in Moltone aforsayd begynyng at a plas ther called the Old Ee goyng
deryctly to Aylwardes Gat & from thens to Seelathes & ther the
water to pas overe the way & frome thens derectly to comone sewer
ys defectyve for lack of scowryng & dyckyng & owght to be scowred
& clensayd by the fruntegers of bothe sydes.

Item the sayd jury sayth that ther ys ane other pette sewer or
drene beginning nere to the howse of Gylbard Wells & so ledyng by
the comone way ther to the howse end of William Harbe & ther the
water to fall into the comone sewer & that the sayd drene is letted
by John Kook of Moltone by reson of the keping of a dry clowe to
the noyans of the sayd drene & the sayd drene owght to be repared
by the fruntegers of bothe sydes.

Item the sayd jury sayth that ther ys ane other pette dren or
seware begining at at[1] Doyse Layke & frome thens derectly to the
landes of John Sheppard genner' called Beells Feld & also on other
pette seware or drene begining at Sottons Gat & it extendes to Ry-
borows & frome thens to the sayd Beells Feld & that the sayd ij
sewars or drens so mettyng go bothe together into the comone
sewere at Kerrells Corner & that the sayd sewas[1] owght to be scowred
& clensed by the fruntegers of bothe sydes.

Item the sayd jury sayth that ther is ane other pette dren or
sewer in Moltone aforsayd frome a plas called Claptone Gat to
Lentonsland End & ther to falle into the comone sewer ys in lyk
defawtt & owghte to be scowred & clensed by the fruntegers of bothe
sydes.

Item the sayd jury sayth that ther ys one other pette drene or
sewar in Molltone begynyng at Betells Holt extendyng betwyne the
landes of the quiens maieste and the landes of Gylbart Lynsay &
frome thens to Claptons Gatt & so falles into the comone seware ys
in lyk defaw[t] & owght to be scowred & clensed by the fruntegers
of both sydes.

Item the sayd jury sayth that ther ys an other pette dren or
sewar begynyng at Est Gatt & so betwyxt the landes of John Cook
and the landes of the ayres of Scarlytes & so extendes to the landes
of Cronwels & so over whart the sayd landes & falls into the comone
seware & owght to be mayd by the fruntegyrs of bothe sydes.

Item the sayd jury sayth that ther ys on heddyng called Mersons
[2]Ease etc.[2] lyeng oppone of the est syd of Moltone Mere betwyxt a
paster now in the tenuere of Thomas Welbe esquiare & a pastor
nowe in the occupacyone of Antone Egere of Flette and one Gammone of Fokyngame & owghte to be repared & mayd by theme three.

Item the sayd jury sayth that ther ys one entre or bank nere to
the sayd merre beyng ane entre to a paster nowe in the tenure of the

---

[1] *Sic.*
[2-2] These two words are interlined and the reading is uncertain.

sayd Thomas Welbe nerre to the marsch & the sayd entre lyes
betwyne Mersons Brygg & the pasters of the sayd Antone & the sayd
Gammone aforsayd ys in uttere rewyng & decay by resone wherof
the watere next the say overflows & rons bacck to the towne of
Molltone to the comone noyans of the inabytans of Moltone & owght
to be mayd in sefecyent hayght & brydth by the sayd Mr Welbe &
Mr Gamon & Antone Egere.

Item the sayd jury sayth that ther ys one dyck or bank ledyng
frome Pyekelle to Brother Howse & from Brother Howse to Clotte
& extends to Crowland ys defectyve for lacce of heyght & bredthe
so that at evre sorgg of watere Weland brekyth overe to the undoans
of the townshep of Moltone & the countre rownd abowght & owght
to be repared & mayd by Spaldyng Cowbytt & Crowland.

[473.XI.33]   209
    (. . .)[1] Rychard Nycolson & his felowes sayethe uppon there
othes that Andrewe Scare of Stamford hath a sartyn banke called
Lowdyke to the valeu of one rood defectyve & fawty in height & in
bradyth & ought to be repared & maded [sic] by the sayd Andrew
Scare.

Item the sayd jury sayeth that the lordes of Moulton hath of the
same banke defectyve from Belsmore to Brother Hous and also
from Brother Hous to Belsmore ageynst the water of Weyland
defectyve as well in height as in breadeth & ought to be repared &
made by the sayd lordes of Multon or his tenantes.

Item the sayd jury sayeth that the quenes maiestie hath of the
same banke from the lords of Multon ageynst the water of Weyland
to Pecayle End defectyve as well in height as in bredeth & ought to
be repared & made by the quens maiestie or her tenantes for the
late house of Spaldyng.

Also the sayd jury sayeth that the quenes maiestie hath an other
banke called Gooll Dyke in Weston defectyve in height & in bredeth
& ought to be repared & made by the quens maiestie or her tenantes.

Also the sayd jury sayeth that Thomas Welbey gentelman hath
of the same banke called Newdyke to the valeu of haulfe a rood
defectyve for lake of height & bredeth & ought to be repared & made
by the sayd Thomas Welbye.

Also the sayd jury sayeth that Mr Ordyn of Whaplode hath of
the same banke to the va[leu] of twoe roodes defectyve as well in
height as in bredeth & ought to be repared [&] made by the sayd
Mr Ordynn.

Also the say that Robert Pulvertofte gentelman hath of the same
banke to [the] valeu of foure rodes defectyve as well in height as in
bredeth & ought to be repared & made by the sayd Robert Pulvertofte.

Also the say Rychard Grenyngame hath of the same banke to

    [1] The left-hand margin has decayed and only two or three illegible letters of the
marginal heading remain.

the valeu thre rodes defectyve as well in height as in bredeth & ought to be repared & made by the sayd Rychard Grenyngame.

Also the say that Cowbyt & Spaldynge have sartyn hedyngs on the west syd of Wykemer which extendeth from Goldyke to the seadyke defectyve in height & bredeth in sartyn places & ought to be repared & made by the lond holders in Cowbyt & Spaldynge which butteth & lyeth agayne the same.

Also the say that the towne of Weston hath sareteyn hedyngs on the est syd of Wyke[mer] which extendeth from Goldyke to the sea dyke defectyve in hieght & bredeth in sartyn p[laces] & ought to be repared & made by the lond holders in Weston which abutteth upon the same.

Also the say that Belsmore to be drened by the same mere from tyme to tyme as the same ned.

Also the say that there ought to be a dam kepet at Baret Gat nere unto the sea for the sault water.

Also the say that yt is nessesary to have twoe dames kepet the one at the Church Brydge the other at Hundell Brydge in Dellgate Mere.

Also the say that the hedyngs on the west syd of the same mere from Gyt Stone to Goldyke [is] defectyve in height & bredeth & ought to be repared & mad by the lond holders [of] Weston which abutteth upon the same.

[473.XI.33*d*]

Also the say that the hedyngs on Multon Mere on the west syd from Goldyke to Bery Homes hedyng is defectyve in height & bredeth & ought to be repard & made by the lond holders abuttynge upon the same by fruntage.

Also we[1] say that ther ys sartyn hedyngs from the sayd Bery Homes hedyng on the west syd to the goote defectyve in height & bredeth & ought to be repared & made by the towneshypp of Multon.

Also the say from Crowland to Spaldyng the mayne ryver of Weyland ys defectyve for lake of dikynge rodyng scouryng & ought to be dyked roded & scoured by the quens maiestie or her tenantes.

Also the say there is a sartyn banke from Dousdalle to Crowland on the north syd of South Ee defectyve for lake of height & bredeth & ought to be repared & made by the quens [maiestie] or hyr tenantes for landes late Crowland.

Also the say that a sartyn banke from Crowland to Brother Hous is defectyve as well in height & bredeth in sartyn places & ought to be repared & made by the quens maiestie or hyr tenantes.

Also the say there ought to be a dore hanged & kepet at Gole Brydge in Weyke Mere.

---

[1] *Sic.*

[473.XI.34]   210
Flette.   The verdeth of the peteryles
queste anno 1568

(11. *The outfalle of the drayne*)   Fyrste the jury sayth upon ther othe, that the outfalle of the drayne from Mages Eye to the gotte is defictyffe for lacke of dykyng clensyng and scoryng, and ought to be dyked clensyde and scored by acar mony of the lordes of Flete & ther fermeres as hath benne accostomed heretofore.

[1](*The fynnes*)   And further the sayd jury saye that ther be ij fynnes, ensydente to the sayd gootte which be defictyffe the one beinge one the weste syde of the sayd gotte and lyeth one Holbyche Marshe, and the other one the este syd on the sayd goot one Gednaye Marshe, and ought to be dyked clensede and scorede by acar monye as they have bene done heretofore.

[1](*The gott*)   And further the sayd jury sayth, that the gote ys defictyffe & ought to be mendede by acar sylver accordynd to the auncyente custome.

(*The eye*)   Further the sayde jury sayth that the eye ys defictyffe for lacke clensyng and scorynge from the gotte to the clowe one the marshe, and ought to be dykede clensed and scorede by acar sylver as yt hath bene accostomede heretofore.

And further the sayd jurye saythe, that the sayd eye is defictyffe for lacke off dykyng clensyng & scorynge, from a place called Hargate Bregge to the Hall Yearde, and ought to be dykede clensed and scored as ys afore sayde.

And forther the sayde jury sayth, that the sayde eye ys defictyffe in sartayne places betwexte Ravens Bredge and Flette Comone, and ought to be dykede clensed and scorede as is affore specyfyede.

(*Dawekynnes Gatte*)   And further the sayde jurye sayeth, that ther ys a gatte called Daukynnes Gatt which is defictyffe for lacke of heaygth, by the meanes whereoff, the water in the same anggle, dessendeth & falleth, from the sea to the fynne contrarye to the lawe of the sewers, which ought to be mendede and made by the lande holders joynnynge to the same.

And forther sayd jurye [saith] that yt is necessary to have one shut to stande at the norre end of a pece of grownd callde Pownd Rege whiche ought to be erected and made made[2] by accar monye.

(*Newedyke*)   And forther the sayd jury sayth, that ther ys a banke callede Newedyke, whiche is defectyffe and ought to be made a stronge bancke for the deffence off the water and to extende from Rovens Gate to the landmere one holle bancke and to be made by comon menworkes.

(*Mylle Bregge*)   Further the sayd jurye sayth, that Mylle Bregge is defictyffe and ought to be repared and mended by acar monye accordyng to auncyente custome.

And further the sayd jury saythe, that the comone sewer is

---

[1] These two paragraphs have been cancelled.
[2] *Sic.*

defictyffe for lacke of dykynge from Weste Plowed Lande to Lang-gredege Craftes Ende & ought to be dyked clensed and scorede by acar mony.

(*Flete the Landmeare*) And further the sayd jury saythe upon ther othes, that therll of Sussex is defictyffe in his landmere to the quantyte of xxx rodes, and ought to be made both of heygth & bredth by Willam Stowe off Holbydche tennante to the same.

Also the sayd jury saye, that Sir William Cordwell ys defictyffe in his landmere xvj rodes both of hygh and bredth and ought to be made by the sayd Sir William Cordwell or his tenauntes.

And further the sayde jury saye, that Sir James Harrentone is defictyffe in his landmere vj rodes both of hygh and bredth and ought to be made by John Thorntone tenaunte to the same.

And further the sayd jury say, that therll of Sussexe is defictyffe in the landmere xlv[1] rodes both of hight and bredth and ought to be made by John Browne tenaunte to the same.

And further the sayd jury sayth that Christover Wilkensone is defictyffe in his landmere xiiij rodes of heygth and bredth and ought to be made by Jhon Thorntone tenaunte to the same.

[473.XI.35]

(12 *The Landmere*) And further the sayde jurye sayth that the wedowe Jacsone of Gednye is defyctyffe in her landmere xxx rodes both off hyght and bredthe and ought to be mad by the sayde wedowe Jacsone off Gednay.

And further the sayde jury sayth, that ther is xij rodes defictyffe of the sayd landmere of hygh & bredth and ought to be made by John Mane esquyere.

Further the sayde jurye sayeth that ther is xxx rodes defictyffe of the sayde landmere bothe off higeth and bredth and ought to be mad, by Symond Browne.

And further the sayd jury sayth, that Lawraunce Clarcke is defictyffe in his landmer iiij rodes and ought to be made by the sayde Lauraunce Clarke of Flete.

Also the sayde jury saye, that next ther is viij rodes defictyffe of hygth and bredth and ought to be made by Jhone Davye jentyll-mane.

Further the sayde jury sayth, that Symone Browne is deffictyffe in his landmere iij[xx] rodes both of hyght and bredth and ought to be made by the sayde Symone Browne.

Further the sayde jury saye that Jhon Negalle off Saynt James is defictyffe in his landmer xx rodes from Symonde Browne to Joyse Dykes End, both of hygth and bredth and ought to be made bye the sayd Jhon Negalle of Saynte James.

And further the sayd jury sayth, that ther vj rodes of the comone landmere is deffictyffe both off high and bredth and ought to be made by comone menworkes as hath bene acostomed heretofore.

---

[1] The margin of the sheet is damaged and the figure is conjectural.

And further the sayd jurye sayeth that Symonde Browne is deffictyffe in his landemer ij hundreth rods both of hyght and bredth and ought to be made by the sayde Symond Browne.

And forther the sayde jury sayeth, that Mr Wiltone parsone of Flete is defictyffe in his landmere viij rods both off hyght and bredth and ought to be made by the sayd William Wiltone parsone of Flete.

And further the sayde jury sayth, that ther is ij rodes off the comone landmere is deffictyffe at Lordes Dykes Ende both of hygh and bredth and ought to be mad by comone menworke as is accostomed.

And forther the sayd jury sayth, that our soveraine ladye the quene and Humfrye Bonevell esquier is deffictyff in ther landmere lxxviij rodes both of hygth and bredth, and ought to be made by William Serventone John Hearne jentellmen, and John Thorntone.

And further the sayd jury sayth, that Sir James Haryntone knyght, is deffictyffe in his landmere xx rodes both off high and bredth and ought to be made, by John Coker and Fraunces Paternuster and Robert Matsone tenauntes to the same.

Further the sayde jury sayth that ther is xl rodes of therll of Sussexe landmere defictyffe both off hig[th] and bredth and ought to be made by John Coker, William Coker Fraunces Paternuster Robert Matsone and John Trotte tennauntes to the same.

Further the sayd jury sayth that our soveraine ladye the quene and Humffrye Bonvelle esquier is defict[yffe] in ther landmer xvj rodes both of high and bredth and ought to be made by the sayd John Trott tenant to the [same].

And further the sayd jury sayth that William Wiltone parsone of Flette is defictyffe in his landmere xiij rodes, both of high and bredth and ought to be made [by] William Willtone parsone of Flette.

And further the sayd jury sayth that John Trott is defictyffe in his owne severall landmere xx rodes both off hygh and bredth and ought to be made by the sayd John Trotte.

And forther the sayd jury saye that the eyers of the Braunshes is defictyve ther landmer xx rodes both off hyght and bredth and ought to be made by the sayd eyers of Braunshes.

[473.XI.36]   211

(13 *The Landmer*)   And forther the sayd jury sayth that the comon l[an]dmer is defectyffe agaynste the comone of Flette xx rod both off high and bredth and ought to be mad by comone menworke, as yt hath bene accostomed heretofor.

And further the sayde jury saye, that Lawraunce Wryte is defictyffe in his owne severall landmere x rod both of hygh and bredth and ought to be made by the sayd Lawraunce Wright.

Further the sayde jury saye, that Sir James Harentone is defictyffe in his landmere iiij rod both of hyght and bredth and ought to be made by William Coker tennaunte to the same.

And further the sayd jury sayth, that therll of Sussexe is defictyff in his landmere xx rodes both of high & bredth and to be made by William Coker, Jhon Coker, Fraunces Paternuster, John Fysher, Robert Matsone and John Trotte tennantes to the same.

And further the sayd jeury saye, that Sir James Haryntone knyght is defictyffe in his landmere xxx rods both off hight and bredth and ought to be made by John Coker and Lawrance Wright tenaunte to the same.

And further the sayd jury saye, that ther is a gatt called Newe Fenne Drove, which is defictyffe and ought to be made by the enhabytours of Flett Fynne Ende by comone menworkes.

(*The defaltes of the hedynges in Byllcers*) Item the sayd jury sayth that the hedynges in Bylsares is defyctiffe v^{xx} rods from Ravens Dyke to Newe Dyke of the weste syde of the Olde Eye, both of hygh and bredth, and ought to be made by Thomas Clarke and Jhon Dagers.

And further the sayd jury saye, that ther is iiij rodes defyctiffe at Newe Dykes Ende both of high & bredth and ought to be made by comone menworke as yt hath bene accostomed heretofore.

And further the sayd jury sayth, that Sir William Cordwille knyght, hath l rods of the hedynges of Byllsars of the weste syde of the Olde Eye is in deffyctyffe, both off hyght and bredth and ought to be made by John Death off Gosbouretownne.

And further the sayd jury saythe that ther is vj rodes defyctiff both of high and bredth and ought to be mad by Thomas Thorntone.

And further the sayd jury saye that ther is iiij rodes of the hedynges in Bylsares defictyffe both of high and bredth and ought to be made by William Serventone and John Hernne jentyllmene.

And further the sayd jury sayth that ther is vj rodes deffyctive, of the same hedynges and ought to be made by John Dagers.

And further the sayd jury sayth that ther is viij rodes of the same hedynges defictyffe and ought to be made by the eayers of the Earbes.

And further the sayd jury saye that Lawraunce Clarke of Gedny have iiij rodes of the same hedynges defficityffe and ought to be made by the sayd Lawraunce Clarke of Gednaye.

And further the sayde jurye saythe, that ther is vj rodes of the same hedynges defyctiffe both of hygh and bredth and ought to be made by Mr John Davye jentyllmane.

And further the sayd jurye saythe that ther is iiij rodes of the same hedynges deffectyffe both off heygth and bredth and ought to be made by William Serventone and John Hearne jentyllmen.

And further the sayd jurye saye one rode defyctyff and ought to be made by comone menworke as yt hath benne accostomed heretofore.

[473.XI.37]

(14 *Myllegatte*) Item the sayd jury sayeth, that ther are vij rodes defictyffe in Myllgate and ought to be made by Cutberde Jacsone and theres off Braunshes.

Further the sayd jury say that ther be iiij rodes in the sayd banke defictyffe and ought to be made by theeres off Braunshes and William Callowe jentyll.

And further the sayd jury sayth, that ther is defictyffe in the sayd banke x rodes and ought to be made by theeres of Braunshes.

And further the sayde jury sayth, that ther is v rodes more defyctiffe in the sayd banke and ought to be made by Sir James Harryngtone knyght and theeres of Braunshes.

And further the sayd jurye sayth that ther be vj rodes defictyfe in the sayd bankes and ought to be made by Sir William Cordall, and the eyres off Braunshes.

And further the sayde jury sayth, that ther be vij rodes defictyffe in the sayde banke and ought to be made by Mr Traforth and the eyers off Braunshes.

And further the sayd jurye sayth that ther be vj rodes defictyffe in the sayde banke and ought to be made by the eyeres off Braunshes and by comon menworke.

And further the sayd jury sayth that ther be vij rodes of the same banke deffectyffe and ought to be made by theres of Hepes and the eares of Braunshes.

And further the sayde jury sayth that ther be ij rodes and a halffe defectyffe of the saide banke & ought to be mayd by eyers of Hepes and by comon menworkes.

And further the sayd jury sayth, that ther is j rode of the sayd banke defictyffe and ought to be made by Willyam Adame esquier and Lenarde Wode.

And further the sayd jury sayth that ther be vj rodes defictyffe off the sayd banke & ought to be made by Larance Clarke and Lenard Wode.

And forther the sayd jury sayth that ther is j rode off the sayde banke defictyffe and ought to be made by John Obbynes and Lenarde Wode.

Further the sayd jury sayth that ther is j rode defictyffe off the sayd banke and and [sic] ought to be made by Thomas Ogulle esquier, and Lenarde Wode.

And further the sayde jury sayth that ther is iiij rodes defictyffe of the sayd banke and ought to be made by John Browne and Lenard Wode.

And further the sayd jury sayth, that ther is vij rodes defyctiffe of the sayd banke and ought to be made by Robert Otterbye and Lenarde Wode.

Further the sayde jury sayth, that ther more iij rodes defictyffe and ought to be made by William Callowe jentyllmane, and the eyers of Nycolas Fostere.

And further the sayd jury sayth that ther is more one halffe rode of the sayd banke defictyffe & ought to be made by John Obbynes.

And further the sayde jury sayth that it is mete and necessarye to have a stronge payere of barres sett one Newe Dyke one the forther

ende next to the landmere for to kepe cattayll of on the sayd land
and ther to be kept and mayntayned by acar mony.

[473.XI.38]

(15 *Flete in Masdykes*) Item the sayd jury saye that ther is vj
rodes in Massedykes next unto Dolles Drove is defictyffe and ought
to be made by Lawrance Clarke.

And further the sayde jury saye that ther is xx rode betwene
Pynne Stocke and Fletes Landes off the weste syd of the Olde Eye is
in deffictyffe and ought to be made by the eyers off the Braunshes
both off hygeth and bredth.

And further the sayde jurye sayth that before this abovesayd
ther is ij rodes deffectyffe and ought to be made by Thomas Thorntone Thomas Cuer and John Thorntone both higth & bredth.

And further the sayde jury saye that the Olde Eye is defictyffe in
sertaytayne[1] places from the Lettyll Brege, to Pynne Stocke, for
want off dykynge and ought to be dyked clensede and scored by the
lande holders of both sydes ajoynyng next unto the sayd eye.

And furthter the sayd jury sayth that from the Lettell Breg to
Pownde Reges Ende the Olde Eye is defictyffe in sertayne places for
went of dykynge and ought to be dykede clensed and scorede by
the land holders of both sydes : as is afore specyffyed.

(*South Eye Banke from the coste of Gadnye, toward the coste of
Holbydche*) And further ther sayd jury sayth that Sowth Eye
Banke is defyctyffe from the coste of Gednye toward the coste off
Holbydche, xvj rodes both of hyght and bredth and ought to be
made by our soveraine lady the quine and Humffrye Bonvell
esquyere.

(*Therll of Sussex*) And further the sayd jurye saythe, that ther
is ij rodes xiiij fott deffectyffe and ought to be made by Symone
Browne both off high and bredth.

And further the sayde jury sayth that ther is j rode iij fotte
defictyffe both of hyghe and bredth and ought to be made by William
Calowe off Holbydche jentyllmane.

Further the sayde jury saythe that ther is xj fott deffictede of
high and bred and ought to be mad by Edward Thomas.

And further the sayde jury sayth that ther is vj rodes deffictyffe
and ought to be made off hyght and bredth by the eyers off Symonde
Whight.

(*Sir James Harytnton*[1]) ... And further the sayd jury sayth that
ther is j rode x fotte deffictyffe and aughte to be made by John
Obbeynes.

And further the sayd jury sayth that ther is v rods xvj fotte
deffyctyffe of hi[ght] & bredth and ought to be made by Symond
Browne.

And further the sayd jurye sayth that ther is j rode deffictyffe of
hight & bredth and ought to be made by Robert Otterbye.

[1] *Sic.*

And further the sayde jury sayth that ther is j rode deffyctyffe & ought to be made by Robert Matsone & Jhon Fysher both of hyght and b[redth].

And further the sayd jurye sayth that ther is j rode xij fotte deffecty[ve] of hight and bredth and ought to be made by Anthony Eger.

And fur[1] the sayd jurye sayth that ther is j rode xij fott deffictyf of high and bredth and ought to be made by John Coker.

And further the sayd jury saye ther is xvj fott deffyctyffe and ought to be made by William Coker both of high and bredth.

[473.XI.39]   212

(16)   And further the sayd jury sayth that ther is . . .[2] rode ij fott deffictyffe and ought to be mad bothe of hight and bredth by John Thorntone.

Further the sayde jury sayth that ther is iij rodes xvj fott deffictyffe both of high and bredth and ought to be made by John Cuer.

And further the sayd jury sayth that ther is xvj fott deffictyffe both of high and bredth and ought to be made by Lawrance Clarke and Robert his sonne.

(*Our soveraine lady the quyne*)   And further the sayde jury sayth that ther is v rode x fott deffictyffe & ought to be made by Jhon Mane esquier both of hygh and bredth.

And further the sayd jury sayth that ther is v rodes x fott deffectyffe bothe off hyght and bredth and ought and ought[1] to be made by Sir William Cordwell.

And further the sayd juery sayth that ther is viij fott deffectyffe both off hyth and bredth & ought to be mad by Addeler Welbye esqueiere.

And further the sayde jurye sayth that ther is x fot defictyffe of hygh and bredth and ought to be made by Thomas Ogulle esquier.

And further the sayd jury sayth that ther is viij rodes x fot deffictyffe both of hyght and bred & ought to be made by the eyers of Dysnyes.

And further the sayd jury sayth that ther is iij rods v fott defictyffe both of hight and bredth & ought to be made by the eyers off Thomas Flete.

And further the said jury sayth that ther is vj rodes v fott deffictyffe of hight and bred and ought to be mad by the eyers of Symond Whight.

And further the sayde jury sayth that that[1] ther is j rode and xiiij fott defectyffe of the sayd banke, and ought to be made by John Harwell of Suffoke.

And further the sayd jury sayth that ther is iij rodes viij fott deficteffe of the sayde b[an]ke and ought to be made by John Davye jentyllmane.

[1] *Sic.*
[2] There is a small hole in the folio.

(*Joyes Dyke*) Furthere the saye that yt ys nessesarye that Joyes Dyke be kyepte and repared bye comone myne work.

(*Holbyche to the Inquerment of the Comitinars*) Furthere the theye[1] saye that Holbyche have of long tyme sufferyd there eye to lye in greate decaye fore lake of dykynge frome a place cauled Egates End to South Eye.

And furthere the saye that the inhabbytans of Holbyche have caste a dame in there eye at a place cauled Holbyche Bryge in the Fene End wherebye the watere ys lettyd . . .[2] course to the se to the greate dangere of the hole countrye nexte adj[oining].

Furthere the saye that Holbyche Eye Brynke ys defectyfe fore lak of heyghte . . . and ought to be mad by the ineabbyetanse of Holbyche frome the Egates End to . . . bryge.

[473.XI.40]

(17 *Holbiche*) The preter illos verdytt for Holbiche at the sessions of sewars kepte at Spaldynge in the x[th] yere of the r[ei]gn of our sovereign lady Elizabethe by the grace of God quene of Inglond France & Irelond deffender of the faithe etc., 1568, Mr Robarte Pulvertofte beynge the foremanne of the said jurye, as followethe.

(*The weste syde of Holbiche Eye* 1) Firste the said jurye saythe that the weste syde of Holbiche Eye frome Chanons Felde Corner to[3] Hye Crosse Bridge lackethe heighte & oughte to be amended by Holbiche by common meane workes.

(*The weste syde of Holbiche Eye* 2) Item they say that the weste syde of the said eye frome Hye Crosse Bridge to Mr Ogles house, nowe in thuse of Richard Holden lacketh highte in some places which oughte to be amended by fruntagers.

(*The este syde of Holbiche Eye* 3) Item they say that the este syde of the said eye frome Cacrow Gates End to Hye Crosse Bridge lackethe highte in dyvers places, and oughte to be made & amended by fruntagers.

(*The este syde of Holbiche Eye* 4) Item they say that the este syde of the same eye frome Hye Crosse Bridge to John Randes house lackethe highte in dyvers places, which oughte to be amended by Holbiche by comon meaneworkes.

(*V bridges* 5) Item they say that one bridge called Hye Crosse Bridge Ravensbridge Maydens Bridge Churchebridge and Garners Bridge ys in decay & oughte to be mayd & amended by acre sylver.

(*Southe Eye* 6) Item they say that the sowthe half of the streame of Sowthe Eye ys defectyve for lack of haffynge & rodynge, which oughte to be donne by the owners of the landes of Thornay syde.

(*Headynges* 7) Item they say that all the headynges of bothe sydes the common sewer frome Randes house to the seabankes

---

[1] *Sic.*
[2] The bottom right-hand corner of the folio is missing.
[3] " Saterday " cancelled.

oughte to be kepte stopte by the fruntagers, and not to be oppeyned but by the consent of the dykegravys.

(*Pety dreyne* 8)   Item they say that ther is a pety dreyne called the Este Pety Dreyne goynge frome Hirdletre Dyke on the sowthe leadynge neare to Damgate to a house of Robarte Thorpes & oughte to fall into the ryver frome Rawlyns in & by a dytche betwene theires of Bawde & Barington & so to Baringtons Gate betwene the land of theires of Mr Flete & the said Baringtons, and so by the gate syde to Puddyng Rigge & over the gate betwene the lorde Dacres & the colledge & ther to fall into the eye.

(*Cranesgate* 9)   Item they say that one gate called Cranesgate lackethe highte frome Ravensdyke to Trynyte Ch . . .[1] Crosse, and oughte to be maid by Whaplode & Holbiche by common meane-workes, and frome that crosse to Ferther Oldegate to be mayd by Holbiche by common meaneworkes, and frome the Ferther Oldegate to Hyndes house to be mayd by Whaplode by common meane-workes, and all the headynges betwene Holbyche & Whaplode oughte to be mayd & kepte suffycyently to the seabanck, frome the said Hyndes house by fruntagers, and also frome Hyndes house lykewyse to Hirdeltre Dyke by the dyvycon of Holbiche & Whaplode the said headynges to be kepte also by fruntagers.

(*A fynne* 10)   Item they say ther is a fynne on the weste syde of Holbiche Hurnegote, which is to be dyked by Holbiche by common meaneworkes, which fynne commethe frome Wearestockes, & fallethe into the Eye by Lytle Cote.

(*Holbiche Eye* 11)   Item they say that Holbiche Eye lackethe dykynge frome Shepardes Bridge to the Hurne Gote which ought to be done by acre sylver.

[473.XI.41]   213
(18 *Ship Eye Banck defectyve in dyvers places as followeth* 12) Item they say that the lorde Dacres hathe iiij rodes in Ship Eye Banck lackethe highte & breadthe, the quene for Crowland iiij roode lykewyse, John Merten for the house of Spaldynge iij roode, the quene for Thetforthe iij roode, the quene for Bridlyngton j roode, Mr Lyttlebery iij roodes, Mr Welby & Mr Davy for Meares ij roodes, Mr Knevytt iiij roode, Mr Callowe for Curson j roode, the Colledge of Tatsall ij roode, Mr Harwell iiij roode, the bysshoppe of Lyncoln j roode, John Thacker of Dammyttes j roode Mr Davy for Henry Tofte ij roodes, Robarte Pulvertofte of Whaplode gent. ij roodes lackethe highte & breadthe.

(*Defaltes in Sowthe Eye Banck in Holbyche* 13)   Item the lorde Dacres vj roodes lackethe highte, the quene for Crowland vij roodes, the quene for Spaldynge iij roodes Mr Harington ij roode, Mr Davy for Waringe ij roode, Mr Gybon ij roode, Mr Harwell iiij roodes, Mr Covell ij roode, and Robarte Pulvertofte of Whaplode gent. iij roode lackethe highte.

---

[1] A small piece of the right-hand edge of this folio is missing.

(Defaltes in Common Dyke Banck in Holbiche 14) Item the lorde Dacres viij roodes lackethe highte & breadthe, the quene for Crowland xij roodes, Mr Tamworthe j roode, John Merten for the house of Spaldyng iiij roodes & xiiij foote, Mr Callowe for Baringtons ij roodes Mr Knevytt v roodes, Mr Davy for Welby of Halsted ij roode, the said Mr Davy for Kyddall & Sergeantes iiij roodes Tatsall Colledge ij roodes, the bysshoppe of Lyncoln j roode, Thomas Sugar ij roodes, Thomas Burnett j roode Mr Harwell iiij roodes, Mr Gybon ij roodes, Thomas Palmer for Glover iij roode, Thomas Scales j roode, Robarte Pulvertofte of Dorc' j roode.

(Defaltes in Ravensdyke 15) Item the lorde Dacres vij roodes lackethe highte & bredthe, Mr Lyttlebery iiij roodes, Mr Knevytt iij roode, Mr Callowe for Upton iij roode, Mr Davy for St. Nycholas Chapell ij roode, the quene for Crowland vj roode Mr Callowe for Barington iiij roode, the quene for Spaldynge house vij roodes xviij foote, the quene for Bridlyngton ij roodes xj foote, the quene for Thetforthe ij roode, Mr Harwell ij roode, Mr Covell iiij roodes & Barre of the Drove iij roode, & Mr Gybon j roode lackethe highte & breadthe.

(Defaltes in Hirdeltre Dyke Banck 16) Item theires of Mr Guddyng & Wm. Stowe ij roodes lackethe highte, Mr Davy for Kyddall & Welby viij roode the quene for Crowland viij roode, the quene for the house of Spaldynge iiij roodes, Mr Callowe for Whittlebery iij roode & xvij foote, the house of Thetforthe v roode, Mr Davy for Bridlyngton iij roode Mr Carsay iiij roode, the bysshoppe of Lyncoln ij roode, theires of Humfrey Carton iiij roodes, Thomas Burnett ij roodes & xv footes, Mr Ogle for Etton ij roodes, Thomas Sugar iij roodes, Mr Ogle for Garner ij roodes, Mr Davy for Lotes iij roodes, Henry Jellowe ij roodes & di., Mr Harwell viij roodes, Mr Davy for Warynge v roodes ix foote, Mr Davy for Sergeantes vj roodes, Mr Gybon vj roodes, Thomas Scotte ij roodes theires of Whyte iiij roodes di. theires of Mr Frankes v roodes, Mr Callow j roode Wm. Cramper iij roodes, Thomas Palmer ij roodes, Mr Covell j roode & di., Barre of the Drove v roodes the lordes of Flete j roode, Robert Pulvertofte of Whaplode gent. j roode, theires of Branches j roode.

(Headynges 17) Item they say that the weste syde of Holbiche Eye frome Chanons Felde Corner to Holbiche Drove Bridge y[s] defectyve in dyvers places in highte which oughte to be amended by fruntagers.

(Cowfeld Gote 18) Item they say that one gote called Cowfelde Gote ys decayed by dammynge of the fynnes which was donne by the fermers of Meares Marsche, nevertheless the said gote oughte to be removed[1] mayd & kepte by acre sylver, and the fynnes to be dyked by common meaneworkes.

(Clowe 19) Item they say that yt ys nedefull to have a paire of clowes at Maydens Bridge to kepe owte the socke of salt water, and the same to be mayd by acre sylver.

[*Endorsed*:] Holbyche preter illos verdytt for the sewars

[1] *Sic.*

F

[473.XI.42]

The verdyt of Robart Pulvertoft gent. & his fellowes of the preter ellowes quest for the sessions of sewers holden at Spaldinge the (?) xxij[1] day of June before Adlard Welby Leonard Irby John Mann Whellum Darbye & Thomas Welby

(19 *South E*)[2] Fyrst the said jury upon ther othes do present that the south side of South Ee which is Thorney side from No Mannes Landes Ende to Parkyns Coote ys defective through out for lacke of haffeinge scowreinge & clensinge and ought to be done by the right honorable Earle of Bedford or by them which have the occupacion of the groundes which perteyned to the late abbaye of Thorney.

(*Great Ship E*) Item dicunt that Great Shipp E Banke from Shipp E Stow to Dowesdale ys defective in dyvers places & ought to be done & amended by joycement by Whaplode & Holbich.

(*Littell Ship E*) Item dicunt that Lyttell Shipp E Banke is defectyve & falty in dyvers places in heygth and ought to [be] done by joycement by Whaplod onely as appeareth in ther joyce booke.

(*Syde Dyke*) Item dicunt that Syde Dyke in Whaplod extendinge from St Katherines Stoone to Moulton Fenn ys defective in many places & ought to [be] made & done wher need ys both [in] [h]eight & breedth by joycement by Whaplod aforesaid.

(*Randall Dyke to the Inquerment of the Commessiners*) Item dicunt that Randall Dyke extendinge from St Katherines Stone to a certayne low pasture belonginge to the lordes of Moulton ys defective in dyvers places both in heyght & breedeth & ought to be repayred made & done by Whaplod & Holbich by common mine workes.

Item dicunt that the said Randall Dyke from the said low pasture to Moulton Hall Rigge ys defectyve both in heyght & breedeth & ought of ancient custome to be done & made by the lordes of Moulton.

(*Ravenes Dycke*) Item dicunt that a certaine banke extendinge from St Katherines Stoone to Fleete Lanmer ys defective in certayne places [&] ought to be repayred & made by joycement by Whaplod & Holbich as in & by th[er] joyce bookes playnely appeareth.

([*O*]*dd measure*) Item dicunt that ther is certayne odd measure in Ravens Dyke betwine Whaplod & Holbich which ought to be made by certayne landes lyinge in Whaplod as often as yt shalbe nedefull by j d. ob. as by ther towne booke playnely is apparan[t].[3]

(. . . *E siddes*) Item dicunt that a certayne banke extendinge from Gayes Hurne to Semans Bridge of . . . of Whaplod E ys in ruyne & decay & ought to be repayred & amended both in . . . by Whaplod by common myne workes.

---

[1] " Eight " has been cancelled. The reading of the corrected date, which is interlined, is uncertain : " xxti " is a possible alternative.

[2] A hand drawn in the margin points to this paragraph.

[3] The bottom left and part of the bottom right corners of this folio are missing.

Item they say that the banke from Gayes Hurne to Asgarsdyke on the east side . . . E ys . . . in dyvers places & ought to be repayred & amended by the land . . . adioyning.

Item dicunt that the banke from Asgersdyke to Gegill Dyke on the . . . [ea]st side of Wha[plod] is defective in dyvers places & ought to be repayred & made by Whaplod with comon min[e] workes.

. . . [tha]t the banke [from]Gegill Dyke to Semans Bridge on the said east side of W[haplod] . . . [oug]ht to be repayred & amended by the landes ther . . .

. . . of Whaplod from . . . to the goote of the same . . . for lacke of dykenge onely & ought to be done by an . . . towne.

[473.XI.43] 214

(20 *E sides*) Item dicunt that the banke from Semans Bridge to Sparrockes Lane on the[1] . . . Whaplod E ys defective in most places & ought to be done & made onely by howse . . . as well the farryners for ther howses or hamstalles as well as thenhabitantes for the partes.

(*Brydges*) Item dicunt that Callowes Bridge Ropers Bridge Semans Bridge & the bridge that goeth over the pety dreane under Lyttell Shipp E which is the high waye to the drove have byn accustomed & ought to be made repayred & kept by acaridge only and the foresaid Callowes Brydge & the bridge leadeinge to the drove ar now at thes presens needefull to be made.

(*The goote*) Item dicunt that the goote of Whaplod ys in ruyne & utter decaye by the meanes of a certayne bank which was made by one Robart Carr esquier by encloseinge of a peece of marsh grond wher a mayne fin was wont to issue through which was the mayntenaunce & only scowreinge [of] Fleete from the goote to the sea.

(*Comon Dyke*) Item dicunt that a certayne dyke called Common Dyke extendinge from Ship E Stow to Holbich D . . . Bridge ys defectyve in dyvers places both in heigth & breedth and ought to be repayred . . . by joycement by Whaplod & Holbich.

(*Cranesgate*) Item dicunt that a certayne way called Cranesgate from Hynes Crosse to Farther Oldgate ys def[ective in] dyvers places & ought to be repayred & amended by comon myne workes by Whaplod onely.

Item dicunt that from Farther Oldgate to Trynitye Crosse ys defectyve in dyvers places in . . . onely & ought to be repayred & amended by the towneshipp of Holbich.

Item dicunt that from Trynitye Crose to Ravens Dyke ys defective in hight one[ly] . . . to be repayred & made by Whaplod & Holbich by comon myneworkes.

(*Pety dreane called Hagbich Hedinges*) Item dicunt that a certayne pety dreane called Hagbich Hedinges extendinge from Lyttell S[hip]

[1] Part of the right-hand edge of this folio is missing.

E to Asgarsdyke ys cleane decayed for lacke of haffeinge dykeinge
& clenseing . . . done by thos which one both sides abutt upon the
same.

Item they say that the said dreane ought to have his passage
under the south [side of] Asgarsdyke & so to fall into the common
sewer of Whaplod through a trenc[h] . . . foote wyde made eyther of
wodd or stone & the same to be made by acaridge.

(*Certayne shuttes*) Item dicunt quod convenit that a trench
eyther of wodd or stone of iij foote wyde . . . be made for dreaneinge
of the feeldes which ly on the west side of . . . north side of Asgarsedyke unto the south side of Ravens Dyke & the . . . laid & made or
sett att Wasshes Brigge Corner & the same to be . . .

(*Order for Barres*) Item the said jury thynke yt convenyent
that ther should [be] x p[ayre] . . . Gayeshurne & Semans Bridge
that is five payre of either s[ide] . . . to be erected & sett upp by
acaridge of the same towne & th . . . the said jury that noe mann
shall neyther ryde or travell to d . . . the E sydes or over the Ee
& that no mann shall drive any ca[ttell] over . . . Barres upon payne
of x s. every one offendinge this order . . . to be removed but att
such tymes as the dyke . . . of the same towne shall thinke yt convenyent.

[473.XI.44]   215
(21 *Certayne shuttes*) Item dicunt that yt ys convenient & very
needefull that a trench eyther of wodd or stone should be made for
dreaneinge of the feeldes which ly on theast side of Whaplod E att
some place wher the townships shall thinke most convenyent and
the same to be done by acreidge.

(*Howse Roodes*) Item dicunt that yt ys needfull that the howse
roodes betwine Goslinge Hurne & the goote should bee dyked which
hath byn accustomed to be done as well by farryners as by the
inhabytante[s] of the same towne both for howses & hamstalles.

(*The gote*) Item dicunt that the goote of Whaplod aforesaid ys
impayred & much falty in dyvers places and ought to be repaired
amended or made by acaridge only.

(*The Fleete*) Item dicunt that the out fall or Fleete from the said
goote towardes the sea ys defectyve in dyvers places for lacke of
dykeinge & ought to be done by comon myneworkes by Whaplod
aforesaid.

(*A new clow*) Item dicunt that yt ys convenient that a clow
should bee erected & sett upp att some convenient place wher the
towneshipp shall thinke meete betwene Callowes Brydge & the
goote fo[r a][1] munycyon or defence to keep the salt water from the
towne & the same to be done by ac . . .

(*Vacant An order for acreadge*) Item they thynke yt meete that
as often as any acarydge ys laid in the said towne that yt maye
be law[full] to and for the dyke reeves of the said towne for the

---
[1] The right-hand edge of the folio is missing.

tyme beinge to dystreyne any one tenaun[t] . . . any lord or lordes within the said towne for the whole sume of acres that the said lord or lordes have within the said towne and that yt may be lawfull to & for the said tena[unt] so dystreyned to dystreyne the rest of his lordes tenantes of & for all such sume or sumes of m[oney] so by the said tenaunt laid out more then his owne amounteth to by the vertue of this ve[rdict] & petunt legem inde fieri.

(*Gould Dyke*) Item dicunt that ther ys a certayne banke called Gould Dyke extendinge from Whaplod S . . . to Moulton E ys defectyve in dyvers places & ought to be repayred amended & made by . . . of Moulton accordinge to ther old custome.

(*Wilsey Gate*) Item dicunt that a certayne way lyinge in Whaplod aforesaid called Wylsey Gate extend . . . Trynytie Crosse to Moulton Hall Rigg Stow ys defectyve in certayne places and ought [to be] repayred & amended by Whaplod aforesaid with comon myneworkes.

(*Pety dreanes*) Item dicunt that ther ys a certayne petye dreane on the west part of Whaplod feelles . . . is in utter decay which said dreane goeth through Cobgate & falleth into Shitt . . . thence hath his passage over the high way right against the church . . . dyscendeth through the landes of William Tassh gen. and by dyvers mens lands . . . the comon sewer of Whaplod aforesaid which ought to be repayred & amended . . . adioyneinge or abutinge upon the same & thosse landes that dren . . .

Item dicunt that ther is a certayne pety dreane goinge from the church gate vyntyn throu . . . leedinge to the markett place & from thence dyscendeth through the church gate . . . passage betwine the tenement of George Chapman & the tenement of . . . And so dyscendeth through the feeldes by dyvers mennes landes & hath his farth[er] . . . the high way into the dyke of a certayne pasture called Pudinge Land and ther . . . the comon sewer of Whaplod which said dreane ought to be repayred & kept from . . . tyme by the groundes which on both sides adioyne or abutt upon the same . . .

[473.XI.45]   216

(22) Item dicunt that all other pety dreanes belongenge to Whaplod which ar not expressed or named in this present verdyt because they ar to us unknowen shalbe suffyciently repaired a[nd][1] amended as they have byn accustomed heretofore.

(*Croyland*) Item dicunt that a certaine banke called Pursam Banke extendinge from Dowesdale to Croyl[and] and from Croyland to Brother Howse & from Brother Howse to Catchcold & from Catchcold to Ship E Stow ys defectyve both in height & breedeth & ought to [be] repayred amended & ma[de] by the queenes maiestie or her fermers of Croyland aforesaid.

(*Moulton*) Item dicunt that a certayne banke from Moulton Gates End to Moulton Low Dyke called the New Causey ys defectyve

[1] The right-hand margin of this folio is missing.

in certayne places & ought to be amended by the inhaby[ta]untes of Moulton.

(*Moulton*) Item they say that a certayne banke from Catchcold to Moulton West Fenn [ys] defectyve in certayne places & ought to be made by joycement by Moulton.

(*Holbich*) Item thei say that a certayne banke on the west side of Holbich fro Common Dyke to Ravens Dyke ys in ruyne & utter decay in dyvers pla[ces] both in heyght & breedeth and ought to be repayred & amended acco[rding] to ther old custome.

[1]Item the saye that it ys convenient that everi towne in Holland as Whaplod H . . . Flite Gedne and Suttone shall make and have one suffeciant bancke one the weast s[ide of] theyr tounes and at theare out (?) reange of thire tounes to beare the weast watre of . . .

Item the saye that it ys conveniant that all the tounes in Holland bequixt the watre of Wh[aplod] and Tyde Sent Marie shall make and have one suffeceant banke one the west side of ever[i] toune to beare the watre of Whelland, the quene for . . . theyrs for here landes as all othere lordes for there lands with thear teanes as all other . . . that oughte to dowe the same by commene menworcke.

Item thei say that from Welse Brige to Trenitie Crosse ys defectie and ought to be maid by Whoplod by m . . .

[473.XI.46]   217

The verdyct of preter illos quest of the townshypp of Moulton holdone at Spaldyng the xxij[ti] day of July

(23   *One crest betwen Belsmore & Turf Pittes in Wesson*) Fyrst the jurye sayth uppon the othes that there ys one chrest or bancke betwyxt Belsmore and the Turfpyts ys in great ruin and decaye for lacke of heyght and breathe from Loedycke to Goulddyke and ought to be repayred and made be the quens maiestyes tenauntes in Belsmore.

(. . . *betwyxt Depedick [and] the Turf Pites*) Also the sayd jurye sayethe that there ys one chrest or bancke betwixte Depedyke and the Turfpyts forom [*sic*] Lodyke to Goulddyke ys in great ruin and decaye for lake of heyght and breathe and ought to be repaired and mayde bye the fruntigers abuttinge uppon the same.

([*Cl*]*ows*) Also the sayd jurie sayethe that there ys one payre of clowes to dreane the Turfpits that ys in ruin and decaye and one newe payre to be made or one sufficient dame to be kepte bye the inhabitants of Mowlton.

Also the sayd jurye saythe there ys one dyke or banke extendynge frome the Turfpyts Clows to Tuns Brygde ys in ruin and decaye for lake of heyght and breathe in divers places and ought to be repaired and mended bye the townshipe of Moulton bye comon minwark.

Also the sayd jurye saythe that there ys one chrest or banke called the Dole Dyke betwixt the Turfpyts and the West Fene

---

[1] This paragraph is cancelled, the following one (itself partly amended) being evidently substituted. These and the concluding paragraph are in a different hand from the rest of the folio.

extendynge frome Lodyke to Gowldyke ys in great ruin and decaye in divers [p]laces for lake of heyght and breathe and ought to be repayred bye our soverayne ladye the quene for the lands late lord[1] . . . rens Dacet.

[Al]so the sayd jurie saythe that there ys one other dyke or banke in Moulton [call]ed the Loedyke ys in ruin and decaye for lake of heyght and [bre]athe in divers places and ought to be repayred and made bye the . . . maiestie and the lords and land howlders of Mowlton as apea[rethe] bye juyse booke.

[Also th]e sayd jurye saythe that there ys one other dyke or banke called the . . . [de]fectyfe in manie places frome Turfpit Clowes to Seyedyke . . . repayred and mended bye our sofereyne ladye the quene . . . land howlders of Mowlton as aperethe bye a juyse book.

. . . sayethe that ther ys one other dyke called Garnerds Dyke . . . ys in great ruin and decaye in divers places and . . . [a]nd made in sufficient heyght and breathe . . . [b]ye the quene and the lords and landhowlders . . . [apere]the bye the juyse booke.

[473.XI.47]   218

(24) *The Ee banke*) Also the sayd jurye saythe that thee Eae bankes be defectyfe for lake of heyght and brethe from the clows to the Newe Brygde one bothe sydes and ought to be repayred and mended bye the inhabytantes of Mowlton bye comon minwork.

(*The New Cawsay*) Also the sayd jurye saythe that there ys one causye called the Newe Causye extending from Lodyke to Gowldyke betwixt the East Fene and the West Fene ys in grea[t] ruin and decaye for lake of heyghte and breathe and ought to be repayred and made bye the towneshipe of Mowlton bye comon minworks.

(*The Ee bankes*) Also the sayd jurie saythe that frome Newe Brygde to Nicals Brygde on the west side one the eae ys defectyfe and ought to be made in sufficient heyght and breathe bye the inhabitantes of Mowlton bye comon minworke.

(*The Ee bankes*) Also the sayd jurye saythe that from Newe Brygde to Nicals Brygde one the east syde of the Eae ys defectyfe in divers places bothe bye headynges and banke and ought to be repayred and made bye the fermers of the Lowe Felde and all other that have lands buttinge uppon the same and frome Nicals Brigde to the goote to be made in like maner of all those that have lands buttinge uppon the same.

(. . . [*pe*]*te drens*) Also the sayd jurie saythe that all suche petye dreans as are in ruin and decaye within the towneshipe of Multon ought to be clensed scowred bye all those that have lande joyninge to theme and bye all those lands that dreans bye them.

(. . . *brigge*) Also the sayd jurie saythe that there ys one brigde cald Poyse Brygde ys in great ruin and decaye for lake of timber and borde and ought to be repayred and made bye the townshipe of Mowlton by acregds.

---

[1] The bottom left corner of this folio is missing.

Also the sayd jurie saythe that there ys certayne hedynges betwixt the sea dike and Northe Medowes ys in ruin and decaye and ought to be repayred and mended bye the land howlders and tenauntes abuttinge uppon the same hedynges & that no mane cut oppene no hedyng withowt consent of the degrevs of Molltone.

Also the sayd jurie saythe that there are certayne wears or wearsteds within the comon sure of Multon ys defectife for lake of widnes and breathe and stopes the freshe water for havinge redye passhade to the goote and that the sayd wers or werstedes be plucte up and made witherd bye those that doo occupie the sayd wersteds.

[A]lso the sayd jurie sayte that there ys one goote in Mowlton called the Owlde Goote [i]s in great ruin and decaye for lake of spedye conveyans of . . . the water to the sea and ougt to be repayred and made bye [the] townshipe of Mowlton bye achrigde.

[473.XI.48]   219

(25 *Weston peterelis*) Fyrst the jury sayeth that the quenens maiestie hath a certayne bancke on Lowedyck to the valew of lx roodes defectyve & fautye both in heyght & breade & ought to be repared made & amended by the quenens maistye.

(*Belsmore Bancke*) Also the said jury sayeth that Belsmore Bancke on the same Lowedycke is defectyve & fautye bothe in heyght & breade & ought to be repared made & amended by the firmore.

(*Lowedycke*) Also the jury sayeth that John Davyson hath a certayn bancke on Lowedycke to the valeu of ij roods defectyve & fautye both in heyght & breade & ought to be repared & made by the same John.

Also the jury sayeth that John Harte of Spoldyng hath on the same Lowdycke to the valeu of ij roodes defectyve & fautye both in heyght & bread & ought to be repared & made by the same John Harte.

Also they saye that Symon Hall hath on the same dyck to the valeu of ij roodes defectyve & fautye both in heyght & breade & ought to be repared & made by the same Symon or his tenant.

Also they saye that Andrewe Scare hath on the same banck to the valew of iij roodes defectyve & fautye bothe in heyght & bread & ought to be repared & made by the same Andrewe Scare.

Also the[1] saye that Thomas Welbye armiger hath one roode on the same banck defectyve & fautye both in heyght & breade & ought to be repared & made by the same Thomas.

Also they saye that Mr Hordyn hath one roode dim. on the same bancke defectyve & fautye both in heyght & breade & ought to be repared & made by the same Mr Ordyn.

Also they saye that Mr Covell hath v roodes on the same banck defectyve & fautye both in heyght & breade & ought to be repared & made by the same Mr Covell.

[1] *Sic.*

Also they saye that Mr Pulvertoft hath iij roodes on the same banck defectyve & fautye both in heyght & breade & ought to be repared & made by the same Mr Pulvertoft.

Also they saye that Sir James Haryngton armiger hath v roodes on the same banck defectyve & fautye both in [heig]ht & breade & ought to be repared & made by the same James or his tenants.

[1]. . . John Leues hath ij roodes on the same banck defectyve & fautye both in heyght & . . . be repared & made by the same John.

[473.XI.49]   220

(26 *Lowe Dycke*) Also the jury sayeth that Thomas Leues hath ij roods on the same bancke defectyve & fautye both in heyght & breade & ought to be repared & made by the same Thomas.

Also they saye that Antonye Heydon hath ij roodes iiij foote on the same bancke defectyve & fautye both in heyght & breade & ought to be repared & made by the same Antonye Heydon.

Also they saye that the lordes of Molton hath ij roodes iiij foote on the same banke defectyve & fautye both in heyght & breade & ought to be repared & made by the same lordes or ther tenants.

(*New Dycke or Ravens Dycke*) Also the jury sayeth that the lordes of Molton hath iij roodes & vj foot on Newdycke otherwise Ravens Dyke defectyve & fautye both in heyght & breade & ought to be repared & made by the same lordes or ther tenants.

Also they saye that Antonye Heydon hath iij roodes & vj foote on the same Newdycke defectyve & fautye both in heyght & breade & ought to be repared & made by the same Antonye Hedon.

Also they saye that Mr Pultoft hath iiij roodes & dim. on the same bancke defectyve & fautye both in heyght & breade & ought to be repared & made by the same Mr Pultofte.

Also the saye that Mr Covell hath ix roodes & xij foote on the same bancke defectyve & fautye both in heyght & breade & ought to be repared & made by the said Mr Covell.

Also the saye that Mr Ordyn hath ij roodes v foote on the same bancke defectyve & fautye both in heyght & breade & ought to be repared & made by the same Mr Ordyn.

Also they saye that Thomas Welbye armiger hath one roode & dim. on Newdycke defectyve & fautye both [in] heyght & bread & ought to be repared & made by the same Thomas Welbye.

[A]lso theye saye that Andrew Scare hath ij roode on the same bancke defectyve & fautye both in heyght & bread & ought to be repared & made by the same Andrew Scare.

Also they saye that Rychard Faukner hath iij roodes on the said Newdycke defectyve & fautye both in heyght & breade & ought to be repared & made by the said Rychard.

Also they saye that John Harte hath iij roodes ix foote on the same bancke defectyve & fautye both in heyght [1][& br]eade & ought to be repared & made by the same John Harte.

[1] The bottom left corner of this folio is missing.

. . . saye that Robert Coolyre hath j roode on the same bancke defectyve & fautye both in heyght & . . . to be repared & made by the said Robert.

[473.XI.49*d*]

(*Spoldyng hye waye*) Also the jury sayeth ther is a certayne common hye waye that ledeth from Shermon Crosse to Wycume Yates defectyve & fautye both in heyght & breade & ought to be reparede & made by the towneshipe of Spoldynge by common mynworke that there water falle not into Wykemere.

[473.XI.50]   221

(27 *Newe Dycke or Ravens Dycke*) Also the jury sayeth that Wylliam Gunne hath ij roodes on Newdycke defectyve & fautye both in heygh & breade & ought to be repared & made by the said Wylliam Gonne.

Also the jury sayethe the quenes maiestye hath xl roode on the same bancke defectyve & fautye bothe in heyght & bread & ought to be repared & made by the quenes maiestye.

(*He deyngs*) Also the jury sayeth ther are certayne hedyngs of the west syde of Molton Mere from Gooldyke to the sea deyke defectyve & fautye both in heyght & breade & ought to be repared by all those that have any lands abuttyng agaynest the same.

([*W*]*eekmeare* [*hea*]*dings*) Also they saye ther are certayne hedyngs on the est syde of Wykemere from Gooldyke to the sedyke defectyve & fautye both in heyght & breade & ought to be repared & made by al those that have anye lands abuttyng agaynest the same.

Also they saye ther are certayne hedyngs on the west syde of Wykemere from Gooldyke to the sedyke defectyve & fautye both in heyght & breade & ought to be repared & made by the towneshipe of Spoldyng by al those that have any lands abuttyng agaynest the same.

Also they saye shalbe drened[1]

(*Damme*) Also they saye ther ought to be a dame or clowe kept in Wykemere at Barryte Gate for the defence of the socke of the sea.

Also the jury sayth ther is a bancke called Olde Fendyke from Molton Mere to Wykemere defectyve & fautye both in height & bread & ought to be repared & made by the towneshipe of Weston by common mynworke.

Also the saye the sea bank from Newcote to Weston Horne defectyve & fautye both in heyght & breade & ought to be repared & made by the towneshipe of Weston by common mynworke.

[Al]so they saye the hye waye from the seadyck to the Churche Bryge to be made by comon mynwork.

[2]. . . sayeth ther ought to be a damme kept betwene the lands of

---

[1] This sentence is left unfinished and the words " shalbe drened " are cancelled.
[2] The bottom left corner of this folio is missing.

John Elward & the lands of Thomas . . . [def]ence of certayne plowed lands.

. . . ought a petty drene to be had at a place called Roods Bryge for the drenyng . . . [a]s it hath bene acostomed where the most of the inhabitors shall thinke it . . .

. . . [saye]th ther ought another petty drene to be had into Scytelond for drenyng of . . . land into Wykemere.

. . . grounds of Symson Morys & Frances to be drened by Wykmere when . . . [r]eceave the water.

. . . angle to be drened into Wykemere.

. . . the west syde from tyme to tyme when nede . . . bryge.

. . . open no gytts over Stone Gatte to . . . into Wyke . . . hole from tyme to tyme.

[473.XI.51]   222

For Spaldyng 1568
anno decimo Elizabeth regine

(29 *The banke of the este syde of the water of Weyland*) Fyrste the jury saith that the greate banke on the este syde of the water of Weyland ys defectyve for lack of height that ys to say frome Brother House to Pycale & frome Pycale to Cubbit and from Cubbit to Spaldyng Towne Ende in dyvers places and ought to be done by the frontagers.

(*The bankes of Lythercotes*) Also they say that the bankes called Lythercoattes Bankes ys defectyve in dyvers places & ought to be made by all those landholders within the said angle.

(*Wykemere hedynges*) Also they say that the hedynges on the west syde of Wykemere ys defectyve in dyverse places and ought to be made by the frontagers.

(*Heigh wayes defectyve in Spaldyng*) Also the said jurye saith that there be certayne heigh wayes in Spaldyng that are defectyve and ought to be exalt[ed][1] . . . height for they be the wayes bothe for passadge and also which doth angle the groundes and will kepe the water in every . . . angle may not be surrounded by another but that every angle to be dreaned after other into Cowhourne Goate . . . the fyrste high way is called Halmer Gate that leadyth to Randall Gate and frome Randall Gate to Wake Dyke betwene We . . . And also one waye or layne called Lawe Gate the whiche wayes we pray that they may be maid . . . and ought to be exalted of sufficient height by common mynworkes by the inhabitauntes of Spaldyng for the passadge of the people . . .

And further more the jury saith that ytt ys necessary that a brydge be made over the dreane that leadyth to Cowh . . . for the passadge of them dwelling in Wyke and also others of the inhabitaunce of Spaldyng & ought to be maide by acre . . .

(*The angle betwene Pynchbeck Lane and the lodge*) And also the said jury saith that the land betwene Pynchbek Lane & the lodge

---

[1] A large part of the right edge of this folio is missing.

of the marshe and Sterfenne Grafte . . . without a dreane by reason of the fenne water in the same grafte ys of suche a heyghte over the same feldes . . . dreane by the same grafte as yt haith bene accustomed therefore the said jury prayeth that the water of Sterf[enne] . . . stopped by the space of foure dayes when nede shall require that the land before named may be dreaned by the same . . . when the greate rage of water by downe fall doth overflowe the same land.

(*A meane for the preservacion for the landyng of Weyland*) Also the said jury prayeth that a lawe may be maide uppon a payne that no maner of person or persones . . . Cubbit and Pycaile that be frontagers of the ryver of Weyland or any other doo lay any maner swepyng of how . . . stofe on the ryver syde or caste any of the same into the ryver and also that every persone or persones . . . the ryver syde that the broken rede in there (?) cates and other suche lyke baggyshe be no[t] . . . that yt be not hurtfull to the ryver and that no man caste no deade carcayses into the . . . do wasshe or clense any paunches of any beastes that haith the donge in them.

(*Takyng of the water out of Weyland*) Also the said jury saith that the takyng of water oute of the greate ryver of Weyland or oute of an . . . Weyland otherwais than for the preservacion of fysshe in fysshe poundes, or for meate water and so tha[t] . . . by any secrete gyttes or trenchis but by such order as haith bene accustomed.

(*The dreane of Lethercotes Angle*) Also the said jury saith that the dreane of Lethercoates Angle ys defectyve for lack of dyk[ing] . . . of Weyland at a place called Pole Grene untyll the fallyng into Hargate Grafte and oughte to be . . . thre foote and the charge of the dykyng of the same dreane for the one moitie therof by all those . . . dreane and the other moytye of the charges of all those that have land lyeng within the same angle . . . the water of Weyland of the este and Westloode of the north and Spaldyng Fenne of the sout[h] . . . dreane ys to be dyked over any heygh waye, and also thorowe Cammell Gate the same to be done by the . . . angle and also at the west ende of Cammell Gate there a brydge to be maid over the heygh way that . . . foote and a halfe and in depeness thre foote and also all vainttes and hollowe tres that shall . . .

[473.XI.52] 223

[1]The verdyt of Robert Pulver[toft] . . . holden at Spaldyng the xxij^{ti} day of . . . before Adlerd Welby Leonard Irsby John . . .

(30 *Pynchbek Sterfen Grafte bankes*) Item the said jurie say that the bankes of Sterfen Graft of bothe siedes . . . to be made by all thos that do abut . . . the same graft every man against his own both . . . and Pynchbek except agaynst the commondes and that to be made by the inhabetantes of Pinchbek and Spaldinge by commond myln wark so muche as lyethe within Pinchbeck & the other by Spalding.

[1] Parts of the right half of this folio are missing.

(*Gytes in Weland*) Item thay say that for as miche as by command experience yt dothe manyfestlye apere that the entringe of the water of Weland towarde the sey by gyttis is very profitable to the mane rever for the depthe therfore thay thinke yt very mete & necessarye that ther be newe gittis made & herafter to be meantened from tyme to tym as nede shall require & the same gittes to be repared & mentened by all thos that dreane by the same ryver of Weyland as well by Kesten as by Holland.

(*The Northe & Southe Fendike*) Item the sade jurie say that the Northe Fendike from Wrightbold Corner to Dove Hurn & from Dove Hurn . . . Halfstowe is defective for lacke of hyght & brede and the same oughte & hathe bene accustomed to [be] made by the quenes mayestye the lordes & owners for ther landes in Pinchbek by acres that is every acre of like muche.

(*Burn Eye & the outfalles*) Item thay say that the outfall from Surflett to the sey ought to be yerly roded skowred & clens[ed] . . . that the same ought to be down twise in the yer at the leaste by the inhabetauntes of Surflet and they think yt mete & very necessarye that all dammes & calfes lefte or made & not taken uppe at the dykinge of the same eye frome Dove Hurn to the outfall at Surflet Seys End be sufficiently tak[en] uppe and amended by them that were charged to the dykinge of the same.

(*Rodinge Burn Eye betwene Est Cote and Godrame Gote*) Item thay say that the rever of Basson Dike or Burn Eye betwene Est Cote and Gotheram Gote . . . roded skowred & clensed in the defalt of Richard Leman beynge fermore to the . . .

(*The dreane at Goderame Cote*) Item thay say that ther is an ancient dreane in Pinchbeck Fenn whiche comethe from a . . . called Goosepites to the lode that comethe from Goderame Cote and so to Black Dyke and from . . . to Sterlode and ought to be diked roded clensed & skowred by the inhabe[tants] of Kesten and Pinchbeck as hathe bene accustomed.

(*Burtefen Graft*) Item thay say that Burtefen Graft which extendes from Lawnscot as . . . Burton Gote ought & hathe bene accustomed to be diked . . . quenes maiestie the lordes & owners of landes in Pinchbek . . . acres . . . accordinge to the valew that ys nedfull . . . to be roded by common menwork . . .

(*Redy Graft*) Item thay say that a graft called Redy Graft extendinge from a place called . . . Gote ought & hathe bene accustomed to be diked so ofte [as] nede shall r[equire] . . . the lordes & owners of landes in Pinchebeck by acres that ys for . . . accordinge to the valewe that is nedefull to be down & to be roded by com[mon] . . .

(*Northe Gate Grafte trenche*) Item thay say that where ther ys a trenche lade under Northe Gate Gr[aft] . . . Burtons Goote for that Stegate Gote is the dreane for the sayde grafte . . . and . . the northe syde of the same grafte : the sade jurie thynkes . . . necessarye that the sade Redye Grafte be dreaned by the Stegate

Goote . . . she will serve and whan she will not serve to dreane by the
. . . to Burtons . . . and not otherways.

[473.XI.53]   224
[1](31 *The gootes*) Item thay say that Stegate Gote & Burtefen
Goote is defectyve for lacke of good . . . made repared & amended
by the quenes maiestey the lordes & ow[ners] . . . Pinchbek by acre
sylver as hathe bene accustomed.

(*The trenche*) Item thay say that the dreane from the trenche
to Redye Graft parsell . . . defectyve for lacke of dykinge rodinge &
skowringe & ought to be dyked by the quenes . . . Pinchebek by
acre sylver and to be roded by comond menwarkes.

(*Basson Dyke*) Item they say that the bankes of bothe sides of
Burn Eye from Est Cote to Neubury . . . in hyght & bredthe &
ought to be repared exalted & amended from Est Cote to Go . . .
by the quenes mayestie the lordes & owners in Burn and from Gotheram Cote to Dov[e] . . . northe syde & from Est Cote to Dove Hurn
on the southe side by the quenes mayestie . . . in Pinchebek as
apperethe by the jose boukes and from Dove Hurn to Neuberye
. . . sydes the same eye ought to be exalted repared & amended by
all thos that . . . any growndes against the same eye by frontage.

(*The drene at West Feld End*) Item thay say ther is a sewer or
lode in the fen is defective in dikinge rodinge & skowringe for . . .
End to the clowes at Wrightbold & ought & hathe bene accustomed
to be dyked ro[ded] . . . by the quenes majestie for hyr landes lyenge
at Wrightbold in Gosbertowne.

(*The Beache Bankes*) Item they say that the banke scalled the
Beache ar defective for lack of height . . . and ought to be repared
exalted & amended by all thos that abut u[pon] . . .

(*The barres & dreftes*) Item the saide jurie thynkes yt very mete
& necessarye that the barres of Basson . . . up shall still be meantened
from tyme to tyme accordinge to the lawes before . . . and no dryftes
shall passe over the same dike but according to the sai[d] . . . made
for the same.

(*The wood growynge of the sewe bankes*) Item thay say that where
dyvers persons have set wod upon the bank . . . Northe Gate Graft
Sterfen Graft as other sewers so thike & so nye the . . . the mener
cannot conveniently be cast upon the bankes of the sa[me] . . . man
convenyently com to the syde of the same rever to rod[e] . . . his
redy course to the sey and therfore thay think . . . of the sade
woodes to cut them upp in su . . . or els that the sade over therof to
be cha . . . so farre as the wood growes . . .

(*The bankes of northe* . . .) Item the . . .

VERDICT FOR PART OF ELLOE WAPENTAKE, 1570
[473.XII.1–20]   *Not printed*   225–244
[A *preter illos* verdict for Fleet (225–7) followed by a verdict
(undifferentiated) for Gedney (228–244). This file may be a detached

---

[1] The foot of this folio and parts of the right-hand edge are missing.

section of the next verdict, since the verdicts for the early 1570s show other signs of past confusion : a folio from a verdict for 1575 (253) appears in the next file which otherwise relates to 1570–1, while folios dated 1571 and 1572 (401, 397, 409) are found in a verdict for 1575.]

VERDICT FOR SKIRBECK AND ELLOE WAPENTAKES, 1570–1

[473.XIII.1]   245

[1](*The verdict of the petrillers inquest in the wapentake of Skirbeck*) The verdict of Anthony Claymond Richard Fryskney Frauncys Reade Henry Hoode Henry . . . Gayre William Roch Richard Dowce Symon Mawer Richard Pynchebeck Richard . . . John Lymme John Bawdrye iunior John Bawdrie senior William Wyldie Roger Grene Richard Larkes Thomas Owresby & Robert Turpyn, taken at Boston the xiiij[th] daie of . . . yere of the raigne of our soveraigne ladie quene Elizabeth before [*blank*]

(*Wrangle fiat lex . . . xiiij[th] Octobre . . .*) Firste they saye upon their othes that the Outfenbankes in Wrangle from Fryskney Barres unto Leake Clowte Rowe called the Floude Eaye and also that their bankes from Dowegrene unto their Outfendike Hurne, are in ruyne & decaye for lacke of height, & are to be repared maide in bredth & height sufficientlie by the landholders of the same towne before the feaste of St Martyn in wynter next comyng upon paine of everie roode xx d., onelie except the frontage from Cooke Garthe Ende unto Floude Eaye & is to be done by William Stevenson before the same feaste upon like payne.

[Item] that William Wyldye is annoyed & taketh great hurte by William Pikeryng in that the said Pikering doith turne his w[ater] . . . de of the said Wyldie a wronge waye & there doith suffer the same water to remayne & will nott convey the same . . . the great losse of the said William Wyldie, and itt is payned that the said Pikering shall convey the same water . . . of twentie shillinges.

(*Leake Fiat lex*) Item they further saye that all the fenbankes in Leake from Clowte Rowe next Wrangle unto Leverton Bank . . . aswell in height as bredth & ought to be repared sufficientlie by the landeholders of the same towne before . . . payne of everie roode [2]xx d. note that this by jusement & the jusebooke to be certyfyed.

(*Fiat lex*) Item they saye that itt is verie mete & expedient & do require ayde of the Comissioners that th . . . from the place where itt standeth nowe, & to be sett in Leverton att a place called Wheat Marshe . . . shall be turned & have the course from Fendike- land End & so to runne under the seabanke unto . . . diked suffi- cientlie by the landeholders of the same towne [2]by acrage.

Item [they] saye that a bridge in Leake beyng John Bussheys in

[1] This folio is in a poor state of repair ; there are several holes, and most of the right margin and foot of the folio are missing.
[2] The concluding words of this paragraph have been added in another hand.

the right of his wief & his wives . . . defective . . . height & bredth,
& is to be heightned & the roof newe turned by them att their
ch . . . free passage, before Michaelmes next upon payne of xl . . .

(*Leverton Fiat lex* . . .) Item . . . that Leverton Gote creeke is
decayed in stoneworke & is to be amended & repared by the land . . .

(. . . *reparetur Fiat lex*) Item they say that all their Yngdike
Bankes from Leake to Bennyngton Yngdike, are defective aswell
in height as . . . repared . . . lie by the landeholders of the same
towne, before Michaelmes next upon payne of everie roode . . . said
bank . . . maide by acridge, ¹Mᵈ they have a levye at the last sessions
of (?) iijᵈ le acre, and . . . more if . . . requier.

(*Fiat lex and the first acreage first to be employed*) Item they . . .
the bankes called Little Mare betwene Bennyngton & Leverton . . .
defective aswell in height . . . repared . . . by the landeholders of
bothe the same townes before the same daye upon like payne & by
acridge.

(. . .) Item they further saye that their seabanke from Crowegrene
End unto their gote is in decaye aswell in height as bredth & . . . is
to be done presentlie upon payne theron ensuyng, ¹pena x s. le rode.

Item they saye that the same order & paynes for their yngdike
is to be observed & done as is afforsaid . . . order towching Little
Mare to be kept & done as afforsaid & by the same acridge, and
likewies . . . narrowe to be diked before the said daye upon payne of
everie roode ij s. vj d., and that the comon . . . Benny[ngton] . . .
Crowe Meere unto their gote is to be diked one spitt deeper before
midsomer² next upon payne of everie roode ij s. iiij d.

(. . .) Item they further saye that their seabankes in many places
are to be skirted & heightned with all spede . . . ensuyng ³. . . le rode
and every fote xij d.,³ and the same order & paynes for their yngdike
is to be done by particularitie, ¹before the . . .

. . . [f]urther saye that theire seabankes from Hallycrofte unto
their gote & so to Tofte seadike . . . [ma]ny places with all spede
possible ³before x August³ upon payne thereon ensuyng ³x s. le
rode³. And itt is agred . . . Richarde Clayes ¹by acreage of j d.
le acre.

. . . & paynes for their yngdike is likewise to . . . defective for
lacke of diking & scour[ing] . . . xx d.

. . . saye that theire seabank . . . [p]ossible upon payne . .

. . . gote is in . . . next . . .

[473.XIII.2]   246
 ⁴(*Pinchbecke*)   The verdycte fo[r P]inchbecke geven & mayde by
      Jhon Wallpoll of Whaplode gent.⁵ and other his

---

¹ The concluding words of this paragraph have been added in another hand.
² " xiiij of October " interlined in another hand.
³⁻³ Interlined in another hand.
⁴ Small parts of the centre of this folio are defective.
⁵ " Jhon Cowell & Ry[ch]ard Huddleston gent." whose names followed have been
cancelled.

fellowes of the preteryll' queste anno domini 1570
and in the xiij[th] yeare of queene Elyzabeth.

(*The north syde of Borne Ea*) Fyrst the sayd jurye sayth that
the north [ban]kes of Borne Ea are defectyve in heygth and breidth :
and ought to be repared, exalted and amended [fro]m Borne to
Goodrham Cote by the queenes maiestie, the lordes and freeholders
of Borne. And from Goodrha[m] Cote to Dove Horne by the
queenes maiestie the lordes freeholders, commonns, and inhabytauntes of Pynchbec[k] as appeareth by the joyce bookes. And
from Dove Horne to Nuberye by everie man abuttynge on the same
by frontage.

(*Basson Dyke*) Item they say that the south bancke of the sayd
ea called Basson Dyke is defectyve in heygth and bredth from East
Cote to Nuberye and the same ought to be mayde, exalted and
amended from East Cote to Dove Horne by the queenes maiestie
the lordes freeholders, owners commons & inhabytauntes of Pynchbecke, as appeareth by the joyce bookes. And from Dove Hurne
to Nuberye by [every] frontager for his frontage, as is aforesayde.
And they thynk yt most needfull, that the sayde bankes, as well of
the north as south syde of Borne Ea & also the frontages aforesayd
to be substancyallie mayd exalted & amended before the xx[tie] day
of October nexte comynge for savegarde of the towne of Pynchbecke,
and the countrie of Hollande.

(*Dryftes*) Item they say that no dryftes shalbe suffered uppon
the south syde of Borne Ea [1]called Basson Dyk[1], for freatynge the
bankes.

(*The North & South Fennedyke*) Item they say : that the North
Fendyke in Pynchbecke from Wrightboll Corner to Dove Horne,
and the South Fennedyke from Dove Hurne to Half Stow be in
greate ruyn and decay for lacke of heygth and breidth : and the
same ought to be mayde or repa[r]ed, exa[lt]ed & amended by
doosenydge, as appeareth by a joyce booke. And they thinke that
it is very needfull that the sayde bankes be mayde with as much
speede, as may be convenyentlie : for yf they shuld breake the
[w]hole towne of Pynchbecke, with greate parte of the countrye of
Holland shuld be surroundede.

(*The Beach Banke*) Item they say that the Beach Banke on the
south syde of the same sewer is in decay of heygh & breidth from the
clowe at the beach heade by Wright Boll to Brymble Hurne, and
ought to be mayd & exalted by frontagers, as hath bene accustomed.

(*The Beach*) Item they say : that the sewer called the Beach is
in great ruyn & decay, for wante of clensynge rodynge and schowrynge : from the clowes at the heade of the sayd Beach by Wright
Boll, to a place called Brymble Hurne : and the sayd sewer ought
to be clensed, roded & schowred both by Gosberkyrke & Pynchbecke
as hath bene accostomed.

[1-1] Interlined in another hand.

(*Gallowe Goote*)   Item the say : that Gallowe Gote is defectyve :
& ought to be mayde the one moyetye therof by the lordes freeholders & owners of Pynchbecke, by acre sylver, and thother moyetye
by the lordes freeholders and owners of Spaldynge, as followeth :
that is to say : the moyetye or half of Gallowe Gote by the landes
in Spaldynge, as hath bene accustomede.

(*The bankes of Starrfenne Grafte*)   Item they say : that the bankes
one both sydes of Starrefennegraft be defectyve, bycause that
Starrefennegrafte is not sufficyentlye dyked accordynge to the
lawes which ought to be dyked by common menworkes of the
inhabytauntes of Pynchbecke, Spaldynge & Deepynge for theyr
commonage in Spaldynge & Deepynge South Fenne, bycause the
sayde bankes, where they are defectyve, ought to be repared by
frontagers & commoners as hath bene accustomed.

(*Makynge of weares*)   Item they say : that it is not meete nor
convenyente that any fysher shuld make any weares in any common
dreanes eyther before any sea gote or fenne gote oneles that the
same be c. foote from the sayd gotes.   Neyther yet to make any
weares in any other of the sayd dreanes, oneles the same be from
banke to banke, that the water be not lettede nor hyndred of his
readye course to the sea.

[473.XIII.3]   247

(*Monye Bridge   Acrag'* . . .)   Item they say : that Monye Brydge
in Pyn[ch]becke aforesayd, is in ruynne & decay: and ought to be
repared & amended by acre sylver of the whole towne.

(*Barres of outerynges, & fendykes & dryftes* . . .)   Item they say :
that it is necessarie from Martlemas to[1] Our Ladys Day in Lent
yearlie,[2] that the fennedykes and outerynges of the townes be
chayned & barred, and that no dryftes or cartynge over them be
used or hadde, for the saftye of the countrye, [3]except ther be other
order taken by trew Commissioners of the Sewers the sheape of the
inh[ab]itauntes of Spalding having common on Pynchbek oonly
exept.

(*Conyes uppon sea bankes*)   Item they say : that it is necessarie,
that ther be no conyes suffered to kepe & breede uppon the sea
bankes, for the saftye of the countrye : and yf ther be any, that it
shalbe lawfull for anye personnes to destroye them.

(*Caves, dennes, lodgynges, & holes in sea bankes*)   Item they say :
that no personnes shall make any caves, dennes, lodgynges or holes
in or uppon the sea bankes : and yf any doe to the contrarye, to be
grevouslye fyned & imprysonede.

(*Repare of seadykes for defence of up grasses . quere* . . .)   Item they
say : that the owners of everie severall marshe or marshes, that
have partycular indykes called inseadykes or waredykes for savynge

---

[1] "Mayday" cancelled.
[2] After "yearlie" the words "and at all other tymes, when there falleth any
greate rayne or waters" have been cancelled.
[3] The rest of the sentence has been added in another hand.

there up grasses, shall mayntayne repayre & kepe the same, in a convenyente heythe & breidthe, as heretofore hath bene usede, & accordynge to the heygth & breidth of the olde inseadykes or waredykes yet remanynge unbroken.

(*Purprestures in Surflet ryver*) Item they say : that some specyall decree & earnest charge ought to be hadde & geven to Jhon Burton, & other his neyghboures of Surflet uppon grevous fynes to be prescrybed by the Commyssionars ; that they, or anye of them shall not hereafter, as they have heretofore done, encroche & straghten the ryver of Surflet by settynge stakes, hedges & other purprestures & devyses to dyverte the water oute of his course. And that they shall do no manner acte, wherby the water by any meanes shalbe dryven oute of his owne channell, & caused to seeke a new channell, which is, & hath bene to the utter decay of the sayd ryver, & the surroundynge of the countrie. And that the inhabytantes of Surflet by a day appoynted shall plucke up and avoyde all the trees stakes & other engynns yet remanynge in the sayd ryver, which are purprestures, & stayes of & for the passage of the water, by reason of beddes of woodes & zilte hangynge uppon the same, by the iudgemente & consyderacons of the offycers of sewers of the nexte towne that may or shall take damage by the same.

(*Weylande from Gallowe Gote outefalle to the meetynge of Bornne & Surflet Ea, to be gitted & perfectede*) Item they say : that it is verie necessarie, this nexte sommer at the furthest, that the outefall of Weyland from Gallowe Gote outefall to the meetynge of Borne & Surflet Ea be gitted, channelled, & perfectede ; and that all purprestures, beddes of sande or zilte betweene the sayd lymytes, be avoyded & clensed, at the costes & charges of them, that owe to doe the same : videlicet by the inhabytauntes of Kesten that have commons, or are commoners in Deepynge Fenne ; for the one moyetye : and by the inhabytauntes of Holland that have commons or are commoners in Spaldynge Fenne, for thother moyetye. And fyrst they thinke yt meete, that such money as alreadye & yet is remaynynge in the offycers handes or inhabytauntes handes, be fyrst expended & bestowede in makynge the sayd gitties and for perfectenge of the sayd outefall, as is aforesayde.

[473.XIII.4] **248**

(*Stygate Gote defectyve*) Item they say : that Stygate Gote is broken & defectyve : and is to be repayred & amended by acre sylver of Pynchbecke : & all those acres in Spald[i]nge that dreane thereby. And is to be landed by the inhabytauntes of Pynchbecke by menworkes, as hath bene accustomede. And yt is necessarie, to be done with all speede, for saftye of the towne.

(*Freshe water dores for sea gotes*) Item they fynde yt necessarye, that fresh water dores be provyded for the sea gotes, bycause of the inconvenyence that contynuallie falleth & ensueth by castynge of earth dammes : which is to the great landynge and choakynge of the mouth and outefall of the ryvers. And that crommes of yron, & other necessary instrumentes be provyded, used & kepte for clensynge of the sayde gotes & outefalls.

(*The headynges of North Gate Grafte*) Item they say : that the headynges one the north syde of North Gate Graft, from North Gate Gote to Gauntes Bridge be defectyve : and ought to be mayde by the groundes lyenge betweene Borne Ea & North Gate as frontagers uppon the same.

(*Norgate Grafte : Laught Bridge Lake*) Item they say : that the common sewer called Norgate Graft is in ruynne & decay, for wante of dykynge roadynge clensynge & schowrynge : and ought to be dyked, roaded, clensed, and schowred from Norgate Gote to Gauntes Bridge, by all them that abbutt agaynst the same, as frontagers. And from Gauntes Bridge to the sea gote, by the hamstalles of the whole towne, eccept those & such as be allreadye charged therein by reason of frontage.[1] And the thinke the same very necessarie to be done before the fyrst day of November. And that Mr Walpoll ought to be charged for all his hamstall in Pynchbecke for the dykynge of Norgate Graft, as other the inhabytauntes of Pynchbecke be with dykynge by hamstalles.

(*Burtyfenne Grafte . . . A clow at Burtyfen Hurne*) Item they say : that Burtyfenne Graft is defectyve in dyverse places, videlicet from Burtyfen Hurne to Burtons Gote, and ought to be done by acre sylver. And they thinke yt very meete, and necessarie that a clowe be mayde & erected at a place called Burtefen Hurne, on the east syde of Borne Ea, there for kepynge backe the salte & freshe water oute of the North Feeldes of Pynchbecke : which at Michaelmas tyme, and after in the wynter hath bene accoustomed to drowne the sayd north feeldes beynge the loweste groundes & feeldes of Pynchbecke. And the same is necessarie to be done before Mychaelmas Day nexte commynge.

(*Borne Ea*) Item they say : that Borne Ea from East Cote to Goodhram Cote ought to be kepte cleane with schowrynge and roadynge from banke to banke yearlie. And now yt is neyther roaded, schowred, nor clensed, but onely in the mydward lyke a troughe, so that the water doth so hange ther in the haffe & weedes both wynter & sommer, that neyther in the wynter tyme the bankes be able to beare yt, neyther canne yt have his ready & speedye course to the sea. And yt ought to be done by [2]Richard (?) Lemon by the right of his . . .[2] And from Goodhram Cote to Nubery yt ought to be roaded from banke to banke by the lordes for there severall pyscharies ; and by the inhabytantes of Pynchbecke for theyr easmente & commodytie in the sayd ryver, as hath bene accoustomed. And they say : that from Nuberye to the sea the

---

[1] The following words " And from thence to Stygate Gote as hath bene accustomede " have been cancelled.

[2]-[2] Interlined in another hand, the original wording " Gregorye More balyf of Borne, or his fermer " being cancelled.

same dreane is not onely foule for lacke of roadynge clensynge & schowrynge : but also is so instrayghtned in many places towarde the outefall in Surflet, that the channell wherin the water runneth is not able to recover & receave the same, & to sende yt readylie & speedely to the sea. And yt ought to be roadede clensed & enlarged by the inhabytantes of Surflet as hath bene accoustomede. And they thinke yt meete & necessarye to be done wyth all expedycion : or els a greate parte of the countrye wylbe in greate daunger to be sourroundede. And that it is necessarie that the outefall in Surflet be twyse roaded & clensed every yeare as heret . . . ede & ordeyned.

[473.XIII.5]   249

Item they thinke yt mete & very necessarye that the woode[1] and haf which is cutte in the ryver of Borne Ea be landede yearlie by the roaders.

(*Sea bankes*) Item they say : that yt is necessarye to have perfecte propps, meates and boundes betwixte towne & towne uppon the seadykes : that every towne may certaynlie knowe theyr owne charge for the saftye of the countrye.

Item they thinke yt necessarye : that there be ij substancyall menworkes everye yeare, bestowed by the commonaltye in Pynchbecke uppon the sayd sea bankes in such places, as by dryfte cartynge or otherwyse are hollowed empayred or mayde lowe by that occasyon : uppon lyke payne & in lyke manner & forme as by the statute for reparacion of highe wayes is prescrybed & lymyted.

(*Hamstall bookes*) Item they say : that it is necessarye to have newe hamstall bookes, joyce bookes, and acre bookes to be perfectlye mayd in everie towne : for bycause that the same are much growen oute of knowledge, & ought to be renewed, & hadde neede to be amended. [2]And especyally in the town of Pynchebeck.

(*A dyke from Goodhram Cote to Blacke Dyke . . .*) Item they say : and thynke yt necessarie, for the better convey of water, and the better dreanynge of the countrie & of the North Fenne of Pynchbecke, to have a dytche mayde of xij fote breidth from Goodhram Cote to Blake Dyke. And the maynour to be throwen all on the south east syde towards Pynchbecke by the commons and inhabytauntes of Pynchbecke & Spaldynge : and to be mayntayned from tyme to tyme as neede shall requyre : and as the same shalbe thought convenyente & profytable for the sayde townes.

(*Gravynge of hassockes or turves*) Item they fynde yt necessarie, that no man shall grave any turffes or hassockes within iiij^c foote under the sydes or bankes of the ryver called Borne Ea, for the inconvenyence that groweth by soccage. And where anye gravynge shalbe hadde or mayde in the marryshes, the same to be taken

---

[1] This word has been corrected in another hand, but the correction intended is uncertain : it may be " weede ".
[2] The rest of this sentence has been added in another hand.

even with the groundes for the inconvenyence that otherwyse may ensue to cattell.

(*Restraynte of reede gatherynge nere the fendykes*)   Item they say : that no manner of personne shall gather any reede, sallowes, hassockes, or flegge wythin ij^c foote of the fennedykes and outerynges : for the same is a greate defence of the fenne waters from the bankes in tyme of storme & tempaste.

(*Bankes from Nuberie defectyve*)   Item they say : that the bankes on the south syde of Borne Ea from Nuberye to the outefall of Burton Gote are very lowe, ryuynous & defectyve : and ought to be mayde by them that are chargede with the same, as hath bene accoustomed : and hadde neede to be mayde substancyallye with speede.

(*Favour of haff*)   Item they say : that it is necessarye for the defence of the countrie, to repulse the vyolence of freshe waters in tyme of rage, and tempaste that there be no haff graven or cut, but onelie for the defence of the bankes, within twoe myles of the sayde bankes or fennedykes : onles it be for the mayntenaunce of fysshynge and bankes.

¹Item they say : yt is necessarye for the bett[er] . . . naunce of Westloode with freshe water in the sommer season, that the loode under the Southe Fendyke . . . before All Hallowe tyde next, from a place called the Half Stowe to the infall of Westloode, by the . . . of Spaldynge.   As hath bene acustomed. ²

[473.XIII.6]   250

(*Spaldynge acres charged to our gotes. Quere*)   Item they say : that it is meete & convenyente, that all the acres in the parrhyshe of Spaldynge which dreyne or are dreyned by the gotes or sewers of Pynchbecke shalbe chargeable and charged with acre sylver to the sayde gotes & sewers : as reason an[d] occasyon doth serve & requyre.

(*Myln Greene dreane*)   Item they say : that the dreyne leadynge from Myln Greene trench unto the outefall of yt into Reedye Grafte, is defectyve, for wante of dykynge : and ought to be dyked, roaded, & schowrede, by the inhabytauntes of Pynchbecke by common menworkes.

(*Reedy Grafte*)   Item they say : that Reedye Grafte is defectyve from the Olde Fennedyke to Steegat Gote, and so to Dunnegate Ende, for wante of dykynge & schowrynge : and ought to be dyked & schowred from the Olde Fennedyke to Stygat Gote, by doosenydge, as hath bene accoustomed.   And from Stygat Gote to Dunnegate Ende, by one common menworke of the whole inhabytantes of Pynchbecke : and by those landes in Spaldynge which dreane thereby : bycause yt is a new charge, and for that they dreane by the same.   And by all the landes in Pynchbecke, by acre sylver.

¹ Part of the foot of this folio is missing.
² The last four words are added in another hand.

(*Norgatgrafte agaynst Bassome*) Item they say : that Norgate Grafte is defectyve for wante of dykynge all alonge agaynste Bassome : and ought to be dyked by the right honorable lord Clynton by reason of his frontage.

(*The trench under Starrefengraft to have a rappyt with a dore. quere*) Item they say : that the trenche under Starrefennegrafte, ought to have a rappyt with a dore, and ij lockes & one bolt, and to be sett at such a reasonable gage, that the water of the sayd trenche shalbe no stoppe nor hynderaunce to the Weste Feeld water, in Reedye Grafte, but that yt may dreane together to Burtons Gote & Stygat Gote. And that the ij keys belongynge to the sayde lockes shall remayne in ij degreves handes the one of Spaldynge & the other of Pynchbecke. And that the sayde trench be gaged by the consente of ij substauncyall and indeferente men one of Spaldynge & thother of Pynchbecke indeferentlye chosen by the consente of the degreves of both townes, and inhabytantes lykwyse.

(*The trench under Norgatgraft to be mayke lyke to Starrefenne-grafte.*) Item they say : that the trench under Norgate Graft by Stygat Gote is in great ruynne & decay : and ought to be mayde and amended in as ample & large manner as the trench under Starrefen-grafte is, videlicet both in breidth & depth, and ought to have a rappyt with a dore : so that the South Feelde water & the North Feelde water may have theyr speedye passage to Burtons Gote together : and ought to be mayde by the lordes freeholders, & inhabytauntes of Pynchbecke by acre sylver, and by those landes in Spaldynge which dreane by the same.

(*Norgatgrafte to be cutt oute. quere. vac'* . . .) Item they say: that yf at any tyme the sayde South Feelde water wyll have anye fall into Norgatgrafte to the measure of an ynche or more : that then the sayde Norgatgraft Banke shalbe cut oute at the trench by Stygatgote : so that the sayde South Feelde water descende to the sea, by the sayde Stygatgote. And the sayde trenche to be abated & set downe so much & so manye ynches, as the sayde trenche hath fall of water into Norgatgrafte when the banke is cut oute : so that the North Feelde may have the better dreane. And the sayde trench to have ij lockes & ij keys, and the one key to remayne in the Fenne Ende and the other in the Seas Ende, eyther with the degreeves, or ij of the moste substancyall men, of those vyntynnes or endes.

(*The dreane under the seadyke* . . .) Item they say : that the dreane under the seadyke from the trench at Norgatgrafte to Dunne-gate Ende, ought to be dyked in breidth x foote, and in depth ij foote : and from Dungate Ende to Burtons Gote ought to be dyked lykwyse in breidth xij foote, and in depth ij foote, where the bankes wyll beare yt.

(*The outefall of Burtons Gote*) Item they say : that the outefall or creeke of Burtons Gote is not of sufficyente breidth : and ought to be vj foote wyde in the buttome : and the maynor to be taken oute in the myddest of the creeke equallye from both sydes of the same.

[473.XIII.7]   251

(*Stygatgote outefall*) Item they say : that Stygate Gote outefall or creeke is not of suffyciente breidth : and ought to be of the breidth of viij foote in the bottome. And that both the foresayde creekes ought to be perfectede before the feaste of Sancte Martynne in wynter yearlie.

(*The clowe in Reedy Grafte*) Item the say : that a clowe ought to be mayde & erected at a place called Penytofte Stowe there for the kepynge backe the salte & freshe water oute of the angle of Fenne Ende, at Mychaelmas tyme, and the same to be done & mayde betwixte this & Martlemas nexte commynge : by all those landes which take commodytie by the same.

(*Seadykes*) Item they say : that the comon seadykes are in decaye : and ought to be mayde & amended in manner & forme followynge : that is : at Gallow Gote ij roodes, by common men- worke, iiij roodes at Stygat Gote, by common menworke, and all agaynste the common marshe, by common menworke, at Dunngat Ende vj roodes by common menworke, at Boston Seadyke Ende iij roodes by common menworke : and the resydue of the sayde seadyke to be mayde by acre sylver.

(*A clowe in Surflet Beach*) Item they say : that there is a clowe in Surflet Beach which stoppeth the water therin that it cannot have the readye passage to the sea, but causeth yt to bowne in the Beach above the sayde clowe, and so overfloweth the bankes towardes Pynchbecke ; and ought to be taken up & nonne such to be there to the annoyance of neyghbours & kepynge backe the water from the sea.

[1]Whereas the inhabitance of Deping and other townshipps in Kevesten [*sic*] have a dren for ther . . . fenes therough the town- shipps of Pynchebeck and Spalding from the first day of Maye unto the last day of October to the utter voidinge of the sayd townshipps therefore the sayd townshipps of Pynchebeck and Spaldinge humbly doth requir your worshipps that the sayd clowe at the hede of the sayd dren shall as heretofore yt hath done stand down. And not opened unto the first day of Aprill and to contynew opene till the first day of October and then to be shytt for the better saftye of the sayd townes and the quenes majesties possessyers. And att the sayd gaige as hath bene acustomede.

[472.XIII.8]   252

(*The Comen drene*) Item they say the drene of Comen wythin Whaplod is decayd & ought to be renewed by acar silver collected wythin the sayd towne.

---

[1] This paragraph is added in another hand.

(*Comen sea banck*) Item they say that the comen sedikes wythin Whaplod ar in decay in diverse places & ought to be amended by Whaplod by comen maynworkes.

(*Marshe banckes*) Item they say that the marshe sedikes wythin Whaplod & Holbeche ar in decay & ought to be repared by the oners of the salt marshes.

(*A shutt*) Item they say that ther wold be a pare of clowes sett at Callowes Bridge to kepe the salt water from the towne the chargis therof to be done by acar mony.

(*Hie ways*) Item they say ther is a hie way leding from the churche to Dikes Bridge whiche is in decay & is to be repared by comen meynworckes.

(*The gote dores*) Item they say ther is a hie way called Spaldinge Gate whiche is to be repared by the quenes mayneworckes & all other hie ways ar to be repared by comen meyneworckes.

Item they say the gote dores be in decay so that they doe receve in salt water & they ought to be repared by acar silver.

(*Barres*) Item they say that yt is requesitt to have of every joise bankes wythin Whaplad ij pare of bares & they to be shutt from the Fest of All Saintes to the Anunciacon of Our Lady the chardgis therof to be done by acar mony.

(*A creste*) Allso the sayd jury say that ther is a crest in Croland hedinge from Ship Eye Stow to Dowsdall in decay & ought to be repared by the quenes majestie or her tenantes of Crolande.

([*W*]*illo Dike*) Allso they say that Willo Dike in Croland is in decay & ought to be repared as aforsayd.

Allso the sayd jury doe request your good worshipes that you wilbe so for the better preservacon of our contre to devise & establishe some good lawes & orders for the better reparinge of all the banckes and crestes wythin the precinctes of Croland & that they may be made & amended at suche tyme as they may come to good menor for the making therof so that they may putt the contre to no more suche hassard in the winter as the last yere they did.

(*Porsham Clow*) Allso the sayd jury thinckethe mete & requesit to have ij lockes & keys for Porsham Clowe the one to remayne wythe the officers of Croland & the other wythe the dikegraves of Whaplod to the end that they may lett in no more water then banckes will well bere & that to be letten in by the consent of bothe the officers.

Allso they doe request your goodnes that you will make some goode and penall law for the dikgraves wythin every towne that they wythin certane space by your worshipes to be apoincted doe make ther accompte to the towne, & make peyment to the new dikgraves of all suche somes remanynge in ther handes upon ther accomptes upon pane.

(. . .) Allso the said jury say that Holbiche Goate whiche lyethe at Cowfeld Stowe is in decay & ought to be repared by the township of Holbeche.

(. . .) Allso they say the drene of Holbiche Horne Goate is to strayte & is to be amended by landholders of Holbiche.

[473.XIII.9a]   253
[1]The verdyt of Robert Ganne & his fellowes maid & geven up the xxvj[th] day of May 1575 et anno xvij[mo] regnie Elizabethe.

(*Crowland streame from the Crosse in the Ee* [2]*fiat lex*[2]) Item the sayd jury say that the streame frome the Crosse in the Eye to the Vachery Were & so to the North Were ought to be rooded in dewe season & that they ought to make stayes for there wede every man within his owne lybertye & to pluck upp the wede once in thre dayes as yt ys nedefull to doo and haith bene accustomed.

(2   *Streame from the North Were   idem*) Item the said jury saith that the streame frome the North Weare to Whyte House & the south syde of the streame frome Whyte House to Brother House ought to be roded by Henry Durrant the fermer thereof & make stayes for the wede as haith bene accustomed.

(3   *North syde of the streame from White House*) Item the said jury saith the north syde of the streame frome Whyte House to Brother House ought to haffed & dydowed[3] as before order was taken & not yet done. [4]Before St Barthelmew Day p. xx[s].

(4   *South Streame idem*) Item the said jury say that the South Streame frome Crowland Towne Ende to Saynt Gudluckes Crosse ought to be rooded by John Durrand & Morrys Bexwell the fermers thereof & to make stayes for ther wede within ther owne lybertye & to pluck yt upp once in thre dayes as haith bene accustomed.

(5   *Streame from St Gudlakes Crosse idem*) Item the said jury saith that the streame frome Saynt Gudluckes Crosse to Thyrty Acres Barr ought to be roded by William Hurne and Morrys Bexwell the fermers thereof & to make stayes for ther wede within there owne lybertye & to pluck yt upp once in thre dayes as haithe bene accustomed.

(6   *Streame from xxx acres*) Item the said jury saith that the streame frome Thyrty Acres Barr to Dowesdall ys defectyve for lack of haffyng & roodyng & ought to be done by William Gayby the fermoure thereof.

(7   *Streame from Dowsdall*) Item the said jury saith that the streame frome Dowsdaill to Perkyn Goote ys defectyve for lack of haffyng & roodyng & ought to be haffed & rooded all the south west syde by my lord of Bedford & his tenauntes the fermers thereof.

(8   . . . *& Holbych north syde of the streame*) Item the said jury saith that the north syde of the said streame ought to be haffed & rooded by thynhabitauntes of Whaplod and Holbych & other but whoo we knowe not.   [4]Fiat lex.

[1] There is a scribbled and barely legible note in the top left-hand corner of this folio which seems to begin " Placed next Spalding & Weston . . . ," the rest being indecipherable.
[2-2] Added in another hand.
[3] *Sic.*
[4] Concluding words added in another hand.

(9 *A pece of a streame*) Item the said jury saith that there ys a pece of a streame decendyng frome Saynt Gudluckes Crosse to Fyned Crosse defectyve for lack of haffyng & rodyng & ought to be done by my lorde of Bedforth the est syde therof & the west syde by thinhabitauntes of Crowland by common menworke. [1]Fiat lex.

(10 *A pety dreane from Kennells Stone*) Item the said jury saith that there ys a petty dreane decendyng frome Kennelles Stone to Fowlers Stake & lyeng betwene Lincoln shyre & Northamtone shyre & hooly within Lyncoln shire ys defectyve for lack of haffynge & roodynge & ought to be done videlicet haffed & rooded by the fishers therof videlicet Richard Weche the elder & Nicholas Bromefeld. [1]Midsomer next xx^d rode.

(11 *A pety dreane from Fowlers Stake*) Item the said jury saith that there ys a petty dreane decendyng frome Fowlers Stake to Graynend Tre defectyve for lack of haffyng & rodyng & ought to be haffed & rooded by the fishers thereof that ys to say Robert Anerton & Thomas Soothe & Rychard Weche junior. [1]consimilis pena.

(12 *A dreane*) Item the said jury saith that there would be a dreane frome Graynyng to Fyncy Crosse for the said dreane that commeth to Graynyng haith no fall forth but turneth back ageyne therefor the said jury thynkyth mete to make the dreane to fall forth at Fyncy Crosse into the Ould Streame, & to be haffed & roded by thinhabitauntes of Crowland by common menworke. [1]Midsomer pena xx d. a rode.

(13 *A pety dreane from Kennels Stone*) Item the said jury saith that there ys another petty dreane decendyng frome Kennell Stone to Crowland Hurne otherwyse called the Dykesend ys defective for lack of haffyng & roodyng & ought to be haffed & rooded by thynhabitauntes of Crowland by common menwork.

(14 *A pety dreane from the Dykes End to White House*) Item the said jury saith that there ys another petty dreane decendyng frome the Dykes End to Whyte House defectyve for lack of haffyng & roodyng & ought to be done by the fysshers therof videlicet Steven Asshby & William Parker Thomas Clerk & William Hurne & Robert Hurne & Henry Durrant & John Cott. [1]All the same ys orderd to be done before Lammas next payne for every roode undone xx d.

(15 *Brodewater*) Item the said jury saith that the place called the Brodewater ys defectyve with slete & haffe & therfore the water cannot have hyr fre course as she ought to have & ought to be repayred & amended by thynhabitauntes of Crowland by common menworke. [1]Before Lammas pena xl s.

(16 *Crowland Hurne banke*) Item the said jury saith that ther ys a banke decendyng frome Crowland Hurne to the Whyte House ys defectyve in serteyne places for lack of height & breadth & ought

---

[1] Concluding words added in another hand.

to be done one half myle by the quenes majestie & the resydewe by the tenauntes. ¹Before Martelmes pena every rode xij d.

(17 . . .) Item we say that ther ys a bank decendyng frome the Northende of Crowland to the Whyte House & frome the Whyte House to Brotherhouse defectyve in dyverse places & ought to be repayred & amended by the quenes majestie. ¹Idem dies & pena.

([1]8 . . .) Also we say that ther ys a bank decendyng frome Brotherhouse to Cathcould Corner & frome Catchcould Corner to Shyppy Stowe & frome Shyppy Stowe to Carefeld Ende defectyve in sarteyne places in height & breadth & ought to be done by the quenes majestie. ¹Item &c.

(19 . . .) Item we say that ther ys a creste descendyng frome Carefeld to Dowesdaill defectyve in height & bredth & ought to be done by the quenes majestie . . . tenaunts. ¹Martelmas pena cuiuslibet rode iijˢ iiijᵈ.

(. . .) Item we say that the bank descendyng frome Dowesdaill to Croyland ys defective in serteyne places for lack of height & breadyth & ought to be repayred by the quenes majestie. ¹Bartulmew next sub pena rode vˢ.

(. . .) Item we say that Brother House Gote ys in ruyne & decay & ought to be repayred by the quenes majestie.

¹Plus in alio veredict.

[473.XIII.10]   255
Anno domini 1571
The vardet for Holbyche preter illos jurie for sewers

(*Holbiche* 1 *See bankes of comentye*) Item we say that our commen see banke from the devision of Whaplode to Holbyche Hirne is defective in heyghte, and bredth and oughte to be maed and repayred as well by everye dweller & inhabiter withe in the towne of Holbyche, as by all others that shall hyer eny ferme, & occupye the same withe in the said towne, because they be teyrers & freters of the said bankes withe ther carryages & dryftes of cattelle.

(2 *Upgrasse Banke*) Item we say that their is an other banke ther, called the Upgrasse Banke beginnynge at the devision of Whaplode, & so ledethe to Cowfyld Corner is defective for heyghte & thyknes & oughte to be maid & kepte by the landholders abuttynge upon the saim as it haithe ben accustomed, whiche is in great ruin & dekaye.

(3 *Ee syedes*) Item we say that all the Ee sydes from the Hirne Gotte to the maen commen see banke is defective in heyghte & bredthe in divers places, and oughte to be maed & repayred by commen menworke as well by every dweller & inhabiter withe in the towne of Holbiche, as by all others that shall hyer eny ferme & occupye the saim, withe in the said town, because they be teyrers and freters of the said banckes withe their carriges & dryftes of

---

¹ Concluding words added in another hand.

cattell, and also to be diked *by vintins &*[1] acre monnay as haith bene accustomed.

(4 *The Hirne Goett*) Item we say that one goett cald the Hirne Goett is defective & rotten, & lyethe to hye by a foett, and is to be taken upe and maid & amended by acre silver.

(5 *Commen sewer*) Item we say that the commen sewer from the ould goett at the Hirne to the comen foett brydge is defective in divers places for lake of dikynge & oughte to be doene by acre monnay, and ther to have a paire of stronnge clowes to be sett by acre monnay.

(6 *Ee syedes & headinges*) Item we say that all the headinges from the commen seedike at the Hirne abothe sydes of the Ee, oughte to be stopped by the digraves or awners of the same ground wheras suche headinges be from tym to tym to John Randes housse in the Fene Ende, to stay the water at all tymes conveniente.

(7 *Ee syedes*) Item we say that from John Randes house to Herdletre Dike the Ee sydes ar to be maid & kept by thoos that lyethe & abuttythe on the weste syde, and the este syed by commen menworke, and oughte to be maed & repayred as well by everye dweller and inhabiter within the towne of Holbyche as by all others that shall hyer eny ferme and occupye the saim withe in the said towne becausse they be freyters and teyrers of the sayd bankes withe their cariages & dryftes of cattelle.

(8 *Ee syedes*) Item we say that from Herdletre Dyke to Ravens Dyke the weste syed of the Ee oughte to be maed repared and amended by commen menwork as well by every dweller & inhabiter within the towne of Holbyche, as by all others that shall hyer eny ferm & occupye the saim within the said towne becausse they be freyters & teyrers of the said bankes with their carryages & dryftes of cattelle, and the este syed of the Ee to [be] maed repayred & amended by the awners or fermers of all thoes groundes that takethe commoditye by the saim banke, & that lyethe betwen Ravens Dyke Hyrdletre Dyke Flett Landmere & the saim banke, & that it is necessarye to have a shutt for a petye dreine for the fyeld & to fall in at Hyecrosse Brydge, and from Ravens Dyke to the Ees end cald Chalensfyeld Corner, the weste syedes to be maed repayred & amended by commen menworke, as well by everye dweller & inhabiter within the towne of Holbyche as by all others that shall hyer eny ferm & occupye the saim within the said towne, becausse they be freyters & teyrers of the said banke with their cariages & dryftes of cattelle, and the este syde to be maed repayred & amended by the awners & fermers of all thos groundes or landes that lyethe within the saim banke, & that shalle repe & take commoditye of the saim. And a shutt to be maed for that fyelde and to falle in at Ravens Brydge.

(9 *South Ee Banke*) Item we say that on banke cald South Ee Banke is defectyve for lake of height & thyknes and oughte to be

---

[1] Words italicized are underlined in the text.

maed repayred & amended by Holbyche from Flett Landmer to the bondes of Whaplod as apperethe in a ioyste bocke their remanynge. befor Mychaellmas next.

(10 . . .) Item we say that their is a banke cald Shipe Ee Banke beginnynge at Dowsdaell Housse defectyve for lake of heighte, and oughte to [be] maed repayred and amended by Holbyche to the bondes of Whaplode, as apperethe in a ioyste boocke their remanyng.

¹(11 . . .) Item we say that there is a banke cald Commen Banke beginnynge at Flett Landmer defectyve for heighte, and oughte to be maed repayred and amended . . . Whaplode as apperethe in a ioyste boocke ther remanynge.

[12] [Item we] say that there is a banke cald . . . defectyve in heighte and ought to be maed by Holbyche from Flett Landmer to the bondes . . . of Holbyche, as by all others that shall hyer eny . . . of the said banke with their carriages & dryftes . . .

[13] . . . to be maed repayred & amended by . . . [rem]anynge.

[14] . . . to be maed repayred & amended . . . remanynge.

[473.XIII.11]   256
Anno domini 1571

(*Holbiche* 15   *Randalle Dike the oute rynge*)   Item we say that ther is an other banke cald Randalle Dyke in Whaplod defectyve and oughte to be maid by Whaplod & Holbyche by commen men-worke, beginnynge at a pastur of the lordes of Molton & so to Ravens Dyke, the one halfe by Whaplode, & the other hallfe to Ravens Dyke by Holbyche, as well by every dweller & inhabiter within the towne of Holbyche, as by all others that shall hyer eny ferm & occupye the saim within the said towne, becausse they be teyrers & freyters of the said bankes withe their cariag[es] & dryftes of cattelle.

(16   *The out rynges*   *Whaplod & Holbyche*)   Item we say there is an other banke there in Whaplode cald Sydyke beginnynge at Ravens Dyke of the northe & extendethe to the mydes of Mollton Fen cald Molton Sydike of the southe defectyve, & oughte to be maid & kept by the inhabitans of Whaplod as they have bene accustomed, and from the mydste of Mollton Fen to Catchecould Corner is to be maede & kept by Holbyche by commen menworke or by sesmentes, as well by every dweller & inhabiter within the towne of Holbyche, as by all others that shalle hyere eny ferm & occupye the saim within the said towne, becausse they be teyrers & freyters of the said bankes with ther carriages and driftes of cattell.

(17   *A bank from Catchcould Corner to Gaisehirn*)   Item we say that from Catchcould Corner to Gaise Hirne & so to the mydes of Great Shepe Ee is defectyve in heighte & thyknes and ought to be maed & kept by Whaplod as they have ben accustomed.

¹ Most of the foot of this folio is missing and only a few words remain at the right-hand end of each line.

(18 *The strem of Southe Ee*) Item we say that Southe Ee from Dousdaille Housse to Flett Landmer is defectyve, for that it oughte to be xxiiij^{ti} foottes wied and is not, and the one halfe is to be kepte by Holbyche & Whaplod, whiche is done, & the other halfe is to be kept by the owners of the housse of Thornaye whiche is not done, and that William Gabye kepethe a were withe in the streme of Holbyche, and so holdethe upe the water at every raige that it bownethe & swellethe a great dell more then it woulde doo, wherfoir we thynke good that no we[re] be kept their under xxiiij^{ti} foottes wied at the leiste.

(19 *Clowes at Garners Brydge*) Item we say that it is necessarye to have a paire of clowes to be sett at Garners Brydge, & the brydge to be maed, that when the winde (?) fetrethe upe the water into the towne being in the southe, for lake of a stay and shutt ther, the saim water returnethe bake into the fen againe and this to be done by acre monnye.

(20 *Petye dreins and shuttes*) Item we say that all suche petye dreins betwen the clowe at Garners Brydge and Ravens Dyke that fallethe in to the Ee shall have shuttes to be maed & sett, to lett the water oute of the fyeldes when it will fall oute, and to kepe it oute of the fyeldes when it will come in, and this to be done by acre monnay of bothe sydes of the ryver.

(21 . . . *petye dren*) Item we say that ther is one old petye drene in Damgaite begynning at Herdletre Dyke & so ledythe to Raulynges & so to the m' of Robert Thorpes & overwhart the way . . . way syd cald Wrotes Gaite & of the southe syd of the saim way to iij acres of Henrye Jellows & overwhart the way of the northe syde of the saim gatt directlye estward to Saultnay Gaite and overwharte the gait to a pastur cald Tylles & so into the ryver, and it is cald of old the est petye dren whiche is to be remeded and kept by frontigers.

(22 *Petye dren for the Upe Grasse quere*) Item we say that all thoese landes betwine the marshebanke & the commen see banke from the devision of Whaplod to Cowefyeld Corner oughte to have a drene, for the drenynge therof at all tymes when as nede shalle requier, and the saim to falle into Whaplod at a place cald the V acre, and so under the marshe banke to Whaplode Ee as it haithe allwais bene accustomed, and for that Holbyche and Whaplod ar lande maettes together.

(23 *Renuing of the* . . . *boockes*) Item we say for as muche as divers mens landes withe in Holbyche be transposed and exchaunged syns the laste renuing of our towne boocke, joyste boocke, & acre boocke, by menis wherof landes will goe oute of knowledge, leste the saim boockes be renued and maed parfecte from tyme to tyme, it is good that the towne of Holbyche do amend and make parfecte, as nere as they can all theis said boockes befor the feaste of Peter Advincula commonly called Lammas next.

(24 *Widnes of brydges and weirsteides*) Item we say that no brydge nor weirsteid that goethe over the commen sewer shalle be

kepte under the wydnes of tene foote at the leste upon paine of every
person that so shalle offende.

(25 *A new . . . for Holbych . . . quere*) Item we say that it is
necessarye to have an other goett for the drenyng of Whaplod
waters & Holbyche for that bothe our waters commethe & runneth
together, and to be maed & kepte by bothe the saim towns by acre
monnaye, and to be laede in suche a conveniente place as shall seme
beste to the commissioners upon their vewe, and the jury to vewe &
treid the saim, and to apoyntte the place with the saim commissioners.

[26] [Item] we say that it is necessarye for Holbyche to kepe
stopped the commen brydge from Chrystenmasse to the laste of . . .
everye yere, . . . to be opened, that the fene . . .

[27] . . . Howsse to Shepe Ee Stowe . . . Crowland withe in them
. . . by the quene or her . . .

[473.XIII.12]   257
². . . of the great inquest called petrellis . . . weapontake of
      Ellowe, in the parties of Holland . . . of Lyncoln made by John
      Wallpowle gent. and his fellowes anno domini 1571

(*Sutton Marie*) In primis the said John Wallpoole gent. and
his fellowes saith upon their othes that they have taken that Sutton
Goate, and Lutton Goate, are defective for lack of brick and other
workmanship, and ought to be made repared and amended, by acer
monay so oft and many tymes as nede shall requyre, accordinge to
our olde auncient custome.

Item the said jury saye that Chappell Brygge, Brownes Brydge
and Loommes Brygg are defective for wante of brick and workman-
shipp, & ought to be made repared and amended by acre mony so
often & many tymes as nede shall requere, accordynge to our olde
auncient custome.

Item . . . seadyke or seabankes, in Sutton is . . . is not yet suff-
[iciently] amended, which ought to be repared made . . . by the
inhabitance of Sutton aforsaid by their common menworke so ofteñ
& many tymes as nede shall requeyre, from the Out Broken to a
certaine place called Polles Cotte.

Item the sayd jurye say, that the fendyke of Sutton is defective
in many places for lack of hight and bredth and ought to be made
repared and amended by the common menworke of Sutton Sainct
Maries so often and many tymes as nede shall requeyre.

[473.XIII.13]   258
³Item . . . meete and necessary to have a trench of stone to be
layd in M . . . gate by Thomas Clarkes house to dreane all those landes
on the east syde of the said gate that the water may fall into Priores

---

¹ The foot of this folio is missing and only a few words at the right-hand end of
each line remain in the final paragraph.
² There are holes at the head and in the centre of this folio.
³ There are holes at the head and foot of this folio.

Fall, and so runne to the goate, and the charges to be borne and done by all those that have landes in the said angle by acre sylver.

Item the said jury say, that Cagate, Dyesgate, Childerhowsgate, and Batemanesgate are common gaytes, and ought to be repared and made by all those that have anny landes abuttynge upon anny of the said gaytes as well on the east as on the west so often & many tymes as nede shall requyre.

Item the said jury say, that all common brigges & spoutes, over all hye wayes and common sewers within Sutton ought to be made and repared by acre sylver so often and many tymes as nede shall requeyre.

Item the said jury say, that wheras many & dyvers officers heretofore by or under color of their . . . have bene alowed their menworkes and not done the same accordyngl[y] . . . [sa]id jury thinke yt very meete, necessary & convenient that fromme henceforth no officer nor officers to be dyscharged of his or theire menworkes, but onely the dikegraves for geveinge theire attendoounce.

[473.XIII.14]   258

[1]Item the said jury . . . henceforth yt shall not be lawfull for anny person or persons within [the] weapontake to make anny trench, grippell or gutter in or upon anny heddynge or aboute anny cloote, set upon the sayd heddynges, upon such payne as the Commissioners shall thinke meete.

Item the said jury thinke yt meete & convenient that wheras ther be many faultes presented to be done, and made by common menworkes, within this weapontake of Ellowe and that dyveres rich menne will sende downe to the said menworkes boyes or other insufficient persons, which are not able to beare out their worke as other pore men do, therfore the said jury praye, that it may be lawfull to and for the officers for that tyme beinge to sende back agayne such insufficient person or persons to set & place such sufficient laborars that be of abilitie to beare out or do the said worke, and allso that it may be lawfull to and for the said officers to dystreine the said parties for his or theire menworke or menworkes. And that yt may be lawfull, to punisshe an[y person] or persons accordynge to the discretion of the said officers or . . . shall thinke convenient, yf that any s[u]ch per[son or] persons shall offende in theire said workes where they shall be appoynted to worke by the said officers.

Item the said jurie saie, that the Ee from Sutton Goate to the fall is defective in manye places, and ought to be diked roded and scowred by all that be joyssed therin, as appeareth by our joysbookes.

(*Lutton in Sutton*) Item the said jury say, that theire is a petie dreane lyinge under the common seadike at Lowgate Ende, which hath tenne roodes defective, for lack of dichinge & scowringe which

[1] There are holes at the head and in the centre of this folio.

H

ought to be made, parte by William Browne, and parte by the inhabiters of Lutton by common menworke.

Item the said jurie say, that they thinke yt verie mete & necessary to have a spowte made of stone, or elles a hollowe tree, and to be layde in a high waye called Mariottes Gate, that a certaine angle maye dreane that waye, to Lutton Goate, which lyeth on the east syde of Pyes Gate, and the charges to be done by acre monye.

[473.XIII.15]   259

[1](*Tydd Saynte Marye*)   The verdytt of the preter illos . . . of the sewers for Tydd Saynte Marye in the parties of Holland in the countye of Lyncoln', John [Walpole] beynge the foreman of the said queste 1571[2] whiche verdytt was gyven up . . . parties & countie afforesaid

(*Common sewer*)   Firste the said John Wallpole & hys fellos say . . . common sewer in Tydd afforesaid begynnyng at a place called Barnardes Bridge at Mylne Gate . . . to the gote, whiche oughte to be dyked, scowred & roded as ofte as nede requyrethe, by all . . . [a]ccordyng to the joyce booke of the said towne, at the cammandement of the dykegreves there.

(*Headynges*)   Item the said jury saythe that frome Barnardes Bridge to the gote, that all the headynges betwene land & land as well on the southe, as also on the northe parte of the common sewer afforesaid, shalbe repared & mayd by the same landholders whose landes eyther joyne or buttes on the common sewer, on this syde the feaste of Saynte Mychaell' tharchangell' next commynge, and so to maynteyne & kepe them suffycyent.

([*Comm*]*on sewer*)   Item they say that the common sewer in Tydd shalbe hereafter roded ij tymes in the yere at the cammandement of the dykegreves of the said towne, upon laufull warnyng gyven unto them in there paryshe churche, upon payne of every roode not so roded to lose xij d.

([*Pety dr*]*eyne*)   Item there ys one pety dreyne within the said towne whiche begynnethe at a place called Whyte Crosse & extendeth by the northe syde of Drodyke, unto a place called Ferrars Bridge, and there yt falleth into the common sewer, which pety dreyne ys & oughte to be frome tyme to tyme scowred & repayred by all the landholders that buttethe or adioynethe upon the same.

([*Pety*] *dreyne*)   Item there ys one other pety dreyne which begynnethe at a place called Crosse Lane, and extendethe by Lowegate on the este syde of the same unto a lane called Hixlane & so passethe by serteyne dyches unto a place called Mottells Gote, & there to be mayd a cundytt of bryck & so to fall betwene . . . John Hunston called [?F]erthen Land, into the common sewer.

(*A pety dreyne*)   Item there ys one other pety dreyne which begynneth at a place . . . ton Lane & passethe betwene the land of

---

[1] There are holes at the head and in the centre of this folio, and part of the foot is missing.
[2] "1570" seems to have been first written.

the manner of Dunton & . . . Lane . . . sewer called Breche Eye, and a cundytt of bryck to be mayd over . . . mondole La[n]e.

(*Pety [dreyn]e*) Item there ys one other pety dreyne which begynnethe at a place called Chapell Gate & so passethe directly betwene the landes of Wylliam Wrighte, & the landes parcell of the manner of Tylnayes, unto the land late belongyng to the chantery of St John the Baptyste unto the northe end of Acres Gate otherwyse called Dentons Gate, and there to go over by a cundytt of bryck on the southe syde of Brodegate & so fallethe into the said common sewer at a place called Barnardes Bridge, at the northend of Mylne Gate, which pety dreyne & all other pety dreynes before naymed, oughte to be frome tyme to tyme dyked & repayred as often as neede shall requyre, at the cammandement of the dykegreves by all the landholders, whose landes there adioynes or buttes upon every one of the said pety dreynes, upon payne of everye landholder that makethe defalte for everye roode to forfeyte xij d., and further that everye one of the said pety dreynes, once by the yere be roded & scowred by all the landholders that eyther joyne or abbuttes upon them or eny of them, at the cammandement of the dykegreves of the same towne, upon payne of every roode not donne iiij d.

[1] . . . said jurey saith that there is a gote called the Gote betwext the Scheres which is in ruen and decay and ought to . . . [re]pared by the landehoulders of Sutton by acredge.

. . . that there ought to be made a cart bryg over the ea betwex the . . . Tydd Bryg, and a nother bryg over the sayd ea at a place . . . Sutton.

[473.XIII.16]   260
[2] (*Seabanck*) Item the seabanck of the said towne whiche extende . . . the gote called Tydd Gote, northeward to a place called Cold Hurne to a place called the Oute Broken betwene Tydd [& Sutton] shall frome tyme to tyme, and as often as nede requy[re] . . . repared & amended by all the landholders of the same towne of Tydd by acre money and further thenhabyta[ntes] . . . for there passage that way shall gyve & make a common meanework day upon the said common seabanck everye yere . . . payne of everye inhabytante that shall make defalte everye day xij d., after knowledge be gyven therof by . . . of the said towne.

(*Owte ryng*) Item we say that frome the said Cold Hurne unto a place . . . Margery Pytt, parcell of the owte rynge of the same towne, shalbe repared maynteyned & kepte in suffycyent highte & breadth at all tymes, by the said inhabytantes of Tydd by common meaneworkes accordyng to the awncyent custome of the saide towne.

(. . .) Item we say that all the headynges frome Sommerleasure Lane End, unto Whyte Crosse & so forthe unto the Pryors Laythe at thend of Masterdyke shalbe suffycyently maynteyned & kepte,

---

[1] The last two paragraphs are added in two different hands.
[2] There are holes at the head and in the centre of this folio.

frome tyme to tyme by Tydd by common meaneworkes for so yt haythe bene accustomed, excepte suche stowes as be occupyed daylye by the owners of the land, which stowes shalbe suffycyently maynteyned by the occupyers of the same landes.

Item we say that Masterdyke frome Grene Drove End unto Brodegate parcell of the owtryng of the same town, shalbe repared mayntey[ned] and kepte in suffycyent highte & breadthe at all tymes by thynhabytantes of the said towne, by common meaneworkes, accordyng to the awncyent custome of the said towne.

Item we say that Brodegate frome Masterdykes End to Badgate & so to Wyllowe Dykes End parcell of the owteryng of the said towne of Tydd, shalbe repayred maynteyned & kepte in suffycyent highte & bredthe at all tymes by the inhabytantes of Tydd by common meaneworkes.

Item we say that there ys a common hye way called Myllgate which oughte to be repayred maynt[eyn]ed & kepte suffycyently in highte so that the waters passe not over ytt in Tylney Feelde by the inhabytantes of the said towne by common meaneworkes.

(*VJ bridges*) It[em] . . . say there are vj bridges over the common sewer . . . [sa]id towne, which oughte to be repayred & amended . . . requyre by acre money.

(*Eye bank*) Item . . . owte rynge of the same towne . . . [f]rome Grayns Hyll to Hix Lane, ys defectyve in dy[vers] pla[ces] & oughte . . . [com]mon meaneworkes.

(*Sowthe Eyey Quere*) Item we say that the banck called Southe Eye b[elon]gyng to the said towne of Tydd ys defectyve in highte & breadthe, which oughte to be mayde & amended by the landholders therof accordynge as ys specyfyed in the joycebooke therof mayd, and all suche persons so charged shall have free & quyett passage over Wyllow Dyke for the repayrynge of the said Sowthe Eye at eny tyme, with takynge meanure of & upon the said Wyllow Dyke quyetly withowte gaynsaynge of eny person for the reparynge of the said banck called Southe Eye, belongyng to the said towne of Tydd.

(*Tydd Gote*) Item we say that the gote belongyng to Tydd St Marye, ys to be mayd & amended as often as neede requyrethe aswell with tymber stone & . . . [w]orcke, by acre money of all the landes in the said towne of Tydd, and the flytte & owtefall of the same ys to be donne also by acremoney.

(. . . *Halls* [*heady*]*nges*) Item we say that all the headynges belongyng to Dunton Hall, beyng defectyve, ys to be amended by Mr Twyforthe fermer therof, as haythe bene accustomed.

(. . . *fynne*) Item one fynne goyng frome Tydd Gote to Colle Hurne beynge defectyve oughte to be dyked by aker money, for the mayntenance of Tydd Dreyne.

[1]Item they say that Tyd Fen ought to drain by the Shire Goat and ought to be charged as Sutton is by acaridge from Willow Dyk to the goat.

---

[1] This paragraph is added in another hand.

[473.XIII.17] 261

(*Sutton Saynt James*) Feyrst the saide jurey saight that the Fendike frowme Saynt Marey Hourne unto Thowrstones Breige and frowme Thowrstons Breyge wnto Maystar Dykes Ende ys in rewne & decaye, for lacke of haight and bredde and owght for to be maide by the parreishe of Saynt James, by ther comman menewarke.

Item the saide jurey saight that Chappell Gatte frowme Richard Rayntons Cornar wnto Eywes Crose and frowme Eywes Crose wnto Rawnes Deikes Ende ys in reune & decaye for lacke of haight and brede and owght for to be maide by the pareishe of St James by ther comman mene warke.

Item the saide jurey saight that Brodegate frowme Eywse Crose wnto Redes Crose and frowme Redes Crose wnto St Edmonds Fendike ys in rewne and decaye for lacke of haight and brede and owght for to be maide by the pareishe of St James by ther comman mene warke.

Item the saide jurey saight that Fendike frowme Redes Crose wnto Teide Howrne Brige ys in rewne & decaye for lacke of haight and brede and owght for to be maide by the parreishe of St James by ther comman meneuarke and frowme Redes Crose wnto Gedney Geyttes ys in like defawe and owght for to be maide by comman menewarke.

Item the saide jurey saight that frowme Maystar Dikes Ende wnto Teyde Howrne Brige and frowme Tid Howrne Breige unto St Edmonds Fendike ys in rewne and decaye for lacke of haight & brede and owght for to be maide by comman menewarke by the parreishe of St James.

(. . . *tes in . . . eley*) Item the saide jurey saight that ther ys sartayn rodes in Eyngeley defectife for lacke of haight and brede and owght for to be maide by theis men folowing that ys to saye the haiars of Richard Blaidewin ix roddes Wylliam Meyson ix rodes John Negall and Richard Mane iij rodes John Negall ij rodes James Bwaldwar iiij rodes Harry Blanke senior xv rodes Thomas Person vij rodes Wylliam Blaidewen xix rodes the haiars of Richard Blaidewen ix rodes Harrey Gleppes iij rodes Lawrans Terington ix rodes Harrey Blanke junior & John Blanke v rodes and in coman for to be maide by coman menewarke by the pareche of St James ij rodes.

(*Bankes in [Bar]linges [Dro]we*) Item the saide jurey saight that ther ys sartayne rodes in Barlinges Drowe defectife for lacke of haight and brede and owght for to be mayde by theis men folowinge that ys to saye Ane Beylleyngame viij rodes John Brete xj rodes Harrey Blanke junior & John Blanke xiiij rodes the chantarre of Sutton xiiij rodes the haiars of Thomas Reche iiij rods Thomas Weytton viij rodes John Cowt and Harrey Cowt iiij rodes James Craxston vij rodes Wylliam Blaidewyn vij rodes Hewe Nordeyn x rodes di. Symond Cowt xj rodes the quenes maigeste for Castelaker xxx rodes comman for to be maide by the parreishe of St James by menewarke iiij rodes.

(. . . in . . . gate)   Item the saide jurey saight that ther ys sartayne rodes in Scales Gatte defectife for haight and brede & owght for to be maide by theis men folowinge that ys for to saye the quenes maigeste for Castelaker ij rodes the haiars of Richard Blaidewynge v rodes Thomas Person x rodes Antoney Edmonde iiij rodes Robart Pawlmar v rodes the haiars of John Mane xiiij rodes.

[473.XIII.18]   262

([De]fawtes in [Do]wrans [Dr]owe)   Item the saide jurey saight that ther ys sartayne rodes in Dowrrantes Drowe defectife for haight and brede and owght for to be maide by theis men folowing that ys for to saye the haiars of John Mane xl rodes Thomas Person xj rodes and coman for to be maide by the parreishe of St James by coman menewarke iij rodes.

([Def]awtes in [Ho]wrsemar)   Item the saide jurey saight that ther ys sartayne rodes in Horsemar defectife for lacke of haight and bredde and owght for to be maide by theis men folowing that ys for to saye the haiars of William Digell x rodes John Elme viij rodes Mawde Wright vj rodes Thomas Wright iiij rodes Gorge Partriche gentilman xviij rodes John Drowe in ij placeis xiiij rodes the haiars of John Mane xxv rodes John Gowneyll x rodes and Wylliam Aneyson v rodes.

([D]efawtes in the [he]ddynges)   Item the saide jurey saight that there ar sertaine heddynges frowme Layseyates wnto Gedney Geyttes and frowme thense wnto Togoodes defectife in sertaine placeies for lacke of haight and bredde and owght for to be maide by theis men folowinge that ys Thomas Blanke xviij rodes Robart Acar xiij rodes di. Harry Blanke senior xx rodes John Drowe xxj rodes James Bawldwar xxxviij rodes Robart Acar xxv rodes John Negall and Richard Man x rods John Negall iij rods Henry Blanke senior v rods heredes John Blanke x rods Richard Man viij rods Henri Blanke senior xiiij rods, Thomas Bateman junior v rods Richard Marchant xiiij rodes John Drowe xij rods Harri Blanke & William Farar j rode Mathew Nicolson one rode Richard Marchant one rode, William Blaidewin ij rodes Thomas Bateman senior v rodes William Blaidwyn j rode heredes John Blanke v rodes John Callow senior xviij rodes wyddow Asteyn viij rodes John Deynes ij rodes.

Item thei saye that the fendike frowme Togoodes wnto Thomas Wrightes ys defectife in sertayne placeis for haight and brede and owght for to be mayde by the pareishe of St James by ther coman menewarke.

[1]Item the saide jurey praiethe that there maye be ij paiar of clowes maide and sett the one paiar at a place called Togoodes and a nother paiar at Thowrstons Brige and the saide clowese for to be maide and sett by acar seylwar.

---

[1] Marginal note in another hand "Vacat" followed by illegible words.

Item the saiede jurey saithe that Bacons Brige Fysheis Breige Redes Brige Tyde Howrne Brige Mownkes Brige Thowrstons Breige Drowses Brige Horsemar Brige a brige at Rawnes Dikes Ende and the brige at Owlde Fendike for to be mendeide so ofte and maney times as nede shall requere by acar seilwar.

Item the sayde jurey praiethe that the watar of the sowthe seide of Chappell Gatte that rowne thorow Bacons Breige maye rowne owar Sutton Brode Gatte into Grete Ee and there a pipe of stone for to be layde for the passage of the saide watar and the saide pipe for to be laide and mayde by acar seylwar and the saide pipe for to be layde betwixe Thowrstons Brige and Battemans Gattes Ende.

[473.XIII.19]   263

(*Sutton Sainte Edmundes*) Sowth Ee otherwayes cauled the Fendike which is defective for heght and [bre]dth with oth[er] . . . inges Middell Fendike with all and singler gattes crosse gates as folowyth . . . particularres

Also we saye that Sowth Ee is defective for [wa]nte of heghte and bredth apone our othe.

Inprimis Edmund Halle esquier has thare x rodes in like maner defective

Item the maner of Gannocke has ther vj rodes in like maner defective	
Item Thomas Macpeace	v rodes in licke maner defective
Item Thomas Johnson	ij rodes in like maner defective
Item heredes Wylliam Hopkynson	ij rodes in like maner defective
Item Thomas Sowter	ij rodes in like maner defective
Item Jeffraye Baldeware	iiij rodes in like maner defective
Item Robart Hille	iij rodes in like maner defective
Item Wylliam Brown	iij rodes in like maner defective
Item Wylliam Stilton	ij rodes in like maner defective
Item James Craxton	ij rodes in like maner defective
Item John Callowe	iij rodes in like maner defective
Item heredes Henrici Mason	iij rodes in like maner defective
Item John Gunwell	iij rodes in like maner defective
Item Wylliam Farrer	iiij rodes in like maner defective
Item heredes Thome Ringe	iiij rodes in like maner defective
Item Robert Raulet	iij rodes in like maner defective
Item John Diggell	ij rodes in like maner defective
Item Robart Thomson	iij rodes in like maner defective
Item John Ranton	iij rodes in like maner defective
Item John Mane esquier	v rodes in like maner defective
Item Adlard Welbe esquier	j rod in like maner defective
Item the quenes maiesti for her lands late perteninge to the chappell of Sante Edmundes	vj rodes in like maner defective
Item Wylliam Coxon	iij rodes in like maner defective
Item Rechart Thomson	ij rodes in like maner defective
Item Edward Johnson	iij rodes in like maner defective
Item Robart Scotred	iij rodes in like maner defective

Item Rechart Marchant ⎫ Jeffraye Baldeware ⎬ James Baldeware ⎭	iij rodes in like maner defective
Item Alexander Coxon	ij rodes in like maner defective
Item the maner of Barlinges	vj rodes in like maner defective
Item Wylliam Lynge	iiij rodes in like maner defective
Item Wylliam Kedbe	ij rodes in like maner defective
The quenes maiesti	xl rodes in like maner defective
Heredes Robarti Allen	iiij rodes in like maner defective
Heredes Johan Blanke	iiij rodes dim. in like maner defective
[Ite]m Roger Morren	ij rodes in like maner defective
[Item] Thomas Johnson senior	iiij rodes in like maner defective
Item Rechart Man	iij rodes in like maner defective
Item Simond Cutte	iiij rodes in like maner defective
Item Rechart Marchante	ij rodes in like maner defective
Item the heres of Wylliam Baldeware	v rodes in like maner defective
Item Wylliam Thomson	iij rodes in like maner defective
Item John Raulinge	iij rodes in like maner defective
[Jam]es Baldeware	v rodes in like maner defective

[473.XIII.20]   264

([L]utton [He]adinges)   Also we saye apone our othe that the hea[dinges] . . . for hegth & bredth as in maner aforesayde.

In primis Wylliam Bladwyn	xij rodes in like maner defective
Item James Baldeware	xx rodes in like maner defective
Item Harry Blanke & Robart Blanke	viij rodes in like maner defective
Item Mr Partriche	viij rodes in like maner defective
Item Laurans Tirrington	iiij rodes in like maner defective
Item Nycholes Harte	ij rodes in like maner defective
Item Eme Pery	iiij rodes in like maner defective
Item Robart Raulet	iiij rodes in like maner defective
Item Edward Jobson	vj rodes in like maner defective
Item Thomas Fessher and James Perkyn	viij rodes in like maner defective
Item Thomas Jeffraye	iiij rodes in like maner defective
Item Thomas Johnson	vj rodes in like maner defective
Item Rechart Raulinge	iiij rodes in like maner defective
Item John Allin	ij rodes in like maner defective
Item James Baldeware	ij rodes in like maner defective
Item the her of Roger Clarke	vj rodes in like maner defective

Also we saye apone our othe that the quenes maiesti has ther xx rodes defective for hight & bredthe

Item Dowmes Daye has	vj rodes in like maner defective
Item Thomas Fissher	x rodes in like maner defectyve
Item Wylliam Seman	ij rodes in like maner defective
Item Robert Raulet	ij rodes in like maner defective
Item Marget Raulinge	vj rodes in like maner defective

Item Laurans Tirrington	iiij rodes in like maner defective
Item John Blanke	iij rodes in like maner defective
Item Laurans Tirrington	x rodes in like maner defective
Item Thomas Fissher	xvj rodes in like maner defective
Item Roger . . . de	ij rodes in like maner defective
Item Thomas Johnson senior	iiij rodes in like maner defective
Item Rechart Thomson	iij rodes in like maner defective
Item Rechart Raulinge	vj rodes in like maner defective
Item Hue Northen	vj rodes in like maner defective
Item James Baldware	xx rodes in like maner defective
Item Thomas Jeffray	ij rodes in like maner defective
[Item] Jeffray Baldeware	iij rodes in lyke maner defective

[Also] we say that the quenes maiesti has in the same gate xl rodes defective for want of highte & brede

[1][Ja]mes Baldeware . . . Fissher

and . . . Seman has	xiij rodes in like maner defective
. . . art Gleppes & Marget Raulinge	iiij rodes in like maner defective
. . . Gleppes . . . ington . . . has	iiij rodes in like maner defective
. . . Gleppes . . . Blanke have	vj rodes in like maner defective
. . . let . . . d . . . have	vj rodes in like maner defective
. . . [Ba]ldeware . . . kes have	ij rodes in like maner defective
. . . Baldeware	vj rodes in like maner defective
. . .	iiij rodes in like maner defective
. . .	ij rodes in like maner defective

[473.XIII.21]   265

[2](. . . *gattes* . . . *gates*) Also we saye that the crosse gate frome . . . Gate and frome Halle Gate to Brodgate and frome Brodgate to Ganok . . . in moste places and is to be mayed by diggre meanworkes.

B[rodgate]

Also we saye that Brodgat is defective . . . places and is to be mayed by comman dayes.

Gannok Gate

Also we saye that Gannoke Gat is defective moste part and is to be mayed by the frantigeres of bothe siddes.

Wyllow Dike

Also we saye that Wyllowe Dike is defective the moste of it for lacke of highte and brede and is to be mayed by the londes liynge of the weste side according to the olde custom and auncyent order.

Fen Dike

Also we saye that the Fene Dike frome Lutton headinges unto Wyllowe Dike is defective and is to be mayed by diggre meane workes the which Fendike goes betwixe Sante James and Sante Edmundes.

---

[1] The bottom left corner of this folio is missing.
[2] Hole at head of folio, and part of left margin missing.

Tid Banke at Sowth Ee

[1]Also we saye that Tide Banke is all defective for heghte & brede which banke belonges to Tide Sante Maris.

Towe payre of clowes

[A]lso we say that it is very nedfull that we of Sante Emundes shulde have ij parre [of] clowes the one parre at Halle Brige at Fene Dike & the other at Lutton Bridge at . . . Dike so that we maye have ij pare of shittes the one at Lutton Gat Bridge & [the] other at Mille Brige.

[2]Item the said jury say the gote & the sewer betwine Cambrydge shyre & Lyncolne shyre ys defectyve and ought [to] be repayred made and amended by the townshipp of Sutton by acreydge as hath byn [acu]stomed so often as nede shall requyre by the quenes maiesty and the tenantes.

[473 XIII.22]   266

Preponit

[3]([Tydd]e St [M]aries. *Ante Johannem Baptiste sub pena ut in lege generale*) Imprimis that[4] . . . suffecyentlye repared amendyd and . . . [hi]gheth and breade bye acaraygs.

(2 *At the discrecion of the Justices.*[5]) Also we say that . . . nne frome the goote, to a place caullid Old . . . ys defectyve, [6]and owght to be made by Tyde and Sutton by acarags as ofte as nede shalbe.

(3) Also we saye that our dames[7] are defectyve, and owghte to be mayde by Tyde & Sutton by acarayges.

(4 *Ante primum Augusti sub pena generale*) Also we saye that our common sewer ys defectyve for lacke of dykyn and to be done by acraige.

(5 *The banke first to be maide equall & the defautes to be amended before mydsomer next*) Also we desyer a newe joysemente to be made for the better reparynge of Soweth Eay bancke.

(6 *Ante primum Augusti sub pena maiore ut in lege generale*) Also we saye that one common bancke frome Graynes Hyll, to Clementes Crosse, ys defectyve in manye places, and owghte to be made by comonag of the towneshipe of Tydde, for the defence of the same towne.

(7 *Fiat*) Also we saye that their ys a gytte upon Maynes Fennedyke, whyche ys the dreane of Gostowefelde and owght to be mayd with a condytte by accaraige.

---

[1] This sentence has been cancelled.

[2] This paragraph has been added in another hand.

[3] This is a small sheet which has been much corrected in more than one hand. Part of the head is missing.

[4] A caret is inserted here, but neither the matter for inclusion nor the next few words of the original text can be supplied as a piece is missing from the head of the folio.

[5] A further marginal note follows in another hand but cannot be deciphered.

[6] The words from here to the end of the sentence have been interlined in place of the following, which is cancelled: "and so maney of Sutton as shall take any benyfyte by the same are to be layd by accarage".

[7] A scribbled interlinear phrase seems to read "mad for the (?)perotayn of our . . ." and to be intended for insertion here.

(8 *Fiat ante Johannem Baptiste sub pena ut in generale lege*)
Also we saye that their wolde be a clowe made at Sewelles Brygge,
by accaraige.

(9 *Fiat ut antea*) Also we saye that yt behowyth a condytte
to be made at Asheholde, beinge the dreane of Redymore Felde,
by accaraige.

(10 *Fiat*) Also we saye that yt ys meyte a condytte to be mayd
betwyxte Hunesegatte & Whytte Crosse, into the petye dreane, by
accarage.

[1](*Sutton ante Johannem Baptiste sub pena in generale lege*) Also
we saye the goote of Sutton bethyxe the Shyars ys nat sufficient in
repare to defend salt water nor for the common passayges.

[*Endorsed*:] Preponit

[473.XIII.23]   267

(*Sowtton Saynte Marie   The new ryver . . . brydge to the new gote
to be dyked & clensed by joyse*) Also the saide jurie saithe that the
newe rewar or sewar of Sowtton frome the owlde rewar or grete
sewar frome a place callede Wickars Brige unto Sowtton Newe Gotte
ys wndikede and owghte for to be dikede rodede and scowrede and
clensede by joysemente accordynge to owr owlde anchente cow-
stowme time owte of minde.

(*Denyelles Bridge . . .*) Item the saide jurie saithe that ther ys
a newe brige to be mayde owar Denyelles Gatte owar the sayde
newe sewar and the saide brige to be mayde by acar seylwar.

(*Other certen brydges*) Item the saide jurie saithe that ther be
other sartayn brigges within the towne of Sowtton and owghte for
to be amendide and reparede by acar seylwar by the quens maygeste
lordes and lande howldars that have aney lands within the towne
by acar seylwar so ofte and maney times as nede schall requere.

(*The fynnes & dames [me]ne work*) Item the sayde jurie saythe
that the petey feines and dames of the marsche schalbe forscene,
kepte reparede and amendide as schalbe thowghte mette by the
baleyffe of Sowtton & and[2] other inhabytans of the same to the
mayntaynans of the grette fine or flette by the inhabitans of the
towne of Sowtton aforsayde by ther comman menewarke so often
and manye times as nede schall requere.

(*A partyclar presentment for the . . .*) Item the saide jurie saythe
that yt ys mette that all hownars fermars & other that hawe aney
proffite of the comman with ther cattell schall cowme holye to ther
comman menewarke so often and manye times as yt schalbe warnede
by the digrifes and that ewerey pore man beynge a cottingar and
hawing no cattell schall cowme and do ther thirde menewarke as
often and maney times as yt schalbe warnede by the saide digrefes
so often & manie times as nede schall requere. And that the
digrifes schall make a trewe accownte of all ownars fermars &

[1] This paragraph is added in one of the correcting hands.
[2] *Sic.*

cottingars that dothe make deffawte in cowmenge to ther menewarke whan that they ar warnede & that thei make ther accownte wnto the balyffe of Sowtton & other inhabitans within one monethe nexte aftar ther departor owte of ther office wppon payne of ewerey digeyffe making defawt to forfayte to the euse of the towne x s.

(. . .) Item the sayde jurie saythe that yt ys mette & nessasarie that Sowthe Ee Banke be newe joyssede accordinge to our owlde cowstome, & also that Sowtton Grette Ee or rewar frome Sowtton Newe Gotte unto Brigelis Brige and frome Brigelis Brige wnto Newe Fendike betuix Saynt James & Saynt Edmonds be joysede also. And also that the Lyttill Ee frome a place callede Newe Stoke wnto Bacons Brige and frome Bacons Brige wnto Newe Fendike betwix Saynt James & Saynt Edmonds for to be joysede also. And also that [So]wtton Ee owghte to be joyssede frowme Lowtton Gotte unto a place callede [To]goodes so ofte & manye times as nede schall requere.

[473.XIII.24]　　　　　　　　　　　　　　　　　　　　268

(3 *Frontagers Sowtton Saynt James*) Also we saye that all those lands that leysse on the northe seide of Yengley Doge Drove and Horsemar owghte to make ther heddyngs agayns Gedney Ee and ewereye man to make there heddyngs or clowtte v fotte wydde in the bottome at the leste uppon payne as yt schalbe thowghte mete by the comisschonars of the sewars.

Item the sayde jurie saythe that all those lands that leyes one the northe seyde of Yengley Doge Drowe and Horsemar schall dyke rodde scowar and clense Lowtton Ee frome a place called Togowdes to New Fendike ewerey man agayns his owne so ofte and maney tymes as nedde schall requere.

Also we say that all those lands that leyse of the sowghte seyde of Eyngeley Doge Drowe and Horsemar schall make the sayde Yengeley Doge Drowe and Horsemar in schefficente haythe and brede so ofte and maney tymes as nedde schall requere.

Also the sayde jurey saythe that Belles Drowe Balkyns Drowe Taylyars Drowe Byrdes Drowe Sondy Gatte and Gowge Gatte ys in rewne and decaye in dywars placis for lacke of hayghte and owghte for to be amendyde by all those that hawe aney landes abowttin a bothe seides of the saide drowes or lanes ewerey man agayns his owne soe ofte and maney tymes as nedde schall requere.

Deffawtes in Horsemar Scales Gatte and
Downneylles Drowe

Iteme the sayde jurie saythe that John Blanke hawe iiij roddes deffectiffe for haythe and bredde in Horsemar, John Man esquiar viij rods in the sayme waye in ij placis in lyke defawte, John Man esquiar ij rods in Scales Gatte agayns Bowlls lande deffectife for haythe, Mr Bowlton ij rodes in the sayme waye in lyke deffawte, John Man esquiar xxiij rodes in the same waye in lyke deffawte in ij placis, the haiars of Richard Blaydewin ij rodes in the same waye in lyke deffawte for lacke of haythe and bredde John Man esquiar xv rodes in iij placis in Downeyls Drowe deffectiffe for lacke of haythe and bredde and howghte for to be mayde by the saide John Man esquiar.

Item the saide jurie saythe that yt ys mett and nessessarie for a gowttar for to be cowtte owar Brode Gatte within Saynt James iiij fotte wide betwixe Robarte Cokexsons and Lawrans Teringtons in tyme of nedde so that the watar of Lyttill Ee seide may fall into Grette Ee and so to Lowtton Gotte.

Deffawts in Yengeley

Item the sayde jurie saythe that John Negall and Richard Man one rode deffectife for haythe John Brokehows one rode in lyke deffawte Harri Blanke di. a rode in the same waye in lyke deffawte.

Item the saide jurie saythe that yt ys mett that Sondigatte and Gowge Gatt schall hawe eyther of them a spowte of stone that the sayde lands of Sondigatte & Gawge Gatte may drayne into Leyttill Ee & the sayde spowts for to be mayd by acar sylwar.

Kalend'

[473.XIII.25]   269

(*Sowtton Saynt Edmonds*) Also the sayde jwrie saythe that Gannoke Gatte in Saynt Edmonds ys in deffawte for lacke of haythe and brede frome a place callede Seynt Edmonds Fendike wnto Welow Dykes Ende and owghte for to be amendiede by all those that hawe aney lands lyeng or abowtting of the same way ewerey man agayns his owne so oft and manye times as nedde schall requere whan menar may be gotton for the saide way.

(*This ys not agreyd upon by the jury untill it may be . . . veyd by vj . . . ssioners*) Item the sayde jwrie saythe that ther ys a place frowme Howndarde Acars Ende wnto Sowthe Ee ys in deffawte for lacke of haythe and brede and owghte for to be amendid by comman menewarke so often & manye times as nede schall requere.

Deffawtes in Sowthe Ee

Item the sayde jurie saythe that Edward Jhonson ij rodes for lacke of backen Robart Acar iij rods for lacke of backen, Antoney Edmonde iij rods for lacke of haythe and bredde, the quenes may-geste for howr manars of Castelaker & Barlyngs iij rods in lyke deffawte the hayars of John Wylkyn iij rodes in lyke deffawte the quens maygeste for howr dowche ix rodes in lykc deffawte, the landhowldars of John Sowtar ij rodes for lacke of backen, Thomas Sowtar ij rods for backen, and that ewerey howndararde schall sett a stone or stowlpe at the ende of ther howndarde betwixe this and Mayday nexte.

Kalend'

[473.XIII.26]   270

[1](2 *Tidde St Mary Brodgat menworkes*) Item we saie that Brodegate from M[aste]r Dike End . . . dgate & so Willowe Dike End parcell of the outringe of the said towne of Tidde shalbe

[1] There is a small hole at the head of this folio.

repeired ma[intained] . . . sufficient heght & breadethe at all times by the inhabitauntes of the saide towne of Tid . . . workes.

(*Willowedike to . . . on minworkes with cartes Jugment*) Item we saye that Willowe Dike from Bad Gate End unto the southe end of Hundred Acras Corner against Harram parcell of the outeringe shalbe repaired mayntayned & sufficiently kepte in hight & breadethe at all times herafter by the land holders of all those landes that lyethe in that place called Tyd Fenne that is to saie from Willowe Dike End unto the southe end of the said Hundred Acres over against Harram with the helpe of one myneworke daye every yere of the wholl inhabitauntes of the same towne as often as nede shall require with the cartes of all them that have & occupie cartes & the rest with spades & barrowes upon payne of ever[y] carte that maketh his defaulte iij s. iiij d. & of every other person besides whatsoever he be that maketh his defaulte xij d.

Item from Hundred Acres Corner aforsaid unto Clowes Crosse shalbe repeired mayntaned & kepte sufficientlye in hight & breadeth at all times hearafter by the inhabitauntes of the same towne with commen mineworkes, & further we thinke very mete & profitable for the common welthe & the preservation of the countrye that the said Willowe Dike at one parte therof shalbe barred from the feaste of S. Martynne in wynter unto the feast of the Appostels Phillippe & Jacob, so that no cartes passe that waie duringe the same at the costes expences & charges of all the the[1] landholders within the same fenne.

Item we say that ther is a common highe way called Millgate which oughte to be repaired & maintaned sufficiently in hight so that the water passe not over it, into Tylney Feild by the inhabitauntes of the same towne by common mineworks.

(*V bridges by acre s*) Item we saye that v common bridges of stone, within the same towne which ought to be repared & amended as often as nede shall require by acre monye.

(*Ee Bancke Tellneis menwork*) Item we saie that vj rodes of the E Bancke parcell of the outeringe of the saide towne over against the manner of Tilneyes which is in great ruen & decaye & ought to be repared & kepte by the inhabitors of Tid aforsaid by common min-workes so that the quens leige people may have theire common passage as ever they have hadd & as the waters belongeth to the said manner of Tilneis & al other land lieinge in the sam felde maie be kepte oute of the said Olde Ee, which is the devisione betwene the sheires of Lincolne & Cambridg[e] except the sam waters maie lawfully & redelye passe derectly from thenc to the sea.

(. . .) Item the sayde jwre saythe that ther ys a banke extendynge frome the Hundrythe Acar Corner wnto Sowthe Ee whyche hawght to be exaltyde and amendede as ofte as nede shalle reqwyre by the inabytans of Tyde Sant Mary by comone menworke.

[1] *Sic.*

(3 *Tydd S. Mary* *Annother pety dren at the commaundement of the degereves to be diked onse in a yere*) Item there is an other petye dreane whiche beginneth at a place called Chaple Gate, and so passeth directly betwene the landes of William Wright & the landes parcell of the maner of Tylneys unto the landes late belonginge to the chauntrey of Saint John Baptist nowe in the quenes maiesties possession unto the north end of Acres Gate otherwise called Deyntones Gate & there to go over by a pype of stone or a hollowe tree on the southe side of Brodgate & so falleth into the comon sewer at a place called Barnardes Bridge at the north end of Milgate, which petye dreane & all other drenes before named whiche ought to be from time to time dyked & repaired as often as nede shall require at the commaundement of the digerevys by all the land holders whose landes dothe there adioyne & abuttes upon every one of the saide petye dreanes upon payne of everie landholder that maketh his defaulte shall for everye rode [not] donne forfaite xij d. and further that everye one of the saide petye dreanes shall ones by the yeare be roded & firmed by all the lande holders that either joyneth or abutteth upon them or any of them at the commaundement of the digereves of the same towne upon payne of everie rode not donne iiij d.

(*The sea banke by acrege by common menwarke once a yere*) Item the sea banke of the same towne which extendeth from the gote called Tydde Gote northwarde to a place called Colde Horne at Outbroken, shall from time to time & as often as nede shall require shalbe repeired & amended by all the land holders of the same towne of Tidde by acre money. And furthermore we saye that all the inhabitauntes of the sayde towne of Tydd for ther easment & passage that waye shal geve & make a comon mynwarke day upon the saide sea banke everye yere yf nede shall require upon payne of everye inhabitur that shall make his default for every daye xij d. after the commaundement & open warninge geven them by the degereves of the same towne.

(*Outbroken by menwerke*) Item we saye that from the sayd Outbroken unto a certayne place called Margerye Pytt parcell of the outringe of the same towne of Tidde shalbe repeired mayntayned & kept in sufficient height & bredth at all times which & by the inhabitauntes of the same towne by common mynwarkes accordinge to the auncient costome of the same towne.

(*Hedinges menwerkes stowes by the owners*) Item we saye that all the heddinges from Sommer Leasur Lane End unto White Crosse & so forth unto the Priors Lathe at the end of Master Dike shalbe sufficienly mayntayned & kept from time to time by common menwarkes according to the auncient costome of the same towne savinge all such stowes as be occupied dalye by the owners of the landes which stowes shalbe sufficienlye mayntaned by the occupiers of the same landes.

(*Masterdike menwerkes*)   Item we saye that Masterdike from
Grene Drove End unto Brodgate parcell of the outringe of the same
towne shalbe repeired mayntayned & kept in sufficient height &
bredth at all time & times hereafter by the inhabitauntes of Tidde
aforsaide by common menwarkes according to the auncient costome
of the same towne.

[473.XIII.28]   272

(4 *Swtton Saynt Marie*)   The saide jurey saithe that yt ys mete
and nesesarey to hawe a trenche or spowte mayde with stone and
to be layde in the heie waye in Maydinhowse Gatte by Thomas Clarke
junior howse at the diches ende that the watar maye rowne owar
the saide gatte into Priars Fawle and so to pase deyreckeley into the
Leytteyll Ee and the chargis thereof for to be done by all those that
hawe aney landes leyeng within the angle that ys to saye frome
Thomas Clarkes wnto Jurdons Gatte.

(*Defawtes in Delfe*)   The said jurey saithe that ther ys x rodes in
Delfe defecketife for lacke of haithe and brede and owght for to be
maide by Rogar Morra Antoney Edmonde John Welles and the
haiars of Rychard Ropar.

(*Defawtes in Deyes Gate*)   The saide jurey saithe that ther ys v
rodes in Deyes Gate defecketife for lacke of heithe and brede and
owght for to be mayde by Robart Rogeman and Symond Deyns.

(*Defawtes in Caye Gate*)   The saide jewrey saithe that there ys
iiij rodes in Caye Gate defecketife for lacke of haithe and brede and
owght for to be maide by Gorge Partriche gentillman Robart Rogeman and John Renowlde.

(*Defawtes in Childerrws Gatte*)   The saide jurey saithe that there
ys vj rodes in Childarrows Gate defecketife for lacke of haythe and
brede and owght for to be maide by Nicholas Reynge and William
Worcheope.

(*Defawtes in Batemans Gate*)   The saide jurey saythe that there ys
ij rowdes in Batemans Gate defecketife for haithe and brede and
owght for to be maide by John Deynes.

(*Defawtes in Lowtton*)   The sayde jurey saithe that there ys a
petey drayne leding frome Powles Cotte to Lowe Gates Ende and
so to Colle Gate defecketife in sartaine placeis and owght for to be
mayde as hereaftar folowithe that ys to saye at Lowe Gates Ende
x rodes parte to be mayde by coman menewarke of the inhabitars
of Lowtton and the other parte by Wylliam Browne.

(*Briges within Sowtton*)   The sayde jurey saithe that all the briges
and spowtes within the towne of Sowtton owght for to be repared
mayde and amendeid by acar money so ofte and maney teymes as
nede schall requere.

[473.XIII.29]   273

(5 *Swtton Saynt James*)   The saide jurye saithe that Horsemer
ys defecketife in sartayne placis for lacke of haithe and brede and
owght for to be mayde by theis parteis polowyng [*sic*] that ys to

saye Ane Bellyngame vj rodes John Mane esquiar xv rodes in iij placis and John Drowe ix rods.

(*Dorantes Drowe*) The sayde jurey saythe that there ys xxij rodes in Dorantes Drowe defectife for lacke of haith and brede in iij placis and owght for to be mayde by John Mane esquiar.

The saide jurye saithe that there ys ij rodes in the same waye defecketife for lacke of haithe and brede & owght for to be maide by comman menewarke by the inhabitars of Saynt James.

(*Scales Gate*) The saide jurie saithe that Scales Gate ys in rewne and decaye in sartayne placis for lacke of haithe and brede and owght for to be maide by theis parteis folowing that ys for to saye John Mane esquiar xviij rodes in iij placis maistar Bowlton vj rodes & the haiars of John Blanke vj rods.

(*Barlings Drowe*) The saide jurie saithe that Barlings Drowe ys in rewne and decaye in sartayne placis for lacke of haithe and brede and owght for to be mayde by their parteis folowing that ys for to saye the quenes maygeste for Castlaker lande vj rodes Hewe Nordeyn vj rods William Blaydwyn ij rodes and John Brete ij rods.

(*Oynley*) The sayde jurey saythe that Eynley ys defectife in sartayn placis for lacke of haithe and brede and owght for to be mayde by theis parteis folowing that ys to saye Harrey Blanke junior & Harri Acar ij rods Lawrans Terington ij rods the haiars of Richard Blaydwyn xj rods in ij placis John Blewicke vj rods James Bawldwar ij rodes John Negall ij rods Richard Mane & John Negall ij rodes to be maide ewerey mane agayns his owne.

(*Bade Gate*) The saide jurey saythe that there ys a waye ledyng frome a place callede Sent Edmonds Fendike wnto Maystar Dike ys in sartayn placeis in reune & decaye for lacke of haithe & brede and owght for to be mayde by comman menewarke of the inhabitars of Saynt James so oft and maney times as nede schall requere.

(*Chappill Gatte*) The saide jurey saithe that there ys a waye leding frome Bacons Brige wnto Rawnes Dike ys in rewne & decaye in sartayne placis for lacke of haithe & brede and owght for to be mayde by coman menewarke of the inhabitars of Saynt James so ofte & maney times as nede requere.

(*Brode Gatte*) The saide jurey saithe that Brode Gate in Saynt James frome Eywes Crose wnto Saynt Edmonds Fendike ys in decaye in sartayn placis for lacke of haithe & brede & owght to be maide by coman menewarke of the inhabitars of Saynt James.

(*Fendike*) The saide jurey saithe that there ys a fendike frome a place callede Godesmans Geytes wnto Redes Crose and frome thens wnto Teyde Howrne Brige ys in maney placeis in rewne & decaye for lacke of haithe and brede and owght for to be mayde by coman menewarke of the inhabitars of Saynt James.

The saide jwrey saithe that the fendike frome Bacons Brige wnto Togoods ys in many placis in & [*sic*] decaye for lacke of haythe & brede and owght for to be maide by the inhabytars of Saynt James by ther coman menewarke so oft & maney times as nede requere.

J

(*Heddyngs*) The sayde jwrey saythe that there ys sartayn heddings frowme Togoods wnto Rawnes Dike that ar defectife in sartayn placis and owght for to be maide by theis men folowing John Deyns Richard Awsten John Callow John Blanke Wylliam Blaydwyn Thomas Bateman senior Richard Marchant the haiars of John Alleyn and John Drowe ewerey man agayns his owne. And frome Rawnes Dike wnto Saynt Edmonds Fendike for to be mayd by theys men Rychard Marchant Thomas Bateman junior John Negall & Richard Man Robart Acar James Bawldware John Drowe Harri Blanke senior ewery man agayns his owne. The rest of the saide heddings for to be mayde by the inhabitars of Saynt James by coman menewarke so oft and maney times as nede schall requere.

[473.XIII.30]   274

(6 *Swtton Saynt Edmonds*) The sayde jurie saythe that Sowthe Ee Banke in Sowtton ys defecketife for haithe and brede that ys to saye Edmonde Hawle esquiar xij rodes the quenes maygeste for howr manar of Ganoke x rodes Thomas Sowtar junior ij rods Robart Hille iiij rods Wylliam Browne iij rods Thomas Sowtar senior iij rods Robart Gybson iiij rods Thomas Fischar ij rods Alyxsandar Cokexson iij rods Jheffarrey Bawldwar James Bawld-war and Richard Marchant iij rods di. Wylliam Kynge iij rods the quenes mayeste for how deuie . . . xx rods the inhabitowrs of Sowtton for ther cherche lands ij rodes ys defecketyfe for haithe and brede and owght for to be mayde by theis parsones aforesayde ewerey mane for his porcion.

(*The heddings*) The saide jwrey saythe that the heddynges ys deffecketife for haithe and brede and owght for to be mayde by all those that hathe lands abowtting of the saide heddings.

(*Lowtton Gate*) The saide jwrey saithe that Lowtton Gate frome the Fendike to the Sowthe Ee ys in decaye in sartayn placeis for lacke of haithe and brede and owght for to be maide by theis partis folowing that ys to saye the quenes mayeste from the Fendike to Owte Gate Brige, and frome Owte Gate Brige unto the Sowghte Ee Banke and owght for to be mayde by the lande howldars abowtting of the saide gate ewerey mane agaynes his owne.

(*Hawle Gate*) The sayde jwrey saythe that Hawle Gate ys defecketife for lacke of haithe and brede and owght for to be maide by the quenes mayeste frome the Fendike wnto Hawle Gate Crose and frome Hawle Gate Crose wnto the Sowthe Ee Banke the quenes maygeste and other tenantes ewerey mane agaynes his owne so ofte and maney times as nede schall reqwere.

(*Brode Gate*) Also they saye that Brodegate ys defectife in sartayne placeis for lacke of haithe and brede and and [*sic*] owght for to be mayde by comman menevarke of the inhabitors of Saynt Edmonds so ofte & maney times as nede schall requere.

(*Ganoke Gatte*) The saide jurey saithe that Ganoke Gate ys

defectife in sartayne placis for haithe and brede and owght for to be
mayde by all those that ar frontagars of bothe seides.

(*Owte Gates*) The saide jurey saithe that Owte Gates in Saynt
Edmonds ys in decaye for lacke of haithe and brede ande owght for
to be mayde by comman menewarke so ofte and maney times as ned
schall requere & frome Lowtton Gate to Hawlle Gate & frome Hawle
Gate to Brodegate & frome Brodegatte to Ganoke Gate to be maide
as ys aforesaide.

(*Lowtton Brige*) The saide jwrey saithe that Lowwtton Ee Brige
in Saynt Edmonds ys in rewne & decaye and owght for to be mayde
by acar seylwar.

(*Clowsse*) The saide jwrey saithe that yt ys mete & nesesarey
that ij paiar of clowse for to be maide and sett the one paiar to be
sete at Lowtton Brige and the other at Hawle Bryge & the saide
clowes for to be mayde & sett by acar seylwar and the saide clowse
to be sett at Sent Edmonds Fendike.

(*Briges*) Also the sayde jwrey saithe that they thinke yt mete
to hawe ij briges stoppede at Mihilmas that ys to saye Lowtton
Brige and Hawlle Brige and for to be latten go whan that the watar
wyll conwaye to the seye.

Also the sayde jurey saythe that frome Ganoke Gates Ende wnto
Sowthe Ee Banke ys defecketife in sartayne placeis in haythe and
brede and owght for to be maide by the inhabtars of Saynt Edmonds
by there comman menewarke so ofte and maney times as nede schall
requere and that the townchepe of Tidde schall hawe there comman
pasage at all times wnto the sayde Sowthe Ee Banke.

[473.XIII.31]   275

(7 *Gedney hedinges pro feodo Pawlect*) First we say that the
quenes majestie of her maner in Gedney called the Pauletts Fee
haithe a hedynge in a place called Parke Doll which is in decaye to
the some of xl^{ti} rodes or more & oughte to be repared by her majestie
of the Pawlett Fee.

(*Hedinges pro feodo Welby*) Also we say that Adlard Welby
esquire haithe of his maner layte Lord Wentworth a hedynge in a
place called Thissell Doll which is in decay to the somme of xl^{ti} rodes
& oughte to be repared by the said Adlard Welby esquire.

(*Ravens Dyke*) Also we say that ther is a serten dyke called
Ravens Dyke which is in decaye to the somme of vj rodes or more
& oughte to be mayd by the inhabitaunce of Gedney by commound
menworkes.

(*Brodegate Brigg*) Also we say ther is a commond way ledynge
frome Ravens Dyke to Broddgayte Brygge which is in decaye to
the some of xx rodes & oughte to be amended by the inhabitaunce
of Gedney by commond menworkes.

(*Common wear dyke*) Also we say that ther is a commond ware-
dyke which ledethe frome Holmes Crose to a place called Towgottes

which is in decaye to the some of vj rodes & ought to be amended by the inhabitaunce by commond menworkes.

(*Benderslaugt Drove*)   Also we say ther is a serten heddynge called Bendersloughte Drove ledynge frome Towgottes to Broddgayte Brygge which is in decaye to the some of xij rodes & ought to be mayd by commond menworkes.

(*Hedinge att Brode Gate*)   Also we say that ther is a sertyn hedynge ledinge frome a place called Broddgayte unto Gedney Gotte which oughte to be mayd as thay have bene aforetym.

(*An unlawfull stow*)   Also we say that the heares of John Bateman ought to kepe a lawfull stowe at a place called Holmes Crosse.

(*Incipiunt le pety dreanes*)   Also we say that ther is a pettie dreayne ledynge frome Stickney Doll Stowe to Burmans Brygge & the commond sure & ought to be scoured & roded by the tennauntes of bothe sydes ther adioynynge.

Also we say that ther is a pettie dreane ledynge from Cowslapp Brygge to Sedyke Brygge & so to Thomas Coney & William Howell pasture & ought to be scowred & roded by the land holderes of bothe sydes.

Also we say ther is a pettie dreane which ledeth frome Thomas Coney pasture and to Kneppell Brygge ought to be roded scowred & clensed by John Watson & Symond Howell.

[473.XIII.32]   276

(8   *Gedney   Blasse Gate Brygg*)   Also we say that frome Kneppell Brygge to Blasse Gayte Brygge & so to the commond sure ought to be dyked & roded frome tyme to tyme by the land holderes of bothe sydes ther adioynynge.

(*Certayne dammes*)   Also we say ther is serten dammes on Lutton Marshe which oughte to be mayd & kepte by the commenty of Gedney by tow commond menworkes in the yeare as by acre selver by the quen majestie lordes & ther tennauntes.

(*The goote*)   Also we say that the commond gotte is in decaie & oughte to be mayde by acre selver of the quen majestie as lordes & ther tennauntes.

(*Communis sewer*)   Also we say that the commond sure frome Southe Ee to Hodgg Hyll oughte to be dyked & clensed frome tyme to tyme by the tennauntes of Gedney by acre selver of the tenorie.

Also we say that the parson of Gedney ought to dyke frome Hodgge Hyll to Brodgayt Brygge when & as often as ned shall require.

(*Brode Gate Brigge faciend' feodo Pawlettes*)   Also we saye that frome Brodgayte Brygge to Clapoll Brygge ought to be dowen by the quens majestie of her maner called the Pawlettes Fee.

(*Abell Tree*)   Also we say that frome Clapoll Brygge to a place called the Awebell Tre oughte to be dowen by Adlard Welby esquire of his maner layte Lord Wentworth.

(*The goote mouth*)   Also we say that frome the Awebell Tre to the Commentie before the gotte mouthe oughte to be dowen by the quenes majestie of her maner called the Abbottes Fee.

(*Yowll Dyke*)   Also we say that ther is a serten way which ledethe frome Yowll Dyke to Ravens Dyke & oughte to be mayd by the inhabitaunce of Gedney by commonde menworkes.

(*Brode Drove*)   Also we say that ther is a sertyn banke which ledeth frome Brodd Drove to a place called Goddesman Gette which oughte to be mayd by the land holders of both sydes of the said banke.

(*Yowell Dyke*)   Also we saye that ther is a sertyn weredyke called Yowell Dyke which is in decaye to the somme of vj rodes or more & oughte to be dowen by the inhabitaunce of Gedney by commond menworkes.

(*Communis sewer*)   Also we say that the commond sure which ledeth frome South Ee Banke to Gedney Gotte ought to be roded as often as ned shall require as well by the quens majestie as by the lordes & ther tennauntes by acre selver.

(*Thissell Dolle hedinge*)   Also we say ther is iiij rodes on the west hedynge which lyeth betwen Thissell Doll & Abbottes Delph which is in decaie & ought to be mayd by the inhabitaunce of Gedney by commond menworkes.

(*A certayne hedinge to be made*)   Also we say that it is convenyent that ther should be a hedynge mayd frome Towgottes to Brodgayte Brygge which lyeth on the est syde of the commond sure & ought to be mayd by the landholderes of the est syde for the more ryder passiage of the same water to the commond gotte.

Also we say that the west hedynge which ledethe frome Suttwell Clowte to Penne Stocke & Pottes Howe oughte to be mayd & kepte by the landholderes of the est syde of the said heddynge.

[473.XIII.33]   277

(9 *Gedney Fen   South E*)   Also we say that our soverreign ladie the quen majestie haith xij rodes at South Ee which is in decaie for lacke of hight & brede & ought to be mayde by her majestie of her maner called the Pawlettes Fee.

(*South E*)   Also we say that John Callowe haithe ij rodes at South Ee Banke which is in decaye for lacke of highte & brethe & ought to be mayde by the said John Callowe.

(*South E*)

The landholderes of John Burton haith xxxix fouttes in the lyke default

Also Nycholas Robertson	xviij foutes
William Read	xxij foutes
Henrie Mason	ij foutes
The armytage of Sutton	j foute
The chaunterie of Sancte Thomas Beckette	vij foutes
The churche of Sutton	iiij foutes
William Lowden	iij foutes
Thomas Neuerton	ij foutes

Alexander Jakson	ij foutes
Thomas Alyn clarke	lvj^{ti} foutes
John Deanes	xxv^{ti} foutes
William Stylton of Lutton	xxv^{ti} foutes
[1]Defaultes at South Ee	
Also James Croxston	x foutes
John Blanke	x foutes
Heares of Thomas Fen	ij foutes
Landholderes of John May	iij foutes
Nycholas Rynge	ij foutes di.
Robert Day	vj foutes
William Day	v foutes
William Browen	xiiij foutes
John Rylie	v foutes
[2]Thomas Wylson	xv foutes

(*West E*)   The defaultes in the West Ee which ledethe frome Southe Ee Banke to the Borden Brygge at Gedney Broddes as foloethe by ther names

Peter Trotte haith which is in decaie for lacke of dykynge & rodynge	xl^{ti} rodes
Symond Coker in the lyke defaulte	xx^{ti} rodes
The quens majestie of the Abbottes Fe	xx rodes
The quens majestie of the Paulytes Fe	iij^{xx} rodes
Adlard Welby esquire betwen South Ee & the Borden Brygge	ix^{xx} rodes
Thomas Fysher	xxv^{ti} rodes
The fefores of Gedney Fen	xl^{ti} rodes
The commentie of Gedney Fen End in the same Ee	vj^{xx} rodes

(*Gedney hedinge*)   The defaultes of Gedney hedynges which is in decaie for lacke of highte & breth a[s] foloeth

The commentie of Gedney Fen End haith iiij rodes in decaie ther & ought to be maid by the inhabitaunce of Gedney Fen by commond menworkes

Peter Trott in the lyke defaulte	vj rodes
Symond Coker	iiij rodes
The quens majestie of the Abbottes Fe	viij rodes
The quens majestie of the Paulytes Fe	iiij^{xx} rodes
Adlard esquire [*sic*]	iij^{xx} rodes
Thomas Fisher	xl^{ti} rodes
The fefores of Gedney Fen End	xl^{ti} rodes

[473.XIII.34]   278

(10   *Gedney Fen End   old clowes*)   First we say that the Old Ee clowes at Leise Yattes is in rew & decaie & we thinke it mett that a pare of newe be sett in stead of them in the commond sure.

(*Old clowes at Old Howse Tree*)   Also we say that the olde clowes

---

[1] The following entries are written in the left-hand margin.
[2] This is the last entry in the left-hand margin.

at Olde House Tre is in decaie & we thinke it mett that a pare of newe clowes be sett in stead of them.

(*Gegill Hurne*) Also we say that ther is a commond way which ledeth frome Southe Ee Banke to a place called Jegell Hurne & ought to be mayd frome tyme to tyme by the inhabitaunce of Gedney by commond menworkes.

(*A pety dreane*) Also we say ther is a sertyn pettie dreane ledynge frome Southe Ee Banke to a place called Penderes Crose which is in decaie & ought to be dyked scowred & clensed as often as ned shall require by the land holderes of the west syde of the same drove & the watere to ronne his course into the West Ee.

(*West Drove*) Also we say ther is a commond gayte called West Drove ledynge frome Southe Ee Banke to Pynderes Crose which is in decaie & oughte to be mayd by commond menworkes.

(*Pety dreane voc' West Ee*) Also we say ther is a pettie dreayne called West Ee on the west syde of West Drove which is in decaie for lacke of dykynge & scowrynge which ledeth frome South Ee to the Borden Brydge at Gedney Broddes & ought to [be] dowen by the lande holderes on the west syd everie man ageanst his owen.

(*A hedinge voc' Gedney Hedinge*) Also we say ther is one hedynge called Gedney ledynge frome Southe Ee Banke to Yowell Dyke which is in rew & decaie for lacke of hight & breth & ought to be mayd by the land holders of the same forlonge.

(*A certayne damme*) Also we say ther is one damme ledynge frome Gedney Hedynges to Sutton Hedynges which is in decaie & oughte to be mayd by commond menworkes to a place called Olde House Tre.

(*A brigg voc' Gedney Brodes*) Also we say ther is on brygge in Gedney Broddes which is in rew & decaie & ought to be mayd by the tennauntes of Gedney by acre selver as well men lord & tenantes.

(*West E*) Also we say ther is a serten ee called the West Ee which lyeth betwen the Borden Brygge & a serten brygg called the Clowes which is in decaie & ought to be dyked & scowred by acre selver of the quen as lord & her tenantes.

(*South E Banke pro domina regina*) Also we say that the quens majestie haith x rodes at Southe Ee Banke which is in decaie for lacke of hight & breth & oughte to be mayd by her majestie of the Abbottes Fee.

(*South E Banke pro Athlardo Welby armigero*) Also we say that Adlard Welby esquire haith x rodes at Southe Ee Banke which is in decaie for lacke of highte & bryd & ought to be mayd by the said Adlard Welby esquire of his manore layt Lorde Wentworth.

[1]Also we say that it is mett that the towen of Flett should kepe a banke frome Flett Landmere to the commond sure of Flett & there to make a pare of klowes within the commond sure betwen Langeredge & Mr Harryngton groundes that John Fysher haith by leays for the defence of Gedney Hedynge ageanst the said commontie for that because the water is so great in the commentie of Flett that

---

[1] The whole of this paragraph has been cancelled.

Gedney Hedynge is not able to withstand it except the head of the same water be kept down by the forsaide clowes & bank within the said (?) marres.

VERDICT FOR ELLOE WAPENTAKE, 1570–1
[473.XIV.1–53]   *Not printed*   279–333
[Much of this repeats information to be found in one or other of the two preceding verdicts, the only difference being that this is a dikereeves' verdict and the others are *preter illos* verdicts. Cf. vol. I, pp. xxvii–xxviii.]

VERDICT FOR ELLOE WAPENTAKE, 1572
[473.XV.1–47]   *Not printed*   334–383
[Consists of a dikereeves' verdict (334–355) followed by a *preter illos* verdict which largely repeats it.]

VERDICT FOR KIRTON, SKIRBECK AND ELLOE WAPENTAKES, 1575
[473.XVI.1–66]   *Not printed*   384–452
[384–7 relate to Kirton wapentake and Bridge End causeway, 388–9 to Skirbeck wapentake, 390–414 to Kirton wapentake, 415–452 to Elloe wapentake. The Kirton wapentake section includes stray folios for earlier years : 397 for Quadring is dated 1572, 401 Quadring 1571, 409 Wyberton 1572.]

VERDICTS FOR KIRTON AND ELLOE WAPENTAKES, AND FOR NESS AND AVELAND WAPENTAKES IN KESTEVEN, 1576
[473.XVII.1–46]   *Not printed*   453–500
[At least two verdicts are included in this file. 453–462 is a verdict for the Rivers Welland and Glen and adjacent watercourses in Kirton, Elloe, Ness and Aveland wapentakes, 27 September 1576. The remaining folios probably all form part of a verdict of March–April 1576 : 492–8 relate to Kirton wapentake, 467–471 to the Welland and Bourne Ea, the rest to Elloe wapentake.]

LAW OF SEWERS FOR MARLODE IN KIRTON WAPENTAKE, 1574
[485.I.1]   501

[1](*Helpringham in comitatu Lincoln'*) AT A SESSIONS of Sewers of our [soverei]gn lady Elizabeth by the grace of God quene of Englond Fraunce & Irelond defender of the fayth etc. HOLDEN AT Helpringham in the county of Lincoln the xxij[th] day of June in the sexteneth yeare of [her majes]ties raygn BEFORE THE ryght honorable Syr Henry Clinton knyght lord Clinton & Saye Robert Carre [esqu]ier Anthony Thorold esquier [Robert] Carre the yonger   Christofer Kelke   Arthur Walpoll   Jhon Lockton   Anthony Kyme   Rowland Sherrard W[illiam Yaxl]ey & Anthony Cawdron esquiers Commissioneres of our sayd soveraygn lady in the sayde county & in . . . borders therof for survay & reformacion of offences in sewers etc. BY

[1] This law consists of two membranes. The head of the first is damaged, and there are a few small holes elsewhere.

VERTUE . . . Commissioners & others directed before them the same day retorned by Robert Sa . . . county WYTH A JURYE of the partes of Kesteven & Holland who did then apper . . . & were sworne & charged then & there to enquire of offences in sewers . . . at the same day & place it is conteyned as herafter followeth

THAT IS TO SAYE 502

(. . . *speciall indented law of anno xiij^{mo}*) WHERE BEFORE this tyme that is to say at Boston in the sayd countye the xxj^{th} day of September in the THIRTENETH yeare of the raygn of our sayd soveraygn ladye the quenes hyghnes A SPECIALL decreed law indented was made for the openynge revivynge & renuinge of the old decayed dreane of Merlode by the sayd lord Clinton by the name of Sir Henry Clinton knyght, Anthony Thorold, Robert Carre, Christofer Kelke, Jhon Lockton, Jhon Busshye & Anthony Robertson esquieres yet livynge UPPON THEYRE view peruse & travell for the survay therof as by the same order law & decre indented under thandes and seales of the same Commyssioners WHEROF ONE part as yet remayneth with Jhon Burton then clerke therunto appoynted AND THE other wyth the ryght honorable Edward now erle of Lincoln hygh Admyrall of Englond accordinge to a late statute of sewers in the xiij^{th} yeare of the raygn of our sayd soveraygn ladye in such case provyded doth & may manyfestly & playnly appeare WHICH LATE speciall decreed law indented the sayd now Commyssioners did advysedly peruse, behold, consider, & deliberatly examyne UPPON WHICH peruse & advised examynacion they were credibly informed that diverse factes by the same late indented decre ordayned were partly practised & put in execution as concernynge the enlarginge alteringe & perfitinge of a perfit dreane & outfall for the sayd sewer of MERLODE & the course therof in & throughe the ee or dreane under the seadykes of Gosberkyrke & Surflette of late beinge the ee of these twoe townes by the lottes & shiftes unto a place called Common Hurne wherof neverthelesse some parte remayneth as yet partly to be perfected from the infall therof at Cockrell Houghe in Gosberkyrke afforesayd in the sayd county unto Laundes Cote & also to Graunge Gate with other small defaltes which are to be reformed AND lykewyse for a new goote by the acredge of Donyngton & Quadringe afforesayd set in the seadyke of Surflet afforesayd wherwith & with all which workes the inhabitantes of the same townes of Donyngton & Quadringe afforesayd by the sayd acredge by vertue of the sayd decreed lawe should stand & be charged & chargable for ever WHICH LATE new goote of soden (?) after thre weekes setlinge therof semynge lykely by all that season instantly the xxiij day of Aprill now last past [di]d sincke downe & was sucked into a quicke sand so as it is dowtfull of the wynnynge agayne of the tonne therof as to the sayd Commissioneres immediatly was related wheruppon A SURVEY view

& travell was taken by Robert Carre thelder esquyer Jhon Lockton
esquier & certayne other of the sayd Commyssioners by whome then
order was taken for the saffegard & takynge up of so much of the
timber of the same goote as then could be won the tonne or botham
as yet restinge & remayninge untaken up by reason of such a quicke
springe as then was at the tyme of searchinge for the same AND IN
lyke maner for the new ee for Surflet & Gosberkyrke with a damme
nye Challeyn Bridge toward the sea dyke of Surflett AND FOR the
clow in the mouth of Merlode at the infall of the fen water redy
framed & apt to be sett and also for the order of the sewer of MER-
LODE from thence by bredth & depth prescribed by all the whole
currant unto Elwold Elmes AND lykewyse for the turnynge of the
same sewer out of the old course therof from Elwold Elmes unto
the late ee of Gosberkyrke afforesayd at Cockrell Houghe WYTH
certayne bridges & diverse other workes not perfected nor done ALL
WHICH workes should have bene perfectly done & finyshed by the
charges of Donyngton & Quadringe afforesayd towardes theyre
which greate charges diverse sommes of mony for that tyme onely
was decreed to be contributed aswell of certayne township pes & the
maner of Sempringham in the partes of Kesteven as by Bykar &
also by the sayd townes of Gosberkyrke & Surflet for the shortnynge
of the new dreane beinge in the partes of Holland for their benefite
& comodytie as in the said speciall law indented of ANNO XIIJ^{mo}
dothe & may appere ALL WHICH decreed law indented of anno
xiij^{mo} with the lawes of Byllingborow & Brigend anno xv^{mo} for the
spedier procedinges of the sayd former law of anno xiij^{mo} supradicto
THE SAYD now Commyssioners uppon the sayd relation & view of
the sayd soden fall of the sayd new goot and of the perfect intelli-
gence of the not settynge of the sayd fen clowe in the mouth of
MERLODE and . . . other imperfections of workes & unfinished
exercises afforesayd which should have bene done by vertue of the
same lawes of anno xiij^{mo} & xv^{mo} before mentioned [503] THEY
DO NOWE order ratifye establishe & confirme aswell the sayd
speciall decreed law indented of anno xiij^{mo} as the sayd other lawes
of Byllingborow & Brigend of anno xv^{mo} so farre forth as is not
repugnant or may stand with the true meanynge of this new &
present decreed lawe with such dayes & paynes & in such maner &
forme as herafter ensueth that is to saye FYRST IT IS ordayned &
decreed by theyre decreed law indented as by statute is in such case
provyded that all & singuler the whole new dreane turned from the
Old Ee of Rysegate toward the seadyke of Surflet afforesayd by
Laundes Mote hereafter to be called the New Ee of Surflet & Gosberkyrke AND THAT the bridge to be buylded newly nye Challeyn
Bridge and the damme therby to turne the water out of Rysegate
Ee with that New Ee shalbe sufficiently finyshed & substantially
perfected & made in bredth & depth accordinge unto the sayd
decreed law of xiij^{mo} and now to be done by the acredge of Donyngton
& Quadrynge afforesayd and by all such & those hundredes thorpes

& hamlettes as hertofore have bene charged or chargable with the same townes or eyther of them in dreanes sewers gootes or other lyke workes unto the same ij townes or eyther of them of auncient tyme belonginge or apperteynynge uppon payne for every rode of the New Ee undone or not sufficiently done sex shillinges eyght pence AND THEN the same to be the proper dreane of Surflet & Gosberkyrke after the same shalbe by Donyngton & Quadringe as is afforesayd once sufficiently perfected by the acredge of Surflet & Gosberkyrke to be maynteyned and kept for ever AND IT IS also decreed & ordayned by this theyre now decreed law indented that the clow at the infall of the fen waters at the mouth of Merlode shalbe substancially set in the same place appoynted by the sayd decreed speciall indented law of anno xiij^{mo} with the necessary shut of the bredth of iij foote & lyke depth for stop of the fen waters by the sayd towneshippes of Donyngton & Quadringe & theyre sayd hundredes thorpes & hamlettes to them belonginge & apperteynynge uppon payne of x li. for eyther towne with the hundredes therunto apperteynynge so refusinge AND THAT the sewer from thence by all the whole currant therof unto Elwold Elmes shalbe sufficientlye & substancially banked dyked scowred & clensed by the sayd towneshippes of Quadringe & Donyngton & theyre sayd hundredes thorpes & hamlettes to them belonginge & apperteynynge ioyntly of the bredth of sextene foote & depth sex foote from the cutt of the bankes uppon payne of fyve shillinges for every rode therof not sufficiently done AND THAT from Elwold Elmes the same sewer shalbe turned & made passable of lyke bredth & depth unto Gosber-kyrke late Old Ee afforesayd by the township of Quadringe afforesayd & by the hundred therof called Quadringe Hundred in Westrop & Northorp in Gosberkyrke afforesayd in lyke order & at such lyke charges as in other sewers & such lyke workes they have bene accustomed with the township of Quadringe And in suche further ordre

in proxima pagina

[485.I.2]
2

And in such further order as by the sayd speciall indented decre of anno xiij^{mo} is ordayned for the same sewer & dreane generally to the towne of Quadringe AND ALSO that the bridges there of new shalbe mayde by the same township of Quadringe & by the sayd hundred in lyke maner as in the same law is provyded & decreed generally by the towne of Quadringe afforesayd uppon payne for every rode of dykinge left undone or not substancially done vj s.
... d. AND IT IS ordayned that at the fallinge in of the sayd new sewer or dreane from Merlode into the sayd late Old Ee of Gosberkyrke the stone bridge by the former indented law decreed shalbe sub-stantially buylded & set there in the quenes hye way AND THE damme made at Perty Bridge by the lyke charges of Quadringe &

Donyngton & there thorpes hundredes & hamlettes uppon payne
for every bridge before mencioned viij li. and for every damme xl s.
[504] AND IT IS also decreed by the sayd Commissioners that the
workes of the same dreane shalbe finyshed from the infall of the
sayd new dreane for Merlode at Cockrell Houghe where the sayd
new stone bridge is to be set from thence in diverse places to Quadringe . . . afforesayd to be fully perfected in dykinge scowringe &
clensinge of the same Old Ee of Gosberkyrke as by the . . . & former
law of anno xiij^mo is ordeyned by the charges of the lordes & landholderes of Gosberkyrke and so to be . . . throughe where nede shalbe
now founde unto the . . . of Surflet . . . & by all the . . . lot & shifte
of Surflet part of the same Old Ee unto a place called Common Hurne
by the lordes and landholders of Surflet where nede shalbe also
found to be in like maner perfected accordinge unto the sayd former
law of anno xiij^mo AND ALSO that from thence unto the north &
east side & end of Sugars pasture the old dreane shalbe by the sayd
townes of Gosberkyrke & Surflet accordingly dyked scowred &
clensed as by the same former law is ordayned & by lyke payne of
v s. the rode as therby is prescribed AND THAT THE same old
sewer afforesayd from the north & est side & end of the sayd Sugars
pasture shalbe also dyked scowred & clensed of the depth & bredth
afforesayd by the acredge of Quadringe & Donyngton & of the sayd
hundredes thorpes and hamlettes to them apperteynynge unto the
place where the goote dyd lye with theyre properties of the same
sewer or dreane & the payne therof accordinge unto the sayd former
decre at Boston afforesayd in anno xiij^mo supradicto ALL THE
PREMISSES now to be done before the last daye of October now
next commynge uppon payne for every rode as before is appoynted
for every bridge not finished eyght poundes for every damme xl s.
and for the clowe not perfected ten poundes AND FORASMUCH
as the same goote now sonken was layde by covenant betwene
certayne the inhabitantes of the sayd two townes of Donyngton
& Quadringe & the workman therof & the cause as yet not prosecuted
ageyne him for the same with the which neverthelesse the šayd
inhabytantes of the sayd twoe townes by theyre acredges generally
by the former decre of anno xiij^mo and theyre hundredes thorpes
& hamlettes by this decre now made for the continuance & enlarge-
ment of the same decre shold & owe to stand & be charged & chargable
for ever [505] THERFORE AT this tyme it is ordayned & decreed
by the sayd nowe Commissioners that aswell for the searchinge &
takinge up of the sonken tonne of the sayd downe fallen goote or so
much of the timber of the same as may be found or other woode for
the new makinge of the sa[id] tonne as also for the new buyldinge
& substanciall settinge of an other new goote for the same late
sonken goote THAT FOURE pence of every acre in Donyngton
afforesayd & in the hundred and hamlet therunto belonginge and
sex pence of every acre in Quadringe afforesayd & of the sayd
Quadringe hundred in Westrop & Norththorp & Gosberkyrke

afforesayd in the sayd county shalbe assessed & instantly collected
for the rebuyldinge of the same goote AND THAT therwith all &
such other sommes as eyther of the sayd townes have now in theyre
handes the same goote shalbe with expedicion of new buylded
ageyne substantially and after the framynge & buyldinge therof
BY SPECIALL advyse & lyke consideracion of perfec[t] . . . worke-
masters & the most expert & discreete persons of the countrye the
foundacion of the same to be very advysedly suffyciently & firmely
wrought AND thereuppon the same new framed & rebuylded goote
to be lykewyse and accordinglye substancially & firmely set & placed
so as yt may not any more fayle AS BY THE sayd former law for
the fyrst goote was intended & ordayned for the good yssuinge &
water course of the sayd sewer or dreane of Merlode and the holdinge
out of the sea water from the same untill such tyme as recovery
may be had uppon the sayd covenant WHERUPPON the mony
so to be recovered (after prosecution of the cause) & recovery had
may be retorned converted & put to such uses & executions AS BY
THE acredges of those twoe towneshippes & the sayd hundredes
thorpes & hamlettes shalbe herafter bestowed by the good consideracion of the now Commyssioners or such others as herafter shall
take the oversight of the accomptes for the same all which newe
workes now to be done as in & about the firme settinge & placinge
of the sayd new goote to be done as afforesayd before the twelfth
day of November now next commynge uppon payne of FYFTY
POUNDES of eyther of the sayd towneshippes & hundredes as by
the former decre was provyded and as by the former law of anno
xiij^mo order is prescribed for the continuance & mayntenance of the
sayd goote and for the dykinge therunto by the acredge of the sayd
twoe townes of Donyngton & Quadringe afforesayd generally now
provyded also to be by the ayde & charge of the sayd hundredes
thorpes & hamlettes unto the charges of the same twoe townes
chargable by accustomed prescription SO IT IS ordayned that
herafter all the same together with the dykinge of all the whole
sewer & dreane for Merlode from the infall at Cockrell Houghe unto
the sayd sea goote when nede shall require after the once well doinge
therof by Gosberkyrke & Surflet in forme bef[ore] ordayned shalbe
done at the costes of the acredges of the same twoe townes of
Donyngton & Quadringe & of the hund[redes] thorpes & hamlettes
before remembred uppon payne of v s. for every rode therof not
done by any conven[ient] day herafter to be set downe & limited
for the doinge of the same by any sex Commyssioners herafter
beinge in Commyssion for the sayd partes of Kesteven & Holland
AND FOR the residewe of the articles orders & decrees set downe
by the sayd speciall indented law of anno xiij^mo consernynge the
residew of the charge of all the whole premysses herin & therin
conteyned & expressed to be the charges of Donyngton & Quadringe
or theyre acredge the same alwayes herafter to be borne by the
hundredes thorpes & hamlettes to them apperteynynge for theyre

accustomed rates & proporcions AND FOR THE property &
propertyes of all the sayd New Ee for Surflet & Gosberkyrke as of
all the sayd dreanes & goote herafter aswell to the same twoe townes
of Donyngton & Quadringe and now to the hundredes thorpes &
hamlettes and theyre continuance of the charges of the place of the
seabanke where the goote was & is to be set downe FOR THE yerly
rodinge clensinge & scowringe of all the sayd dreane of Merlode
from the infall therof at the fen clow unto the sayd seagoote by
theyre lottes & shiftes casten & taken or to be agreed uppon for the
bankinge & kepinge of the headinges of the same [506] THEXECU-
TION of any the former decrees in defalt of the owners by the other
coparteners or by the officers for the course of the water runninge
by the clowe at the infall of the fen waters for the continuance therof
with water not to be diverted or taken away by any of the partes
of Kesteven AND FOR ALL other necessary & convenyent articles
orders & decrees in the former decre mentioned herby not altered
shalbe in lyke maner ratifyed confirmed & establyshed BY vertue
of this decre at this tyme nowe made by the sayd Commyssioners
as by the former decre of anno xiij^{mo} or of anno xv^{mo} was ordered
decreed & provyded AND NOWE further decreed & ordayned to
stand be & continue in force & effect for ever as parcell of this lawe
AND for the drawinge of this decre the indentinge & ingrossinge of
the same for the copie therof to be made to eyther of the sayd townes
for them & theyre hundredes and for the travell of the clerk taken
in & about the same at this tyme & hertofore it is ordayned by the
sayd Commyssioners that the dykereves of the sayd twoe townes
& hundredes afforesayd shall of the sayd acredge pay unto the sayd
clerke for eyther towne xl s. the one halfe presently within one
weeke of the receyte of theyre warrantes for the same acredge and
the other halfe uppon the receyte of ther copies of this our order &
decre IN WYTNES whereof we the sayd Commissioners have
caused this our decree to be engrossed & indented and aswell to one
parte herof remaynynge with the sayd Jhon Burton the clerke
therunto appoynted as to the other parte herof by us appoynted
to remayne with the sayd honorable Henry lord Clynton one of the
sayd Commyssioners at his castell of Tattershall, have set to the
same sunderly our seales & handes the day yeare & place in the
first parte of the same now indented lawe mentioned & declared
[*Signed above seal tags* :] ¹H. Clinton
 Robert Carre Antony Thorold Jhon Lokton Wylliam Yaxlie
 Anthony Kyme Antony Cawdron Burton²
[*Endorsed*:] (i) No officers to be sued but in sessions of sewers.
 [*contemporary hand*]
 (ii) 28. Marlode [*contemporary*]

---

¹ The two membranes are fastened at the foot with 8 seal tags. It would appear
that not all the commissioners attested.
² The clerk.

(iii) Marlode. Donington Quadring Gosbertown & Surflet. 22
June 16 Eliz. 1575. [*17th century hand*]

GENERAL LAWS OF SEWERS FOR HOLLAND, 1576
[458.a.8–12]   *Not printed*   507–533
[These laws are dated April 1576. They differ little from the
next set of laws save in being rather shorter and less specific.]

GENERAL LAWS OF SEWERS FOR HOLLAND, 1576
[485.II.1]   534
(*Boston in the county of Lincoln*) CERTAYN GENERALL
lawes ordres and decrees consydered provyded ordayned
decreed establyshed sett downe and indented att the sessyons
of sewers of our soveraigne ladye the quenes majestie that now
ys Elizabeth by the grace of God quene of England Fraunce and
Ierland defendour of the faythe etc. houlden att the town or
borow of Boston afforesayde in the sayde countye of Lincoln
the xxj daye of Auguste in the xviij^th yere of her highnes reigne
by Richard Bollys William Hunston esquires Robart Carre
the yonger esquire [*blank*] Richarde Felde gent. maior of Boston
for the tyme beinge William Watson William Yaxlay Arthur
Walpoll Anthony Caudron Richard Hyltoft
Henry Adam esquires of her majesties Commyssyoners of Sewers
in the sayde countye of Lincoln and in the confynes and borders of
every parte therof thought very necessary uppon the view of the
sayde Commyssyoners and peruse of the presentmentes of the jurors
before the sayde Commyssyoners and others FOR THE PRESERVA-
TION and common welth of the sayde borowgh of Boston aforesayde
and of the weapentakes of Skyrbeck Kyrton and Ellowe thearunto
adiacent in theis partyes of Holland in the sayde countye and of the
borders and confynes of the same partyes BY VERTEW of her
highnes Commyssyon of Sewers too them and others dyrected very
necessary and profytable for the defens and safegarde aswell of the
same towne and borowgh of Boston aforesayde as of every towne
towneshippe and hamlet appartaynyng untoo the same borow or
untoo eny the towne or towneshippes within the sayd wapentakes of
Skerbeck Kyrton and Elowe in the same parties of Holland in the
same countye NOT ONLY agaynst the daunger of the sea but allsoo
for defens of the perill of the sorrounde by the freshe waters by spede
and remedy too be provyded by and wyth the good and substancyall
repaire of all and all maner the bankes and owteringes about the
same and other defensable bankes wythin the same and the good
ordre of kepinge the sewers in and throughe the same wyth clensyng
scouringe and wythowte impedymentes as hearafter followeth, that
is to saye
                                                       535
FIRST WEE the said Comyssioners doo now ordre and decree &
constitut that all and all maner of seabankes or other defensable
bankes mayde for and agaynst the rage of the seawaters knowne by

the saide names or by the names of seadikes or bankes gootes, scotes oute marshe bankes haven bankes wharfes stayth and frontages within the saide borowghe of Boston or abowte the terrytoryes of the same or abowte any terrytoryes of the townes of and in any of the said wapentakes of Skerbeck Kyrton or Ellowe beinge all the tyme of this owr decree, or whiche hearafter shalbe jused bankes too be mayde by the agyssed or cessed bookes whearby every person is too know his owne particuler banke defalt and charge in every of the same bankes or els too be mayde by any frontagers for their frontages accostomed or by comoniage shalbe from tyme to tyme well and sufficyently repayred amended mayde and maynteyned aswell in hight bredeth in the toppe and whole skirted att the bottom AS THE best or GOOD BANKES of and in the lymyttes metes or devysions of the bankes in the same towne or towneshippe where the said banke or bankes is to be mayde (allowed by the sayd Commyssyoners v iiij or iij whereof one of the quorum) by sutche person and persons corporacions and comonialltyes or comonages as owe too doo the same by suche daye, dayes and tymes as is or shalbe by lawe ordre or decree of sewers prescrybed appoynted or lymytted uppon the payne of forfayture of ij d. for every foote nott repared accordinglye too be levyed too the quenes majesties use her heires and successoures of his or their goods and cattalls landes and tenamentes whear soo ever they shalbe founde.

(*In defalt of owner by dykerevys adhuc seabankes*) AND YT YS further ordered and decreed that yf any suche landholder owner or owners appoynted and ordered by jusement or frontage shall nott repaire and maynteyne from tyme too tyme his and their bankes as is afforesayde att and by the daye or dayes too him or them lymytted and appoynted or hearafter too be lymytted and appoynted THATT THEN the dykereves or dykereve of the same towne or townes where the sayde bankes shall lye soo unrepaired or amended shal repaire and amend the same att and by suche tyme or tymes as shalbe too them lymytted and appoynted by ordre of sewers.

(*Sallary iij foot j d. costes*) AND HE OR they too have for the makinge or amendment of the same defaltes for his sallarye and travell of the proper goods of suche person or persons bodyes politike or corporate that owght too doo the same by law and ordre of sewers beinge in defalte as is afforesayde for every iij foote ONE PENYE over and besides suche costes and charges as he or they shall dysburse and laye owte in or abowte the makinge or amendment of the sayd banke or bankes soo by him or them too be mayde repayred or amended too be levyed of their goods and cattalls landes and tenamentes as is aforesayde.

(*In defalt of dykerevys surveyours*) AND IF THE sayd dykereve or dykerevys of the sayd town or townes shall not repaire and amend the sayde defaltes in any of the sayde bankes as is aforesayde by suche tyme or tymes as too him or them shalbe lymytted and appoynted by ordre or decre of sewers THATT THEN the sur-

veyour or surveyours for the tyme beinge wythin the lymyttes too
him or them lymytted and appoynted shall repaire and amend the
same defaltes and offences by suche daye dayes tyme or tymes as
too him or them is or shalbe lykewyes appoynted & lymytted by
order of sewers.

536

(& one other peny of the goodes of the dykerevys over his costes)
AND HE OR THEY too have for his or their paines takinge in and
aboute the saide warkes (one peny) for every iij foote soo beinge in
defalt and by him or them maide of the proper goods and cattalls
of the person or persons bodies politike or corporate that ought too
doo the same and further the sayde surveyour too have ONE
OTHER PENY of the goods and cattalls of the dykerevyes of the
said towne or of any of them for every iij foote by him mayde being
in defalte as afforesaide OVER AND BESYDES his charges and
expenses too bee dysbursed for the same repaire too bee levyed of
the goods and cattalls lands and tennamentes of suche owner or
owners aforesayd and of suche dykerevys and dykereve aforesayde
as owghte too have doone the same.

(Seabankes & bankes of owteringes by acrage   the dykereve   payn
the rode iij s. iiij d.)   AND YTT YS allsoo ordered and decreed
that whear any seabankes or any other bankes of charge or importaunce beinge owteringes or pryncypall defences of ryvers or mayne
dreanes are too be mayde by acrage the same shalbe maide by the
dykereve or dykerevyes of the towne or townes whear they doo lye
and be by suche daye & tyme or tymes as too him or them shalbe
lymytted and appoynted uppon payne of forfayture of iij s. iiij d.
for everye roode nott mayde or repaired too be levyed too the use
of owr sayde soveraigne ladye the quenes majestie her highnes
heires and successors as is afforesaide and soo for every foote under a
rode accordinge to thatt raytte.

537

(The dykerevys defalt by the surveyour)   AND YF THE said
dykereve or dykerevyes shall nott repaire and make the foresaide
bankes in suche maner and forme as shall too him or them be
lymytted and appoynted and by suche daye and tyme and tymes as
is or shalbe lykewyse agreed and ordeyned YTT YS ORDERED
and decreed thatt the SURVEYOUR OR SURVEYOURS shall
make repare and amend all and every suche defalte in all and every
the saide bankes whiche the dykerevys ought to have doone.

(xij d. sallary)   AND HE OR they too levye of the proper goods
landes and tenements of the saide dykerevys for his and thear
sallarye and paynes takinge in and abowte the sayde warkes xij d.
for every rode by him or them repaired mayde or doone being soo
in defalt over and besides his costes and charges expended abowte
the sayde warkes WHICHE MONEYE soo by the surveyours too
be hadd of the dykerevys goods for the costs onely by them bestowed
shalbe too the sayde dykereve or dykerevys ALLOWED BY THE

K

acrage of the saide towne chargable untoo the makinge of the sayd defalt beinge in his or their handes or possessyones.

FOR LACKE WHEROF a levy too them the sayd dykereves too be graunted by the Comyssyoners for the tyme beinge for their repayment of the same costes and expenses for the same defectyve bankes. And ytt ys further ordered

in defalt of surveyours

[485.II.2]　　　　　　　　　　　　　　　　　　　　　　　538

(*In defalt of surveours　payn for defalt in surveyours ij s. rode*) AND YT YS further ordered and decreed that yf the sayde surveyours or surveyour shall omytt and neglect their dewtyes and nott repayre and amend suche bankes and defalts as ys afforesayde by suche daye and tyme as too them shalbe lymytted and appoynted THEN they and every of them too forfayte for every roode not repayred and amended as ys aforesaid too the use of the quenes majestie use her heires and successors ij s. too be levyed of their proper goodes and cattals lands and tenementes and soo ratablye for every foote as is aforesayde for his and their defaltes and negligenses abowte the same.

(*Commyssioners*) AND YTT YS further ordeyned and decreed that as many of the sayd Commyssioners & others soo they be ij in nomber wharof one of quorum as shall in defalt of the owner or owners dykerevys or dykereve surveyour or surveyours or any of them cause too be repaired and amended by them selves or by their deputyes or assignes by warrant under their handes and seeles suche banke or bankes or other workes aforesayde new sett downe or hearafter too be ordayned too be doone as by the same Comyssyoners or their deputies shalbe founden defectyve

(*For every rode*) SHALL HAVE & TAKE for every rode by them or any of them mayde being defectyve as afforesayde too their owne uses aswell of the proper goodes of the owner or owners and dykereve and dykerevyes as before lymytted unto the surveyours AS ALLSOO OF the proper goodes of the surveour or surveyours in lyke maner omyttinge their dewtyes for everye of the same defectyve roodes.

(*By warrant　except forfature*) AND SHALL HAVE full power and auctoretye by them selfs or by warrant as aforesaid too any offycer deputyes or assignes dyrected too levye collect and gather all and every parte of the somes of monye soo by any of the sayd owners or offycers lost for salaryes stypendes and travels or for costes charges or expences by any of them in and aboute suche woorkes within any the sayde towne townes thorpes or hamlettes whear suche defaltes shalbe by them or eny of them founden EXCEPT suche forfaytures and losses as ys or shalbe forfayted or lost unto the quenes majestie her heires and successoures.

(*Too receyve & bestow*) AND THAT YT shalbe lawfull too any ij of the said Comyssyioners as aforesaide makinge any the repare aforsayd too receve and take in too theire handes the monye soo collected and to retayne and kepe therof for ayther of them too their owne use for every daye thatt any ij of theym shalbe soo occupyed in those travells iiij s. AND ALLSOO att their will and pleasure too gyve and bestowe of all and every suche other person and persons as shall take paynes in and abowte the same woorkes soo muche thearof and as to the dyscressyons of the same Comyssyoners shall seme good.

539

(*Forfaytures*) AND TOO THEND the quenes majestie may be duly answered of all and every the paynes and forfyturs lost and forfayted unto hyr highnes hyr heires & successors by any person or persons by force of any order or decree heartofore new mayde or hearafter too be ordayned.

(*By defaltes to be certefyed*) YT YS ORDERED & decreed thatt as well any ij of the said Comyssyoners as aforesaid shall present as their deputyes by warrant allsoo before prescrybed AND IN LYKE maner the dykereve or dykereves surveyours or surveyour and every of them particulerly shall exprese and declare in wrytinge all and every suche defaltes and offences together with the quantetye and quantytes of every of theym and the names and surnames of the offendours as from tyme too tyme shall grow or happen and be knowne unto any of theym in their vyew & travels and by them or any of them mayde repaired or amended AND SHALL CERTEFYE the same as aforesayde in wryting att the next generall sessyons of sewers too be houlden for those lymyttes beinge a full courte of Comyssyoners vj in nomber wherof iij of quorum

(*& examyned & all other inquisicions and verdyttes and all forfaturs mete & requisyte extracted & indented one parte intoo the exchecker*) AND THAT THEN the same Comyssyoners there beinge present uppon their exact examynacyon of the same shall cause the clerke of sewers for the tyme being forthwyth to receyve the same and all other inquisycyssions verdytes and presentmentes of any jurours yelded taken and presented before them att the same sessyons AND THERUPPON all suche paynes losses and forfaytures as by the same Comyssyoners then and there shalbe adiudged and decreed and shall seme mete and requisyte too be lost and forfayted too the quenes majesties use her heires and successours the same too be by the same clerke as aforesaid extracted AND THE SAME extract so mayde and indentcd to be sygned with their proper handes whearof oone parte to be sent or delyvered in too the quenes majesties courte of Exchecker.

[485.II.2*d*]
540

(*Staythes wharfes & frontages in or nigh Boston*) AND YT YS further ordayned and decreed by the sayde Comyssioners that all and all maner staythes wharfes and frontages too be now mayde and hearafter too be repay[red and a]mended by and with stone or tymber pyling jetting or hedgynge or suche seabankes or haven bankes abowte the haven in or nygh the towne and borow of Boston Skerbeck or Skerbecke Quarter or elles whear wythin the precynct of the sayde borowe.

(*As within eny the sayde weapentakes*) OR WITHIN ANY of the sayd wapentakes of Kyrton Skerbecke & Ellow or in or aboute any gootes clowes or brydges in eny towne wythin any of the same weapentakes whear any suche lyke woorkes have bene used or shalbe nedfull too be used practysed or provyded.

(*Strongly buylded doble paynes doble valew of stypendes*) SHALBE sufficientlye stronglye and substancyally framed buylded sett mayde and doone by such person and persons lordes landhoulders bodyes politike corporacyons dykerevys for comoniages and acrages as shall owe too dooe the same according as by the law and order of sewers is or shalbe from tyme to tyme established ordered and decreed uppon the doble paynes penalties and forfaytures to be forfayted too the quenes majesties use and uppon the payne of payment of suche doble valew of stypendes sallaryes and satisfactions for the paynes and travels of the Comyssyoners and their deputyes and assignes & of all other offycers & mynysters.

(*To be taken*) TOO BE FROME tyme to tyme by them taken and levyed of and uppon the goodes catalls lands and tenements of all and every person and persons corporacions comonialties and owners offycer or offycers in theis defaltes and in suche maner order and forme as is before lymytted and appoynted for the lyke paynes and forfaytures too the quenes majesties use as is before expressed lymytted appoynted & sett downe for seabankes and other owtringes too all intents and purposes.

(*For workes to be done by comoniage*) AND YT YS further ordered and decreed that in all and every former bankes and all and all maner lyke woorke and woorkes too be wrought and doone by comoniage or the common menwoorke lyeng and beinge within the precinct of the towne or borow of Boston or within the lymyttes and precinctes of the wapentakes of Skirbeck Kirton and Ellowe or eny of them by the daye and tyme now sett downe or too be hearafter lymytted and appoynted

(*Warning by the dykerevys festyvall day*) THE DYKEREVE or dykerevyes shall give reasonable and convenyent warning before the doyng of the sayd woorke or woorkes in the churche uppon some festivall daye as heartofore hathe bene comonly used after service and common prayer ys doone for the good knowlidge of the commoners by whome the same is too be downe.

(*For lack of warninge payn xx s. & x s.*) AND FOR LACKE and defalt of suche knowlidge and open warning given as befor the dykerevys and every of them shall forfayte to owr soveraigne lady the quene for every suche defalt of warninge nott geven towchinge suche chargeable bankes xx s. and towchinge other woorkes of lesse charge of importaunce x s.

(*And every comoner offending*) AND FURTHER yt is ordered
and decreed that every person and persons uppon suche oppen
warning geven of the daye or dayes tyme and tymes appoynted and
of the place and places for the sayd common woorke & woorkes too
be doone not attendinge and dutyfully not doing or observinge
his daye woorke att the daye and place soo published accordingly
as is or shalbe appoynted and prescrybed by the dykereve or
dykerevyes

(*Chargable too attende carte xl d. slede xvj d. defalt xij d.*) EVERY
OF THEM soo chargeable too be attendant beyng in defalte too
forfayt for every carte or corte wyth horses and the guyder thearof
xl d. And for every defalt or lacke of horse and sleade xvj d.
And further ytt ys ordered that every inhabitant comoner person
and persons chargeable too be thear making defalt and not attendinge
in his and their owne person or some able person or laborer for him
too be allowed by the sayd offycer or offycers too forfayte too the
quenes majestie her heires and successoures for every daye soo
makinge defalte xij d.

(*Nevertheles the woorke too be performed and wrought by the dyscres-
sons of the offycers att the costes of the offenders to be levyed which the*)
AND NEVERTHELES the sayd dykereve or dykerevys surveyour
or surveyours or suche other as arre before lymytted shall cause soo
mutche of the woorke afforesayd as the proporcion or allotment of
soo many as shalbe founden too make defalt att that daye and tyme
soo appoynted too bee wrought perfected and doone by their convenyent dyscressyons and consyderacions be ytt for the loedes
caryage by cartes or cortes by daye woorke of horses and sleades
or by eny proporcion of roode or roodes of banke making or sewer
or dreane dyking rodinge scouryng or clensyng or other lyke woorke
by their co[n]venyent dyscressyons and consyderacyons to be rated
taxed or cessed att the costes and charges of hym and them soo
makinge defalt of his and their goods and cattalls by the same
offycers too be levyed in forme before remembered for their whiche
travels and sallaryes uppon certyfycatt of such paynes penaltyes
and forfaytures as before ys prescrybed too and for the quenes
majesties use they too take and receyve soo mutche for the same
as by the Comyssyoners uppon their certyficat therof att the next
sessyons of sewers shalbe too them lymytted and appoynted.

(*For joyse bankes betwen towne & towne*) AND ALLSOO THATT
all suche bankes as be agysted by specyall joyse booke or be frontages
or headinges and bankes provyded to be defensable betwene one
towne and another to keppe the surplysage of every water wythin
the owne towne from surrounding the next towne.

(*And devydinge the low groundes or any quarters*) AND ALLSOO
ALL suche bankes as be agysted within any particuler towne too
devyde and preserve the fenne marshes and lower growndes from
the hygher parte of the same towne OR DEVIDING eny quarters

hamlets or lymyttes of the same towne by accostomed kept bankes
of and by joyse dykes or by headinges or frontages

(*Sewer bankes   half payne forf'*)   AND THE BANKES of the
comen sewers in any towne heartofore mayde maynteyned and
kept by ioysment or as afforesayde SHALBE ACCORDYNGLY
mayd preserved and mayntened from tyme too tyme by suche person
and persons corporacyons or cominalties as owe too doo the same
att and by the lyke dayes and tymes as before is lymytted or hearafter shalbe sett downe & appoynted uppon the moyte or half paynes
before prescrybed for the bankes of the more charge and importaunce
in all forfaytures

(*Lyke rate of sallary*)   AND THE LYKE rate for sallary or
sallaries of every of the sayde officers as well dykereve surveyour as
deputye or assignee of the ij Comyssyoners which shall fynde eny
suche banke defectyve as before too be levyed for every of them

Sodeyn breaches
in tercia pagina

[485.II.3]   542

(*Tertia pagina Sodeyn breaches*)   AND TOO THE INTENT that
spedy and present order may be taken for sodayne breatches it is
further ordeyned by the sayde Comyssyoners thatt where any
within the sayd borow of Boston or eny the sayd weapentakes of
Ellow Kyrton or Skerbeck seabankes haven bankes freshe water
bankes or fenne bankes or adioyning unto any of them or too any
fennes or marshes nye unto eny of them is or shalbe broken and not
forthwith repaired & amended by them who ought too doo the same

(*Howses   the inhabitantes   damyaged*)   AND THERBY eny
howses feyldes commons or common fennes shalbe anoyed or
surrounded thatt it shalbe lawfull too and for the inhabitauntes of
eny the sayd towne or townes or eny of them receavinge damage
thearby or whiche shalbe anoyed by the same breatche or breatches
eyther in their howses townes or feyldes commons or common
fennes forthwith too repaire and amend the same breatche or
breatches

(*To repair to towe Comissioners an accompt*)   AND AFTER suche
repaire soo by them or eny of them mayde in and uppon the sayd
defaltes or breatches and by them relayted too ij next Comyssyoners
of Sewers wherof one too be of the quorum toogeather with an
accompt of suche monye as hath bene bestowed in and abowte the
sayde woorkes

(*Warrante to be graunted to levy the same*)   YTT SHALBE LAW-
FULL for the said two Comyssyoners forthwith too graunt there
warrant under their handes and seales too the sayd person or persons
as hath layde forthe or bestowed the monye in and abowte the sayd
woorkes too levy the same of the goods & cattalls of suche person
or persons that owght too have doonne the same in what place soo
ever the same arre too be found within the county of Lincoln or ells
wheare soo mutch hath bene expended

(*With salurye or comitt person*) TOOGETHER with reasonable stypend and sallary for their paines as by their dyscressyons shall seme good or ells too commytt the sayd person or persons too the next common gaole there too remayne withowte bayle or mayne pryce untyll he have satysfyed contented or paied suche money as shalbe due too him or them thatt layde owte the same or shall take suche order as they shall lyke of and allowe.

543

(*Dyking of sewer for the dames the payns*) AND WHEN any dykinge of eny sewer or dreane shalbe appoynted it is ordered & decreed thatt all suche towneshippes of Kesteven or of Holland as have accostomed to make the estople dame or torninge of the same mayne sewers ryvers or waters shall att all tymes lymytted and too be lymytted by order of sewers make the said estoppell damming or torning in places thought mete and requesyte for the same by the officers havinge charge of the same woorkes uppon payne of forfayture of and for every person & parsons soo making defalte too make the sayd estoppell turning and daming both owner commoner & officer too all intentes and purposes as is before prescrybed and lymytted for common woorkes

(*After eny begining of dyking enter in workes the next to procede payne in defalt one dykereve*) AND ITT IS further ordered and decreed thatt assoonne as eny person or persons shalbegine too dreane estoppe or dame any waters for the makinge of any woorke or woorkes assoonne as any parcell thereof shalbe entered intoo or sett uppon they thatt be the next adioyning shall follow and procede in order as the lye one by the other thatt the one may nott be a lett or hinderaunce to the other too proced or gooe forwarde in their sayd woorkes uppon payne and forfayture of every parson and parsons soo makinge defalte or neglecting orderlye too procede for every roode v s.

(*Ryvers haffing & inlarging the payn*) AND FOR THE good usage and order of all great sewers & mayne dreanes & lykewyse of all commen sewers as dreanes and other water courses itt is ordayned and decreed by us the sayd Comyssioners that the same and every of them shalbe well and sufficyently haffed scoured & enlarged from tyme to tyme as nede shall require where any nede or stratnes shalbe untoo a sufficyent bredth and wydnes as the most parte of suche great sewers or mayne dreanes and in lyke maner the other commen sewers & dreanes for their proporcyons shalbe and accustomably and allowably have bene used too be by suche as owe too doo the same att & by suche day & tyme as by order of sewers is or shalbe lymytted uppon payne for every rood in mayne dreane nott perfected accordingly v s. and in every commen sewers for every rood therof iij s. iiij d.

(*Rooded thryes*) AND ALLSOO FROM tyme too tyme yerely shalbe well and sufficiently rooded hooked & clensed of the flegges sedges & other noysome weddes growing or springing in any of them

(*Wedes landed*) AND THE SAME weddes soo rooded and hooked or by eny other meanes comming intoo them or eny of them too be plucked upp or landed in every parte porcion or lott lymytted & knowne in every suche mayne ryvers sewer or common dreane by suche person & persons bodies politike and corporate as owght too doo the same uppon payne and forfaytur for every rood defectyve in roodinge and scouringe and for the nott doinge of the same yerly by suche dayes & tymes as shalbe from tyme too tyme by order of sewers provyded for every roode xij d.

[485.II.3*d*]   **544**

(*Gootes & clowys*)   AND THAT ALL & synguler gootys buylded & sett in any . . . any owtefall toward the sea AND all & all maner off CLOWES sett . . . and for the recytt of any fenne or fresshe waters to passe in through or by any sewer or dreane in any terry-toryes apperteynyng to the said borough of Boston or within any towne toward any suche former seagoote

AND ALL & every other clowes and shyttes sett in any lyke sewer or dreane to holde & kepe any the waters severally in any quarters of any towne for for [*sic*] any tyme thought good, of or by the dykerevys OR for any specyall defens for the whiche the same was provyded

(*Bridges*)   AND ALSOO all & every bridge and bridges of stone or tymber sett in any suche ryver or mayn sewer commen ee graft or dreane within the said parties of Holland aswell for the good yssuyng of the water course in the same as for common passage of the quenes majesties lyege people in and by the same

(*Dykerevys searched & amendyd paynes*)   WHETHER they be to bee maynteyned by acrage or by comonage YTT YS ordeyned ordered and decreed that the DYKEREVE and dykerevis shall shall [*sic*] cause the same and every of theym from tyme to tyme to be well surely and suffycyently by theym vyewed & considered and yf nede be to be searched and soo perfectly to be repayred and amended from tyme to tyme by by [*sic*] suche dayes and tymes as ys or shalbe lymyted and appoynted att the costes & charges off the owner and owners & of such as ought to doo the same uppon PAYNE and forfayture for every goote clowe or shytt v li. AND for every bridge over mayne dreane iij li. vj s. viij d. and for every bridge over commen sewer xx s.

545

(*Weares & purprestures*)   AND THE said COMMYSSYONERS doo further ordre and decre that no maner of parson or parsons shall make or sett weare or stampe or levye any purpresture annoyaunce or impedyment to the yssuyng in any of the sayd mayn ryver or ryvers sewers common dreanes ees or graftes or any of theym in any of the said townes terrytoryes or hamlettes of Boston aforesaid or of any of the said wapentakes of Skyrbek Kyrton and Ellow or any of theym

(*Severall fisshinges*) AND THATT SUCHE as have severall fysshynges or lybertye of fysshyng in any of the said dreanes mayne ryvers or waters nott to fysshe ther too the stoppyng or annoyaunce of the water course OR LEVYE any purpresture in any of the said dreanes or waters uppon payn of forfayture for every such offence xx s.

(*Annoyauns by unlawfull nettes*) AND WHERE any suche annoyauns or purpresture shalbe in any ryver mayn dreane or commen sewer by reason of suche fitching wyth any nettes YTT SHALL and may be lawfull to & for the officer and officers to take suche nettes and engynes for fysshyng beyng any lett or hynderaunce to the course of the water and the same to detayne withoutt allowans of replevye as a forfayture to the use of the quenes majestye ONELESSE by the next sessyons of sewers in those partyes ytt shalbe otherwyse by law ordered

(*Lycenced weres*) AND YFF any suche weares or stampes shalbe hereafter lycencyd by orders of sewers the same in every mayne sewer to be the breadeth of xxiiij foote att the least and in every common sewer of the breadeth of xij foote or from banke to banke WITHOWTE ESTOPPLE and DYSTANT one from every other by the space of [*blank*] rodes or more but no lesse uppon payn for every parson offendyng to forfayt for every weare or purpresture sett or permytted to stand contrary to thys ordre iij s. iiij d. and for every nett whiche shalbe sett in suche place of impedyment in every mayn sewer x s. and every other defalt in common sewer eeas or graftes x s.

(*Pluck upp*) AND THATT ytt shalbe lawfull to and for every dykereve or dykerevys within theyr lottes or offyces to plucke upp and cause to be caryed awaye suche unlawfull nettes and the weares stampes or other impedymentes as is afforesaid uppon payne for every suche offens xl d. not performyng this decree by the tyme to hym or theym lymyted

Tertia pagina
Warrantes for doinge of worke

[485.II.4]   546

(*Fol. 4 Warraunt for doyng of workes & for colleccions*) AND FURTHER ytt ys ordeyned thatt when any dykereve or dykerevys surveyour or surveyours or other offycer mynyster or mynysters of sewers shall have eny warrant or precept for the doyng or workyng of any worke or workes OR FOR the levyeng gatheryng or collectyng of any acrage OR of assessement of any comonage OR of any somme or sommes of money for costes chargys salarys or expencys ayther used occupyed and layd owte for owners OR offycers for offencys in workes of sewers OR to be dyspendyd in and abowte any labours or workes to be done by acrage or by comonage

(*Under handes & seales*) THAT THE same warraunt shalbe under the handes and seales of vj v iiij or thre Commyssyoners of Sewers whereof oone to be of quorum beyng of the said law makers

(*REFUSALL of paymentes   DYSTRES as appereth*) AND
THEN in every suche case uppon eny refusall of eny suche payment
or paymentes ytt shall and may be lawfull to & for suche dykereve
or dekerevys surveyour or other offycer or mynyster or mynysters
of sewers to distreyn the owner & owners or others chargeable to
the said workes   OR HYS or theyr tenaunt fermour or grounde
occupyer of convenyent quantyte of any theyr goodes & cattalles
IN ENY his or theyr house or grounde   OR IN ENY common or
fenne grounde where they shalbe founden

(*Not urgyng the pore*) PROVYDED allway and ytt ys decreed
thatt eny poore tenante shall not tbe urged for for [*sic*] the chargys
of any owners AND that every owner dwellyng in place where the
offens ys or shalbe founden or other dutye to be paid as afforesayd,
shalbe oonely charged for all the offences of hys bankes and workes
of sewers and hys or theyr dutyes AND none of hys or theyr tenaunte
or tenauntes   ONELES any of theym be specyally charged with
suche chargys and yett then att the electyon of the offycers or
mynysters

(*iiij dayes impounded*) AND THAT the dystres so taken shalbe
deteynyd in open pounde by the space of iiij dayes withowte allowans
of replevye

547

(*The thyrd day unpaid*) AND YFF the owner or owners or any
of theyr tenantes doo nott satysfye the said money or moneys
distreyned for to the said officer or officers mynyster or mynysters
then end of the thyrd day of impoundement

(*Present sale*) THEN UPPON the iiij^th day or any tyme after
ytt shall and may be lawfull to & for the said offycer or offycers
mynyster or mynysters then presently to sell the said dystres too
any person or parsons to be praysed by iiij indyffyrent parsons

(*Surplysage*) AND thatt they the said offycers shall yelde to the
partye dystreyned be he owner tenaunte or grounde occupyer or
eny of theym the surplysage of the money over & besydes the charge
and dewtye att that tyme dew WHERUPPON the offycers shall
take viij d. for every distres aswell for the day of takyng as att the
sale thereof

(*With a byll*) AND SHALL also delyver to hym or theym a byll
mencyonyng the somme or sommes by eny of theym receyvyd and
the cause of the takyng for his or theyr allowans att the quenes
majesties handes or hir highnes officers or att the hande of his or
theyr landelord chargeable unto the same charge accordyng unto
former statute therein provyded

(*And every officer in his lymytt by office*) AND THAT ALL and
every dykereve and dykerevys surveyour and surveyours or any of
theym within theyr lymyttes for suche costes chargys salarys or
expencys as any of theym shall paye or bestowe or shalbe due to
any of theym in or abowte eny the workes off sewers afforeseid
doone or to be doone by ordre of sewers now ordred or hereafter to

be ordeyned and decreed SHALL use lyke levye by dystres and sale
EX OFFicio and in lyke maner & forme as before ys ordeyned and
decreed to theym & to others offycers and mynysters for theyr levye
by warraunt as afforesaid to all intentes and purposes by vertue of
thys our generall decree

548

(*Uppon suche warrant within iij dayes a supers' by the grauntes
under theyr handes & seales*) PROVYDED ALSO and ytt ys
further decreed thatt ytt shall & may be lawfull the said Comyssyoners that shall make any suche warraunt att eny tyme within thre
dayes after the takyng of suche dystres to make a supers' and to
dyscharge any suche offycer or officers mynyster or mynysters for
the sale thereof YF YT SHALL seme soo good to theym uppon any
reasonable consideracion by theym allowed att the sute of the
partye or persons dystreyned SOO THAT the same warraunt of
supers' and discharge be also under theyr handes & seales who dyd
dyrect the same warraunt for dystres and sale and delyvered unto
eny the said offycers or mynysters within the same fyrst three dayes
after the takyng and impoundement of the same

(*For warrauntes for levyeng or workes justyfyable . . . questyon*)
AND YTT YS furthermore ordered and decreed thatt all & every
warraunt and warrauntes precept or preceptes for the levyeng
gatheryng or collectyng of any dett dewtye paymenttes for costes
chargys expencys or salarys or for acrage or any assessement for
comoniage OR for the doyng of eny worke or labours of sewers beyng
under the handes and seales of vj v iiij or thre Comyssyoners whereof
oone of quorum SHALBE as good and effectuall in law to bynde all
& every person and persons and bodyes polytyke and for the offycer
offycers mynyster and mynysters TO JUSTYFFYE by force of the
said warraunt & warrauntes all & eny acte & actes thyng & thynges
by theym or any of theym doone or executed by force of suche
warraunt or precept AS the same hadde bene decreed in open
sessyons of sewers AND AS YF every worde in the said warraunt
conteyned were in this our law and decree partycularlye declared
mencioned and recyted ANY AMBYguyte dowte or questyon to the
contrary notwithstondyng SOO THAT the said offycer or offycers
doo nott excede the contentes wordes and meanyng off the sayd
warraunt

[485.II.4*d*]   549
[1](*For fermours or others distreyned frehoulders charged or others
should uppon complaynt Comyssioners to dyrect ratably*) AND
BYCAUSE ordre ys prescrybed that no fermour or ground occupier
may be dystreyned for all the charges for eny owners dewtye as
afforesaid YTT YS therefore ordered and decreed that when and
as often as eny person or persons beyng . . . or otherwyse shalbe
dystreyned . . . or somme of money for acrage or other . . . of costes

---

[1] The head of this membrane is badly stained with gall.

chargys . . . workes founden defectyve or hereafter to be defectyve
when the freholder . . . shalbe chargeable to the said workes OR
WHERE any others fermour . . . owner or owners or other person
or persons arre or shuld be charged with the same aswell as the
parties charged or distreyned IN EVERY suche case uppon compleynt thereof made the person . . . charged or distreyned to twoo
of the next Comyssioners . . . oone to be of the quorum YTT SHALL
and may be lawfull to & for the said Comyssyoners . . . suche ordre
or dyrect . . . shalbe . . . and nedefull that the . . . any other for . . .
chargeable or charged as the . . . in equall degre of . . . every way
charged for his & theyr . . . AND NOT oone to paye the whole or an
others dutye withoute recompens.

(*Theyr ordre in open sessions by sale estople or otherwyse for
recompens by warr'*) AND whattsoever the said ij next Comyssyoners shall doe therein itt shalbe as good & effectuall in law as yf
the same hadde beene made or doone in open sessyons of sewers be
ytt SALE of lease or leasses for yeres of theyr landes and tenementes
sale of theyr goodes & cattalles estopell defalcacion or reteyner of
rent or rentes imprisonorment of hys or theyr bodyes or otherwise
whatsoever by the said ij next Comyssyoners shalbe thought mete
requysytt or convenyent by theyre wysedomes & dyscressyons to
make the sayd recompens to any person or persons dryven or
enforced to paye more then his or theyr own dewtye or dett PRO-
VIDED allwayes that the said law of recompens be made by warraunt
under theyr handes and seales beyng of the said ij next Commyssioners.

(*For spedye workyng*) AND FOR the more spedy & better ex-
pidycion of the makyng workyng doyng or repayring of any the
said fen bankes or any other bankes or of any other maner of woorkes
of sewers herafter or herafter by theys or eny other decrees ordres
or lawes of sewers ordered or to be orderyd and decreed of new to be
mayde wrought & doone repayred & amendyd

(*Of workes of sewers*) IN OR ABOWTE any gootes clowys
shyttes brydges or new dyking scouring or clensing or of haffyng
roding or hooking of mayne ryvers sewers or commen dreanes or of
eny other woorkes of sewers of whatsooever kind within the sayd
borow or within eny the sayd weapentakes

(*By eny order*) AYTHER BY specyall decree specyall warrant
particuler commaundment or generall ordre of the sayd Comyssyoners or of eny other vj wherof iij of quorum or of eny ij Comissioners
as before prescrybed uppon their vyew and by their warrant as befor
ys ordeyned & sett downe

(*To officers of & by office & others ministers by warrant*) THAT
YTT shalbe lawful too and for eny the sayd dykereve & dykerevys
surveyour or surveyours as of office and for all other mynisters
person & persons as shalbe attorysed as deputy mynisters or assignes
of eny ij the sayd Comyssyoners as afforesayd by warrant under their
handes & seales for the repaire and making of any the sayd woorkes

ordeyned too be doone or hearafter decreed too be doone accordingly
by vertew of this owr decree

550

(*To take for new woorkes or others all workmen*) TOO TAKE from
tyme to tyme as nede shall move them for the new woorking of eny
new woorkes or for the perfecyon of such woorkes as shalbe founden
defectyve by eny of suche officers or ministers wrought or doone as
well as they hadd specyall woorkes by warrant too take all and all
maner of artyffycers woorkmen and laborers soo too doo accordingly
by statute wages or by the good consyderacyon of the next Comyssyoner Justice or cheyff constable

(*& necessaryes with caryages*) AND LIKWYSE too take all
& all maner of necessaryes apte and mete for suche woorkes as eny
of them shall cause too be doone att and by indifferent pryces or by
the aprysement of [*blank*] and all suche charges as shalbe nedefull
for the acrage of the same where they may be convenyently hadd
and founden presently to be payed for according untoo agrement or
by the good consyderacyon of the next Comyssioner or others as
afforesayd

(*For ponishment of offendours by ymprisonament*) AND thatt
the dykerevys or other officer or ministers surveyeng or having charge
of any woorkes of sewers finding any laborer or woorkeman dys-
obedyent stubburn or eny wilfull person or persons abusing them
selves toward any suche as shall have the oversight of eny the sayd
woorke or woorkes thatt then they the sayd dykereve or dykerevys
or other offycer or mynister or any of them shall presently ponyshe
the same offender or offendours att his or their dyscressyons by
imprysonament in the stockes by the space of one hole daye & a
night or lesse

(*Reconsyllyacyon*) AND UPPON reconsilliacion shall & may
remyt hym or them and yf eny person or persons persever in his
or their dysobedyens then the said officers or mynisters or eny of
them to bring the same soo dysobeing as is afforesayd before the
next Comyssyoner or Justice too be ponyshed according too the
quantety of the offens by the discressyon of the same Comyssyoner
or Justice of peace before whome he or they shalbe brought

For accomptes of charges

[485.II.5]   551

Quinta pagina

(*For accomptes of chargys wekely*) AND MOREOVER ytt ys
ordeyned and decreed thatt the dykerevys and every of theym
whiche now or hereafter shall take uppon theym any collectyons
or receyttes of acragys or off assessementes off comoniages to be
expendyd concernyng any workes as aforeseid SHALL WEKELY
or twyse in one month att the furthest duryng the tyme of suche
workes make a declaracion of theyr partyculer paymentes and
chargys by any of theym or to be made for the same workes

(*Warnyng for the hearers in tyme of memory*) AND SHALL gyve

warnyng thereof openly in the paryshe churche on a festyvall day
in due tyme whereby the lordes of the town or theyr officers and
others owners and dyscrete persons of the town and place where the
workes be or shalbe hadde & wrought att the tyme of suche worke,
may attend and be present att the hearyng of the same for theyr
better remembrans and understondyng the truthe of the same
reconynges and that uppon payn of forfayture by every dykereve
for every offens thereof or not gyvyng warnyng of the same iij s.
iiij d.

(*And a perfect accompt exhybyted*)   AND WHEN the money shalbe
expendyd or the worke fynysshed then a perfect and a whole
accompt shalbe by theym & every of theym exhybyted and made
of all theyr hole charge and receyttes and of all theyr former partycular paymentes

(*Within a month after the workes ended respytyng a weke for the
better hearyng of the same*)   THE SAME to be doone within oone
month next after the workes fynysshed or the money of the acrage or
comoniage shalbe expendyd and before the lyke lordes or theyr
officers owners & dyscrete persons of the said town or paryshe
AND the lyke open warnyng as before ys appoynted respytyng the
tyme oone whole weke next after the warnyng SO AS they or suche
as shalbe mete and wyll heare the same may have suche knolege
thereof as they the better may attend and be present att the hearyng
thereof and thatt uppon theyr further payn and forfayture of
[*blank*] every of theym offendyng this ordre and decree

(*Deliberatly herd & perfectyd*)   AND THE sayd accompt beyng
delyberatly herd and advysedly consydered as before ys ordeyned
the same soo perfectyd then by xij viij vj or accordyng unto the
nombr of the hearers of the moost dyscrete persons aforeseyd shalbe
subscrybed with theyr handes or markes testyfyeng the same

552

(*Then by ij Commissioners exactly examyned*)   AFTER THE
perfection whereof in maner and forme befoore remembred THE
SAID dykerevys shall within oone other month or lesse tyme then
next ensuyng tender the same accompt unto ij the next Commyssyoners whereof oone of quorum by theym to be exactly examyned
& tryed soo farre as they can or may by questyons trye the same
AND FOR testymony thereof shall sygne ytt wyth theyr own handes
and names under the same

AND THEN thatt the sayd dykerevys shall certyfye the said
accompt unto a full nombr of Commyssyoners in open courte att
the next sessyons of sewers to be holden within the said borow or
wapentake where the workes aforeseid were doone

(*The office of a dykereve*)   AND FURTHER ytt ys ordered and
decreed thatt for the offyce of the dykereve thatt no person or persons
hereafter shalbe dykereve or shall take uppon hym to execute the
same offyce ayther by hym selff or by his deputye or deputyes oneles
he so chosen to be dykereve have landes and tenementes freehold or

coppyehold to the cleare yearly value off fouretye shyllynges OR BE worth in goodys fouretye poundes OR THATT twoo Commyssyoners whereof oone of quorum shall lyke and allowe of hym and thatt uppon payn of forfayture of [*blank*] to the quenes maiesties use v li.

(*For deputyes*) AND BYCAUSE som person or persons beyng chosen of suffycyent valew dwellyng owte off the precyncte of the lete where he shalbe chosen OR shalbe dysposed to serve by a suffycyentt deputye THAT suche deputye shalbe advysedly consydered by the next Commyssyoners or twoo of theym whereof oone of quorum and by theyr dyscrete wysedomes the same to be allowed OR som other by theyr good dyscressyons to be appoynted

(*Salarye*) AND YFF there shall happen any varyans for the salary of suche deputye then the same Commyssyoners to sett down the stypend of suche deputye OR TO commytt the ordre thereoff unto the next sessyons of sewers in those lymyttes next to be holden there to be determyned by the Commyssyoners in open courte

(*& dyscharge of penaltyes*) AND YTT ys ordeyned that suche deputye assigned by any suche dykereve allowed as aforeseyd or appoynted by any twoo Commyssyoners or more as before also prescrybed SHALL take uppon hym to dyscharge his master of all suche paynes penalltyes and forfaytures as by vertue of that office he ys to be charged and shall beare and paye every oone of theym whiche shall happen in his defalte

(*The dykereve refusyng forfaytt*) AND YTT YS ALSO further ordered and decreed thatt all & every person and persons chosen to be dykereve in any leete or courte baron as ys aforesaid beyng of suffycyent value accordyngly and dwellyng within the same town refusyng to take uppon hym the exercyse of the sayd offyce & the executing of the same by hym self or his suffycyent deputye to be allowed by the twoo next Commyssyoners within xij dayes after Mayday in any yere hereafter shall forfaytt to the quenes maiesties use fyve markes

(*Outt of the precynct to forfaytt*) AND YFF HE dwell owte of the precyncte of the sayd leete or wold appoynt a suffycyent deputye on his behalf then he to exercyse & execute the sayd office by hym self or his lawfull deputye within oone month next after his seid choyse and election and publication thereof in the churche made where the said lond lyeth uppon som festyvall daye and thatt uppon payn of the forfayture off fyve poundes to the quenes maiesties use hir heyres & successours

[485.II.5*d*]   553
(*The dykerevys entre their office on Madaye*) AND FOR the better knoledge when any person chosen shall enter uppon the sayd office of dykereve YTT ys ordered thatt every parson chosen dykereve shall enter in the said office att Mayday yerly and to cowntynew and hold on for a yere

(Though chosen before) AND THAT though eny suche dykereve shalbe appoynted or chosen in any lordship as befoore in the leete at Mychelmes or in any courte baron att thatt tyme in any yere hereafter thatt he shall nott enter otherwyse then uppon his own voluntary wyll ne be compellyd to execute eny suche office before Mayday then followyng butt the old to contynew officer tyll the seyd fyrst day of May

(But the old dykereve) AND EVERY old dykereve as is aforeseid refusyng to serve accordyngly the same shall forfaytt unto the quenes maiesties use iij li. vj s. viij d.

(shall publishe newe election uppon payn) AND YTT YS ordered and decreed that yff the old dykerevys where the land lyeth doo nott publyshe in the paryshe churche of that place wythin sex dayes next after the choyse & election of the newe dykereve or dykerevys theyr election together with theyr names & dwellyng placys whereby they may have knoledge by theyr tenantes they or theyr frendes then thatt the same old dykerevys for deffalt of publyshyng of the same as afforeseid on som festyvall day in the tyme before prescrybed every of theym to forfaytt xx s.

(New dykereve not over ij yeres & to accompt) AND THAT every suche dykereve new chosen shall execute his offyce oone hoole yere yerely after Mayday and thatt he shall nott contynew ne occupye the same office above twoo yeres AND SHALL make his accompt of all & synguler suche money or moneys as he ys to be charged wyth nott accompted for oone hole month before the end of his yere uppon payn of forfayture of fyve poundes

(For acrebookes and ioysebookes) AND IN AS MOCHE as dykereves havyng great changys apperteynyng unto theyr offices to be wrought in dyverse townes and places within the seid borow & wapentakes as well in & uppon the sayd seabankes and other bankes aforeseid as in dreanes ryvers & sewers and in and abowte the repayre and amendement of gootys clowys brydges and others devyses of sewers to be doone aswell by acrage as by joysement or agystement

554

(For perfection of workes) WHICHE WORKES can nott be dewly wrought and perfectyd in dyverse townes & hamlettes within the seyd lymyttes for lack of perfect acre bookes and jusebookes hytherto reteyned & deteyned from this courte of sewers imperfectyd & nott certyfyed into the same courte by dyverse townshyppes within the said lymyttes contrary unto ordres & decrees for the same heretofore provyded & ordeyned

(Anno xiij^{mo} incerteyntees) WE THE SAYD Comyssyoners therefore perusyng a decree in anno xiij^{mo} doo ordre and decree thatt the same ordre shalbe revyved for the makyng of townebookes acre bookes and ioyesebookes as herafter followyth thatt ys to saye THE incerteyntees then perceyvyd as now may be well considered in dyverse acre bookes and ioysebookes with dyverse alterations in the

tymes by dyverse of the said townes and hamlettes WHICH owe
to be exactly & trewly made & putt into perfect certeyntee

(*xij discrete*) DOO NOW ordre and decree thatt xij discrete
persons of every town & hamlett OR accordyng unto the quantyte
of the nombre of the place where the want of suche bookes shalbe
to be nominated by the dykereves or dykereve of suche towne or
place to be tendered unto twoo the next Commyssyoners whereof
oone of quorum and by there consent the same persons and every
of theym within oone weeke after warnyng geven openly in the
churche in oone festyvall day in due tyme by readyng of theyr
names shall instantly repayre unto the next Commyssyoner Justice
or steward in any courte where eny of the landes & tenementes of
that town or place shalbe holden

(*To take othe*) AND SHALL take his & theyr othe & othes to
perfect suche acre bookes & iuse bookes accordyng unto his & theyr
knoledge & knoledges and thatt uppon payn of every of theym soo
to doo refusyng to forfayt unto the quenes maiesties use to be
levyed xx s.

(*& by due examynation peruse old bookes*) FOR THE doyng
whereof they & every of theym shall forthwyth faythefully enquyre
and dewly examyn and peruse all suche olde and auncyent acre
bookes as shall or may com unto theyr syght for the makyng of the
new acre booke AND lykewyse the olde ioysebookes when they
shall procede to & for the makyng of new joysebookes

(*With attendans the payn*) AND THE said dykereves and every
of the said jurours shall from tyme to tyme attend att suche daye
& dayes place & places as the forman appoynted before the said
Commissioners shall assigne untyll the same acre booke & joysebooke
and ayther of theym shalbe fynyshed & perfected and thatt uppon
payn for every of theym refusyng or nott attendyng not beyng syck
or lyke suffycyency of excuse havyng to forfaytt for every defalt
xij d.

555

(*For doubtes*) AND THAT for any dowtefull places within any
the lymytes of suche town or place accordyng unto theyr dyscrete
wysedomes aswell by tryall & examynation of any the said bookes
or others terrours olde evydences or other bookes of antyquyte &
credytt whereof they shall or may have syght as by wyttnes of any
auncyent persons takyng othe before the next Commyssyoner or
Justyce or by measure vyew or treadyng eny grounde or groundes
in questyon & by all convenyent wayes & meanes whiche by theyr
wysedomes knoledges they can consydre accordyng unto theyr othes
ayther by consent of the partyes to whom the doubt shall apperteyn
to make a fynall determynation or to certyfye suche as shall remayn
(by a full courte of sewers att the next sessions to be herd with the
circumstaunces to theym apparaunt in theyr examynations of the
same) by the Commissioners there to be determyned

AND FOR all other alterations of possessyons or propertyes in

L

bankes or other jusementes, by any deathes, dyscentes, gyftes or bequestes, or by any purchases, exchaunges, or other devyses, the same in the new acre booke or ioysebooke to be sett down by expresse manyfestation & declaration of the same

And the same booke or bookes

Quinta pagina

[485.II.6]   556

Sexta pagina

(*To be indentyd & oone parte thereof to be presentyd & every person charged*) AND THE same booke or bookes by theym exactly and iustly made and perfectyd to be indentyd in parchement whereof oone parte engrossed subscrybed with there handes & markes to be yeldyd & tendered unto the cheyff jurours in those lymyttes att the next sessyons of sewers by theym to be considered and uppon theyr allowans of the same by theym also to be presentyd unto the Commissioners att the same sessyons to remayn emongst the recordes AND every person & persons by the same to be charged untyll by the Commissioners in full courte of sewers eny other ordre uppon further mattier shewid be ordeyned and adiudged

(*Notes of devysions for a town booke*) IN WHICHE travelles for the certeyntye of all the acres in every of the said townes & hamlettes where no perfect terrour or good town booke hathe bene heretofore of late made, notes & entres to be made of the severall boundes & devysyons in every quarter & lymytt of the same town and the true nombre of acres of every person & persons in every of the same lymytes & boundes whereby the rather an exact & perfect town booke may also be made of all & synguler the acres of every person with good & perfect metes and boundes for the whiche town booke so to be perfectyd & to remayn in every of the same townes in sure & saffe kepyng fur ther tyme hereafter to be appoynted

(*Untyll the which no person or inheritans charged but for the tyme & receyvyd in courte by tryall all the former bookes att the chargys of*) UNTYLL WHYCHE towne booke shalbe exactly made no enherytans of eny person or persons to be otherwyse charged then for this tyme of the makyng of these new acre bookes or iuse bookes SO AS every person & persons uppon compleynt of any overcharge or wrong charge by eny of the same new bookes they & every of theym shalbe receyvyd in open courte att the next sessyons after theyr greyffes or wronges perceyvyd and theyr allegacyons & proles by the Commyssyoners for tyme beyng then & there to be exactly examyned & tryed and theruppon suche order by theym to be sett down as by theyr dyscrete wysedomes shalbe consydered adiudged or determyned

557

(*And thother parte of the acrebookes & joysebookes to be examyned & found agreable to be sygnyfyed suff' untyll further ordre*) AND OF THE sayd acrebookes & ioyse bookes in forme before remembred tendered presentyd and in courte receyvyd indendyd the other parte or counterpayn of every of theym att the request of any the dykerevys or offycers of any the sayd borow or townes shalbe by the clerk of sewers for the tyme beyng examyned wyth the parte or partes of suche booke or bookes as shalbe founden presentyd by the jurours or receyvyd by the Comyssyoners in full courte of sessyons off sewers beyng in his custodye by ordre of the same courte AND UPPON the exact examynation off every of the same bookys FYNDYNG theym or any of theym agreable with the part or partes indentyd beyng in his custodye shall sygnyffye uppon every of theym by the subscription of his name as offycer of the courte of sewers THATT THE OTHER PARTE or partes or counterpaynes of suche booke or bookes be receyvyd and doo remayne emongst the recordes of those sessyons when & where they were presentyd or receyvyd WHYCHE sygnyfycation in forme aforesaid shalbe suffy-cyent unto every dykereve and offycer or mynyster for collectyon off acrage and lykewyse for the chargyng of eny person or persons by booke of joysement by vertue of this our generall ordre and decre UNTYLL further order shalbe hereafter sett down as before ys ordeyned and prescrybed

(*For knolege of offences*) AND THE SAYD COMmyssyoners also consyderyng the inconvenyences whiche may hereafter aryse and growe whiles the new joysebookes shalbe of new certeynly perfectyd unto the dykerevys and offycers whiche now be or hereafter shalbe of new electyd and chosen DOO ORDEYN & decree thatt the dykerevys whiche now be or whiche shalbe hereafter from tyme to tyme shall with the consent of the surveyour yff he shall then be in place uppon warnyng to be geven in the churche in due tyme att day and place by theym or any of theym to be assigned & appoynted examyn suche booke or bookes of ioysement or agystament of the bankes sewers or dreanes AS WELL of moost importaunce FYRST by theym advysedly to be forseene, att suche day & place treadyng and measuryng theym with poll & roll or ioysebooke then and there to be redde

558

ATT THE WHICH examynation and declaration of every person and persons lott or lottes in every of the same banke bankes or dreanes YTT YS DECREED thatt every person of ten shyllynges yerely value of enherytans or frehold in his own person or oone dyscrete person of his or there household or householdes ayther oone honest labourer able to take the knoledge and dyscharge of his burdeyn therein or thereuppon AND every other person also havyng charge att the same daye & place shall attend in person uppon payn of forfayture every oone nott attendyng att every suche excercyse att the day & place lymyted for every offens

[1]ASWELL to take . . . of theyr owne charge as elles to have under-standyng and knoledge of suche . . . to be doone for the preservation

---

[1] Part of the foot of this membrane is illegible owing to a gall stain.

& . . . of the same towne . . . adiacent in and uppon the same day &
travell

ATT WHYCHE . . . exercyse the surveyour of that lymytt . . .
of his charge advysedly to be . . . att the tyme of theyr vyew & survey
beyng . . . AND . . . with the consent of the dykerevys or dykereve
WHOO also in his . . . surveyours shall also commaund all suche
ground as shalbe specyally . . . to be of moost quantyte off whose
soo ever possessyon the same shalbe to be staked stoned or marked
with stullp stone or stake for the better knoledge of the same

[485.II.6*d*]   559
[1](. . . *placys to be . . . ked   by owners* . . .)   AND LYKEWYSE
thatt the grounde and groundes moost defectyve in eny the said
bankes beyng joysed iused or agysted shalbe stoned staked or
marked with stulp stone or stake by the owners of suche defectyve
bankes within . . . dayes then next ensuyng for the good knoledge
thereof by the same owners to be . . . all officers or mynysters whoo
shall have the charge off & for the . . . of theyr . . . of offices &
mynystration of examynation of reformation of suche defaltes and
suche . . . for . . . [th]ereof to forfaytt for every marke nott sett as
before ys prescrybed . . .

(*Or dykerevys takyng iiij d. & forfaytt*)   AND THE DYKEREVE
then the owners tyme expyred, to cause the same to be doone and
to take & levye of suche owners goodes & cattalles ex officio for
every stake soo by hym sett iiij d. of the bankes of moost quantyte
not severed by knowen marke or in & uppon eny defectyve place
or placys of eny person or persons severall banke or bankes not
knowen by lyke metes or marke WHICH YF the same shall nott be
doone by the dykereve . . . every of theym omyttyng the same shall
for every stake or marke omytted forfaytt other iiij d.

(*Surveyours*)   AND in theyr defalt the surveyours or eny of theym
shall cause every of the same stakes or markes within lyke tyme to
be sett doown att the owners charge with lyke salary and uppon the
lyke payn

(*Commissioners*)   AND EVERY OF theym neglectyng theyr
dutyes & offices the assignees of any ij Commissioners as aforesaid
aswell to perform this ordre & decree as to cause all former ordres
& decrees to be fully perfectyd and duely performed after offens
founden by eny the said Commissyoners or ij of theym whereof one
of quorum

(*Attendaunce of officers*)   ATT WHOSE commyng aswell the
surveyours as the dykerevys to attend with poll & roll for the perfect
tryall of all suche offencys in all & every the sayd ioyse bankes or
other defectyve places ioysed or agysted WHICHE by signes or
markes sett may & wyll save great labours in & abowte the often
measuryng of the same

(*Uppon new ioysement   equalyte of workes*)   AND THAT att

[1] Part of the head of this membrane is stained by gall.

every new ioysement or agystament of any banke or dreane where
any shyft or alteration by commen consent shalbe made within any
the sayd lymytes of the said borow or any the sayd townes within
any the said wapentakes YTT YS ORDERED thatt a perfect
equalyte shalbe made by every owner accordyng to order prescrybed in & uppon every suche place soo to be altered or shyfted
OR ATT theyr chargys by the sayd offycers to be doone in forme
before ordeyned

560

(*& ordre for stakes from tyme to tyme*) AND WHEN the same
new agystament shalbe fynyshed and the booke thereof fully
perfectyd and allowably certyfyed in forme before remembred
THEN uppon the exact tryall of the same new booke by the poll of
mesure mesured by the dykerevys or any of theym as before ys
ordeyned THE SAYD ORDRE for stakes & markes to be practysed
& sett accordyng unto the tryall of the measure by the same new
booke AND the same from tyme to tyme as decayes of any of theym
shall happen to be renued & of new sett in lyke ordre and uppon
lyke paynes to be forfayted and lyke paymentes unto the offycers
& mynysters as before ys ordeyned & provyded

(*For knoledge of dayes & tymes*) AND FURTHERMORE to the
entent thatt aswell the owners dykerevys & surveyours as all others
offycers & mynysters off sewers shall & may knowe the dayes &
tymes att or before the whiche all & all maner of defaltes & offencys
in bankes dreanes & in & abowte others workes of sewers now to be
made repayred or amendyd shalbe accordyngly reformed and doone
accordyng unto the former ordres and decrees

(*This somer parte*) SPECYALL DAYES for the somer parte of
this present yere for dyverse consyderations be appoynted ordered
and decreed by us the said Commyssioners in maner and forme
followyng that ys to saye

(*For seabankes*) FYRST thatt all and all maner the former seabankes fennebankes owteryngbankes and other defensable bankes by
whatt so ever name they be or shalbe called or knowen

(*& others workes*) AND ALL & synguler ryvers common dreanes
and water courses GOOTES clowes shyttes bridges AND ALL and
all maner of kyndes of others workes of sewers what so ever heretofore ordeyned to be doone or hereafter to be decreed accordyngly
in maner & ordre before mentioned in the tytle or artycle of every
of theym

(*Doone by owners September*) SHALBE accordyng unto the
same former ordres suffycyently made doone repayred reformed and
amendyd by all & every person and persons bodyes polytyke
corporations and comonialties now charged or hereafter by ordre of
sewers to be charged to & with the makyng or amendement of any
of the same att or before the fyrst day of the month off September
now next commyng

(*Dykerevys October*) AND YFF suche owners shall make defalt or eny of theym then the dykerevys or dykereve of the town or place where suche offens shalbe founden after the daye aforeseid expyred shall & maye cause suche defalt or offencys to be well repayred & amendyd att or before the fyrst day of October then next ensuyng

Sexta pagina

[485.II.7] 561

Septima pagina

(*In def' of dykereve for owner or propre SURVEOUR November*) AND IN LYKE mener yff the dykerevys and every of theym shall omytt the tyme to theym lymyted & appoynted ayther for reformation of suche defaltys as were left undoone by eny of the said owners OR FOR any theyr own chargys and dewtyes by every of theym neglectyd concernyng theyr own offyces THEN the surveyours or eny off theym within his or theyr lymytt shall & maye cause all defaltes by eny of theym founden to be well repayred & amendyd in ordre before sett downe att or before the fyrst day of November

(*And by all defaltes then Commissioners or there mynysters from tyme to tyme*) AND THAT in and by the defaltes of every of the said owners dykerevys & surveyours omyttyng and neglectyng every of theyr dewtyes in & abowtt eny of the seyd workes in bankes ryvers commen dreanes or other workes of sewers whatt soo ever THEN the COMMYSSyoners or eny twoo of theym whereof one of quorum by theym selffes or by warraunt unto eny their deputyes mynysters or assignees as before is prescrybed after the sayd fyrst day of November SHALL and may from tyme to tyme for the performans of theys ordres and decrees make the reparation & amendement of all suche workes afforeseid as they shall fynde nedefull to be repayred or amendyd by eny of the fornamed owners & others offycers or eny of theym omytted & neglectyd

(*Yerely reparation of all defaltes*) AND LYKEWYSE ytt ys further ordered and decreed thatt all & synguler the same forenamed seabankes fennebankes owterynges and other the said defensable bankys AND ALL & all maner the said ryvers common dreanes & water courses gootys clowys shyttes bridges and all others workes of sewers afforeseid whatt soo ever FOUNDEN defectyve and not thought suffycyent in repayre accordyng unto the intendement of theys ordres and decrees in any yere hereafter for the preservation & defens & common weale of the sayd borow or of any the townes or hamlettes in any of the sayd wapentakes

(*By owners SEPTEMBER*) SHALL ALSO BE yerely from tyme to tyme for ever hereafter as before ys sett down by former ordres suffycyently made doone repayred reformed and amendyd by all & every the said person and persons bodyes polytyke corporations and comonialtyes in maner and forme before mentioned att or beffore the lyke fyrst day of September in every yere hereafter

(*Dykerevys October*) AND IN & by the defalt of eny owner or owners THE DYKEREVYS or dykereve where any defalt as afforeseid shalbe founden within his or theyr offyces shall & maye cause the same forthwith to be repayred and amendyd att or before the fyrst daye of OCTOBER then next ensuyng also in every yere hereafter

562

(*Surveyours NOVEMBER*) And also in & by the DEFALTES of the dykerevys and every of theym after tyme to theym before lymyted THEN the surveyours or eny of theym as afforesaid shall and maye cause the defaltes founden in eny of theyr lymyttes instantly to be repayred & amendyd att or before the fyrst day of November then also next followyng in every yere hereafter not protractyng eny tyme ever havyng regard unto the moost daungerous place or places fyrst to be doone

(*After which tyme COMMYSSIONERS*) AFTER WHICHE tyme & tymes ended yerely & every yere hereafter ALL & ALL MANER of defaltes in any the said former seabankes or other the bankes afforeseid whatt so ever and in lyke maner all & synguler the defaltes in any other the fornamed ryvers or water courses or in any other the forsaid workes of sewers of what soo ever kynde founden by the said Commyssioners or eny ij of theym as before ordeyned

(*From tyme to tyme*) SHALL & may be by theym or by theyr deputyes mynysters or assignees as before prescrybed yerely in every yere hereafter from tyme to tyme repayred reformed and amendyd in ordre and maner as also before ys decreed and provyded

(*After wynter wastes & decayes*) AND BYCAUSE the wynter weather and stormye tempestes doo the many tymes impayre frett and waste the weake placys and dyverse other partes of the sayd sea bankes fenne bankes & owterynges and also dyverse other defensable bankes AND ALSO many tymes doothe or may yerely impayre and endamage dyverse other the forsayd workes off sewers as afforesayd

(*All former workes of sewers then necessary to be amendyd*) WE THE FORSAYD Commyssyoners doo moreover ordre decree and establysshe by these our lawes and ordynaunces indentyd that all & all maner the forenamed seabankes & other bankes whatt soo ever and all & synguler the before mentioned workes of sewers whatt soo ever soo weakened hurted or impayred or whiche shall be founden or thought insuffycyent & necessary to be then repayred reformed or amendyd accordyng unto ordres of sewers heretofore ordeyned or whiche hereafter shalbe ordeyned to be doone

shalbe yerly

[485.II.7*d*]   563

(*Before APRILL owners*) SHALL BE YERELY and from yere to yere herafter suffycyently repayred made and amended as before ys sett down for the ordre and maner of the same workes & every of theym in theyr degrees att or before the fyrst day of APRYLL from tyme to tyme by all & synguler person & persons corporations and comonialtyes as arre now charged or herafter shalbe charged with the same or eny parte thereof by ordre of theis owr lawes ordres and decrees of sewers or others hereafter to be ordeyned and decreed to be doone

(*And in defalt DYKEREVYS before Maye*) AND YFF SUCHE owner or owners in eny yere hereafter shall omytt the tyme to hym or theym prescribed and shall & wyll permytt theyr defaltys to remayn nott reformed then after suche tyme passed the DYKE-REVYS or any of theym shall cause the same defaltys to be repayred and amendyd in maner before remembred att or before the fyrst day of MAY yerely and in every yere hereafter

(*In their defaltes*) BEFORE WHICH fyrst day of Maye yerely and in every yere hereafter YFF the dykerevys or dykereve shall nott performe all and synguler theyr dutyes in reformation off offencys of owners or apperteynyng unto their own offices

(*SURVEYOURS before June*) THEN AFTER the same day yerely and in every yere hereafter THE surveyours or eny of theym within theyr lymytes shall & may cause all offencys concernyng any of the premysed workes of sewers by theym then founden unrepayred & nott amendyd to be reformed & perfectyd att or before the fyrst day of June yerely in every yere hereafter then next ensuyng

564

(*After which tyme THE COMMYSSIONERS from tyme to tyme*) AFTER the whiche fyrst day of JUNE yerely and in every yere hereafter YFF ENY Commissioners beyng twoo in nombr as before ys ordeyned shall fynde eny defaltes or offencys in any the forsaid seebankes or other former bankys sewers dreanes or eny maner of other workes before mentioned then necessary or nedefull to be repayred then the same COMMYSSyoners or eny ij of theym whereof one of quorum theyr deputyes mynysters or assignees by theyr warraunt as before provyded shall & may cause all & all maner of defaltes aforesaid whatt so ever to be repayred & amended in forme before provyded from tyme to tyme yerely and in every yere hereafter as the necessyte thereof shall or may requyre

(*For owners workes ones at eny tyme doone*) PROVYDED always and ytt ys ordeyned and decreed by us the said Commyssyoners thatt when and after thatt any the said person or persons owner or owners of eny the premysed workes of sewers SHALL HAVE mayd & amendyd any maner of defalt in any of the same forenamed bankes dreanes or other workys of sewers whatt soo ever before mentioned OR reformed any offens whatt so ever in any yere heralter OR ENY offycer or offycers for hym or theym

(*For the somer parte*) FOR the whiche he or they shalbe att eny tyme herafter presentyd THE defalte certyfyed the costes payd or fynes forfayted in this somer parte of this yere OR in eny yere hereafter

(*Or wynter parte*) OR FOR eny lyke makyng or amendement of any defaltes afforeseyd in any yere hereafter by eny of the sayd owners in the wynter parte or after the wynter wastes wearynges

frettes or decays by theym mayd and amendyd as affore ys mentioned OR by any the said officers for hym or theym as before ys
prescrybed

(*Not to incurre eny damage*) THATT SUCHE person or persons
corporations comonialtyes or bodyes polytyke shall nott incurre or
be indamaged by reason off any suche offens founden by any the
sayd offycer or offycers mynyster or mynysters for any of the sayd
paynes penaltyes or forfaytures

565

(*Oneles warnyng*) ONELES publike warnyng thereof shalbe
hereafter gyven by any dykereve or other offycer or mynyster in
the churche or otherwyse for the repayr or amendement of suche
defalt or offens to be doone within sex dayes after suche warnyng
gyven

(*Or urge*) OR AS THE URGE or daunger of eny peryll lyke to
ensue may move eny the seid offycers or mynysters presently to
admonyshe the partye by warnyng or relation made whereby he or
they may understond or heare of the same instantly or in shorte
tyme to provyde therefore

(*And then lyable to former ordres*) WHEREUPPON yff suche
person or persons shall omytt any tyme lymyted or soo to be
appoynted thatt then the same worke of suche lyke of peryll omytted
by suche owner or owners to be thens lyable to all former ordres of
reformation and repayre thereof as heretofore ys provyded &
ordeyned or att eny tyme hereafter by ordres of sewers shalbe
decreed or estabylyshed

(*After workes wrought*) PROVYDED ALSO and ytt ys decreed
as aforesaid that after the makyng repayre or amendment of all
and synguler the former workes in bankes ryvers sewers dreanes and
all and all maner of workes as before expressed mentioned provyded
and ordeyned or to be hereafter ordred & decreed to be doone in
maner & forme prescribed in this present somer parte of this present
yere OR ATT eny other partes or tyme of eny yere hereafter

(*To be maynteyned*) THATT ALL and every person & persons
bodyes polytyke corporations and comonialtyes now charged or
hereafter to be charged by ordre of sewers to & for the makyng
reparation or amendement of any the seyd workes of sewers whatt
so ever in this present yere or in eny yere hereafter

SHALL FROM tyme to tyme suffycyently preserve and con-
tynually as the necessyte of the decay of eny of the former workes
shall appere repayre maynteyn and uphold the same accordyng unto
all and synguler the former orders & decrees and also accordyng
unto suche others ordres of sewers as hereafter shalbe provyded
ordeyned and estabylisshed for and concernyng the commodyte &
common weale of the said borow of Boston & of all the townes &
hamlettes in every of the sayd wapentakes of Skyrbek Kyrton &
Ellow in the partyes of Holland oone of the conffynes of the said
countye of Lincoln

Septima pagina

[485.II.8]　　　　　　　　　　　　　　　　　　566

Octava pagina

(*For mytygation of paynes*)　AND TO THEND and entent that no rygour or extremyte shall or may be used hereafter toward eny person or persons for towchyng or concerning any paynes penaltyes losses or forfaytures OR BY any law artycle or thyng in theis presentes conteynyd THEREFORE be ytt knowen that the entent and verey true meanyng of the said Commyssyoners now att these sessyons and assemble for and concernyng all & every law ordre artycle thyng & thynges in theis presentes conteyned ys now and every of theym hereafter shalbe taken receyved used and hadde in maner and forme hereafter mentioned especyfyed and declared that ys to say

(*Ordre*)　YTT YS FURTHERmore ordered decreed and fully agreed ordeyned estabylysshed and determyned by us the said Commyssyoners by thyse presentes thatt ytt shall & maye be lawfull to & for sex of the said Commyssyoners or others whereof thre to be of quorum att eny tyme hereafter in theyr next sessyons of sewers to be holden & kept within any the said lymyttes WHERE or after any certyfycat presentment or inquysytion of any the defaltes or offencys before mentioned expressed or declared shalbe yelded geven in or taken before theym in full courte of sewers as aforeseid

THAT THEY from tyme to tyme in suche open sessyons as aforeseid shall & may by theyr dyscrete wysedomes and dyscressyons consyder lesson mytygate or qualyfye all and every payn and paynes penaltyes forfaytures and losses whatt soo ever whiche by vertue of theis presentes shall fortune att eny tyme hereafter to be certyfyed presentyd or founden by any inquisition to be lost payd or forfayted by any person or persons bodyes polytyke corporations or comonialtyes what so ever to our soveraigne ladye the quenes maiestie to hir heyres or successours

SO THATT no somme or sommes of money further losse forfayture or penaltye shall be taken or adiudged by force and vertue of thyse presentes to be forfayted lost or due unto hyr maiestie hir heyres or successours by eny person or persons as aforesaid BUTT ONELY that and so moche as shalbe allowed taxced cessed ordered adiudged and determyned by the same Commyssyoners in theyr said sessyons of sewers as afforesaid provyded ANYE law artycle ordre decre thyng or thynges in theis presentes conteyned to the contrarye thereof in any wyse notwithstondyng

567

(*For ambyguytees　after the ingrosement & indentyng*)　AND MOREOVER ytt ys furthermore ordeyned decreed provided determyned & estabylysshed by us the said Commyssyoners THAT yff anye ambyguyte doubt quere or questyon shall or may fortune att eny tyme hereafter to be hadde moved or to grow for or uppon theys our present lawes ordres constytutions and decrees now engrossed indentyd accordyng unto the forme and effect of the late estatute of sewers in the xiij[th] yere of the reign of our said soveraygn lady the quenes maiestie that now ys after the ingrossement indentyng and sealyng of the same accordynglye OR IN FOR or uppon any clause artycle sentens tytle poynt thyng or thinges in eny off the same lawes ordres and decrees conteyned especyfyed or mentioned OR BY IN for or uppon any other law ordre or decree indentyd or to be indentyd heretofore or hereafter to be in suche wyse for the sewers decreed constytuted and establysshed

[1]OR IN . . . any lyke artycle clause sentens tytle artycle poynt thyng or . . . conteyned or . . .

OR IN for or uppon . . . uppon theys our former decrees or . . . or hereafter to

[485.II.8*d*]
[2]be grauntd dyrectyd . . .

OR IN . . . same lawes or decrees or if the law makers of . . .

(*To be adiudged*) THAT THE same . . . consydered ordered ended adiudged and determyned before & by sex of the same law makers in open courte of sessyons of sewers

(*& determyned*) AND FOR LACKE of suche nombre of the lawe makers THEN by sex Commyssioners in lyke maner in open courte of sewers from tyme to tyme to be considered expounded used interpreted expressed explayned devysed dyscussed determyned and ended and nott otherwyse

AND THAT suche consideration construction explanation interpretation exposition end judgement and determynation as they the said Comyssyoners in forme aforeseid SHALL consydre expound interpret construe expresse explayn or determyn UNDER theyr handes & seales

SHALBE adiudged taken and determyned accordyng unto the same theyr prescribed ordre of construction interpretation and determynation as aforesaid

(*The verey intent*) AND THE very true intent and meanyng of the said lawes ordres constytutions and decrees and of the lawe makers of the same

AND lykewise of any warraunt precept or commaundement uppon the sayd former decrees dyrectyd or any others lyke ordres hereafter to be grauntd and dyrectyd

(*Avayllable*) AND SHALBE good avaylable and effectuall in law AND pleadeable iustyfyeable and suffycyent in law

AND OTHER law construction exposition adiudgement or determynation to the contrary of the same in any wyse nott withstondyng

[*Endorsed*:] 18th Eliz. 1576

---

[1] A small part of the foot of this membrane is illegible owing to a gall stain.
[2] A small part of the head of this membrane is illegible owing to a gall stain.

INDEX OF PERSONS AND PLACES

The numbers relate to pages.

Place names are indexed under their modern forms wherever these are known, but minor names, e.g., of fields and petty drains, usually appear under the spelling in the text. Where no county is given after the name of a place, it is in Lincolnshire.

Abbottes Delph, delfe called the Abbottes [in Gedney par.], 55, 121

Abbottes Fee manor [in Gedney par.], 121, 122 *bis*, 123

Abell Tree, Ambell Tree, Ambyll Tree, Awebell Tre [in Gedney par.], 54 *bis*, 120 *ter*

Acar, Henry, 117
    Robert, 106 *bis*, 113, 118

Acreland, Acrelande, Acraland, Acerland [in Sutterton par.], 46
    Stowe, Staw, 2, 3 *bis*, 5, 38, 45, 47

Acres Gate [in Tydd St Mary par.], 103, 115

Adam, Adame, Henry, 131
    William, 64

Alderlod [in Crowland par.], 14

Aldyke. *See* Alldyke

Algarkirk, Allgarkyrke, Algerkyrke, Algarkirke, Algarkyrke, Algerkerke, Allgarkyrke, 1-5 *passim*, 22 *ter*, 38 *ter*, 45-47 *passim*
    gote, 47 *bis*
    parsonage, 47

Alger Hundreth, 45

Alinson. *See* Allinson

Alldyke, Aldyke Fyllede, 10
    Lode, 10 *ter*

Alleinson. *See* Allinson

Allen, Allin, Alleyn, Alyn, John, 108, 118
    Robert, 108
    Thomas, 122

Allenson. *See* Allinson

Alleyn. *See* Allen

Allgarkyrke, Allgerkerke. *See* Algarkirk

Allin. *See* Allen

Allinson, Allenson, Alinson, Alleinson, Rankin, 27, 33
    Thomas, 26, 28, 32, 34

Allson, Thomas, 55 *ter*

Allythorpe, Thomas, 19

Almondbecke. *See* Hammond Beck

Alyn. *See* Allen

Ambell Tree, Ambyll Tree. *See* Abell Tree

Ammone, James, 18

Anarton, Anerton, Robert, 15, 95

Andrew Grave, Androe Gravye, Androwe Grave, 4, 6 *bis*

Anerton. *See* Anarton

Aneyson, William, 106

Angote, Angotte, Angte [in Quadring par.], 9, 10 *ter*, 48

Anthony, John, 25, 32

Antro. . . . , Mr., 18

Ape Dyk, Ape Dick [in Leake par.], 28, 34

Armon, John, 1
    Nicholas, 1
    Thomas, 1

Asgarsdyke, Asgersdyke, Asgarsedyke, 71 *bis*, 72 *ter*

Asheholde, 111

Asperton Bridge, 4

Asshby, Stephen, 95

Asteyn, widow, 106

Atkinson, Atkynson, Attkynson, Edward, 20
    Richard, 19
    Robert, 20
    Thomas, 19
    William, 18 *bis*, 21 *bis*

Aveland wapentake, 124 *bis*

Averye, John, 19

Awebell Tre. *See* Abell Tree

Awsten, Richard, 118

Aylwardes Gat [in Moulton par.], 57

Bacon Tofte, 6

Bacons Brige, Bacons Breige [in Sutton St James par.], 107 *bis*, 112 *bis*, 117 *bis*

Badgate, Bad Gate, Bade Gate [in Sutton St James par.], 104, 117
    End, 114

Baker, Lawrence, 37

Baldeware, Bwaldwar, Bawldwar, Baldware, Bawldware, 109 *bis*
    Geoffrey, 107, 108, 109, 118
    James, 105, 106, 108 *passim*, 109 *bis*, 117, 118 *bis*
    William, 108

Butterwick—*cont.*
  Gote, 28
  Hundreth, 28, 34
Bwaldwar. *See* Baldeware
Bycker. *See* Bicker
Bygott, John, 15 *bis*, 16
Bykar, Byker. *See* Bicker
Byllcers. *See* Bylsares
Byllingborwgh, Byllyngborrow. *See* Billingborough
Bylsares, Byllcers, Byllsars [in Fleet par.], 63 *passim*
Byrdes Drowe [in Sutton St James par.] 112
Bytes, the, 6

Cacrow Gates End [in Holbeach par.], 67
Cagate, Caye Gate [in Sutton St Mary par.], 101, 116 *bis*
Callow, Callowe, Calowe, Mr., 68, 69 *passim*
  John, 52 *bis*, 53, 54, 55 *ter*, 106, 107, 118, 121 *bis*
  William, 64 *bis*, 65
Callowes Bridge, Brydge [in Whaplode par.], 71 *bis*, 72, 93
Calwell, William, 20
Cambridge, Cambrig
  St Johns College, 15
  'the college', 68
Cambridgeshire, Cambrydgeshyre, 110, 114
Cammell Gate [in Spalding par.], 80 *bis*
Canttlatt Rowgth [in Bicker par.], 37
Carefeld, 96
  Ende, 96
Carre, Carr, Mr., 29, 30
  George, 12
  Robert, 71, 125, 130
  Robert, senior, 124, 126
  Robert, junior, 124, 131
Carsay, Mr., 69
Carter Grene, 28
Carter, John, 19
Carton, Humphrey, 69
Castell, 1
Caster, William, 19
Castle, Leonard, 26, 28 *ter*, 32, 34 *ter*
Castle Acre, Castelaker, Castlaker, co. Norf., 105, 106, 117
  manor, 113
Catcate Bridge, Catcate Brydge, Categate Brige, Kitgate Brige [in Swineshead par.], 4 *bis*, 37, 38 *ter*
Catchcold, Catchecold, Kashcould, Kachcould, Cathcould Corner, Catchcould Corner, Catchecould Corner, 14 *passim*, 73 *bis*, 74, 96 *bis*, 98 *ter*
Cate Bridge. *See* Kate's Bridge
Categate. *See* Catcate
Cathcould. *See* Catchcold
Caudron. *See* Cawdron
Cave, Thomas, junior, 7

Cawdron, Anthony, 124, 130, 131
Cawode, Mr., 11
Cawsse, the. *See* Moulton
Cawthorpe [near Bourne], 8
Caye Gate. *See* Cagate
Chalensfyeld. *See* Chanons Felde
Challeyn Bridge, 126 *bis*
  new bridge near, 126
Chanons Felde Corner, Chalensfyeld Corner [in Holbeach par.], 67, 69, 97
Chapel Bridge, Chappell Brygge [in Sutton St Mary par.], 100
Chapel Gate, Chappell Gatte [in Gedney par.], 54 *bis*
  pits, 54
Chapel Gate, Chappell Gatte, Chappill Gatte [in Sutton St James par.], 105, 107, 117
Chapel Gate, Chapell Gate, Chaple Gate [in Tydd St Mary par.], 103, 115
Chapman, George, 73
Cheal, Chele [in Gosberton par.], 42, 43, 44 *ter*
Childerhowsgate, Childerrws Gatte, Childarrows Gate [in Sutton St Mary par.], 101, 116 *bis*
Churchebridge [in Holbeach par.], 67
Church Brydge, Churche Bryge [in Weston par.], 59, 78
Chyntofte Stone, 9
Clamond, Claymon, Claymond, Anthony, 29, 30, 83
  George, 1
Clapooll, Clapoll, Clapowll [in Gedney par.], 52, 54
  Bridge, Brygge, 53, 54, 120 *bis*
Clapton Gate, Claptone Gat, Claptons Gatt [in Moulton par.], 57 *bis*
Clarke, Clarcke, Clerke, Clerk, Laurence, 61 *bis*, 63 *bis*, 64, 65, 66
  Richard, 19
  Robert, 66
  Roger, 108
  Thomas, 63, 95, 100
  Thomas, junior, 116 *bis*
Clarkson, Clarkeson, Lettice, 54
  Solomon, 24 *bis*, 31
Claxby, William, 20
Claxson, Edmund, 20
Clay, Claye, Richard, 28, 31, 84
Claydicke, Clay Dyk [in Leake par.], 26, 32
Claymond, Claymon. *See* Clamond
Clementes Crosse [in Tydd St Mary par.], 110
Clerke, Clerk. *See* Clarke
Clinton, Clynton, Edward, 9th baron Clinton and 1st earl of Lincoln, 91, 125
  Henry, 10th baron Clinton and 2nd earl of Lincoln, 124, 125, 130 *bis*
Clinton and Saye, lord. *See* Clinton
Clonys. *See* Cloynes
Clotte [in Crowland par.], 58

M

INDEX OF COUNTIES

INDEX OF SUBJECTS

J.W.
RUDDOCK
& SONS LTD
PRINTERS
LINCOLN